JESUS IN THE NEW UNIVERSE STORY

JESUS
IN THE NEW UNIVERSE STORY

CLETUS WESSELS, O.P.

ORBIS BOOKS

Maryknoll, New York 10545

Founded in 1970, Orbis Books endeavors to publish works that enlighten the mind, nourish the spirit, and challenge the conscience. The publishing arm of the Maryknoll Fathers and Brothers, Orbis seeks to explore the global dimensions of the Christian faith and mission, to invite dialogue with the diverse cultures and religious traditions, and to serve the cause of reconciliation and peace. The books published reflect the views of their authors and do not represent the official position of the Maryknoll Society.

To obtain more information about Maryknoll and Orbis Books, please visit our website at www.maryknoll.org.

Library of Congress Cataloging-in-Publication Data

Wessels, Cletus.
  Jesus in the new universe story / Cletus Wessels.
      p. cm.
Includes bibliographical references (p.   ) and index.
  ISBN 1-57075-465-9
  1. Jesus Christ—Person and offices. 2. Cosmology. I. Title.
  BT205 .W456 2003
  232—dc21
                          2002013556

CONTENTS

PREFACE

Within the historical tradition of the Christian Church and throughout its history, salvation has been a central theme. The great sweep of history flows from creation to the fall, from the fall to redemption, and from redemption to new life. Christian life is a constant struggle to overcome the sinfulness and evil that is part of human life in order to be saved, and the final act of salvation is found in the fullness of life in the resurrection of the dead.

At the center of this theme stands the figure of Jesus Christ who is seen as the savior of the world. Jesus redeems the human race by shedding his blood and overthrowing the powers of evil. In his resurrection this man Jesus is made Lord and Christ, and he is the source of life for all nations. Christian life is modeled on Jesus and his message of salvation.

The background for this story of salvation and redemption is a cosmology and a story of creation that emerged in ancient Jewish tradition. According to this story, as found in the Book of Genesis, the universe was created out of chaos by God about five or six thousand years ago. The culmination of this creative act was the creation of the human species from the Earth and the creation of Eve from the side of Adam. They were created in a state of original justice and placed in a garden of paradise. But our first parents sinned by eating of the tree of the knowledge of good and evil, and this original sin was the source of our fallen nature. Then God expelled them from the garden of Eden.

Thus the underlying story of creation calls for a savior, Jesus Christ, in order to bring salvation to a broken world and to a fallen human race. This has been the foundational story of Christian life for two thousand years.

Within the last eighty years, a new story of the universe has emerged. It both challenges our Christian faith and theology and opens up new horizons for a synthesis of this new universe story with our ancient Christian story. Some Christians are frightened by the new story, and some are excited by its possibilities. My own recent book, entitled *The Holy Web: Church and the New Universe Story*, is an effort to integrate modern physics and Christian theology into a new and positive vision of the church. Since that book was published, I have often lectured and given study days and retreats on this new vision of the church. Every time I have presented these ideas someone will ask, "Well, what about Jesus? Where does he fit into this new universe story and this new cosmology? What does this story tell us about Jesus?" My answer to these questions is found in this present work, *Jesus in the New Universe Story.*

On the one hand, this is a modest book. It does not attempt to treat all the current christological issues that are found in a book like Roger Haight's *Jesus Symbol of God.* On the other hand, this is a more difficult and a riskier book than my first. It attempts to re-think the meaning of Jesus in the context of a new world view, that of an emerging universe. As we will see, there is a greater difference between the stories of the biblical universe and the emerging universe than there was between patristic theology and the theology of the Middle Ages, which was interpreted within the philosophy of Aristotle. Moreover, biblical teachings as well as the thought of Aristotle and Thomas Aquinas were based on an archaic story of a "created" universe, and it was in this context that the story of Jesus was articulated to the modern world. Our challenge is to maintain the underlying reality of the biblical story of Jesus while reinterpreting that story through the new lens of an "emerging" universe and to articulate that story in images and language understandable within the context of the twenty-first century.

This work is not a complete integration of the story of Jesus and the story of the universe, and it is not a final word on this subject. It is a partial and initial attempt to interpret Jesus in terms of an emerging universe. This book may raise many questions, perhaps more questions than answers, and it may sometimes come to some tentative conclusions on matters that might challenge ordinary church teachings. My image is that of an amoeba that has a shape but no definite shape. When the amoeba approaches a piece of foreign matter, it surrounds it and, if the matter is edible, assimilates it, but, if it is not edible, it rejects the matter. Theology today, and especially Christology, has a shape but no definite shape. Some of my ideas may be like foreign matter to the church's traditional Christology because they emerge from a new vision of reality. Hopefully, the believing community will surround my ideas, examine them openly and honestly, and, if they are compatible, embrace them. If they are found to be incompatible, the community will reject them. I know that the believing community and the guidance of God's Spirit within that community will join in the discussion and judge prudently and well.

This is a book that does not simply set out to prove its thesis or impart new information to the reader. Its purpose is to awaken in the reader a new way of thinking. I will use stories and examples to touch readers in a way that will help them discover and probe more deeply the new universe story, and this paradigm will offer an exciting and experiential vision of Jesus in an emerging universe.

In a work like this, the words *symbol* and *symbolic* are often used and they are easily misunderstood. Many people tend to say, "This is *only* a symbol." What they mean is that a symbol is something empty or external and therefore unimportant. This is not the case for me. A symbol is a sensible event or thing that both points us to and contains what is symbolized. If we take as an example the story of the man born blind in chapter 9 of the Gospel of John, the blind man who receives his sight is a symbol of the Jewish Christians who receive the gift of faith, a gift of sight. The symbol is the blind man receiving sight and that which it points to and contains is his own new faith as well as the new faith of the Jewish Christians. In this story the blind man seeing symbolizes the Christians believing, and this symbol contains the reality of a new faith. Moreover, in this symbolic event the Christians believing is more important than the blind man seeing. There is always a deeper spiritual dimension to a symbol, which is its reality, and in this passage that reality is new faith of the believer.

Another example is found in chapter 6 of John's Gospel in the story of the bread of life. Jesus says that "he who eats my flesh and drinks my blood abides in me and I in him." After hearing this, some of his listeners take his words as a literal eating of flesh and drinking of blood, and they reject him. They do not see the deeper meaning in this symbol, namely, the new life that we receive from the presence of Jesus abiding in us. The eating and drinking contain the very life of Jesus. Then Jesus says to them, "It is the spirit that gives life, the flesh is of no avail; the words I have spoken are spirit and life." Thus we can see in these two examples that the symbol contains the reality symbolized. These are not empty symbols, but symbols that embody a deeper spiritual dimension. Ira Progoff in his book entitled *The Symbolic and the Real* comes to the final conclusion that the symbolic *is* the real.

When we say that Jesus is the symbol of God, we are not talking about an empty symbol. We are saying that Jesus, in his mission and his message, in his death and resurrection, not only points to the presence of God but also contains within himself the presence of God. Jesus is the presence of God. In my use of the word "symbol" I mean that the symbolic is the real.

All the biblical quotations in this book are my own translations. I have tried to use language that does not exclude and yet maintains the sense of the original texts. This is not always possible, because the original texts arose within a patriarchal culture.

This book is not intended primarily for scholars. Its audience is the educated Christian who is open to an experience of Jesus in a new way and who is willing to look at Jesus in light of an emerging universe. It is not an easy read, and I do not avoid difficult and controversial matters. With diligence, readers can find themselves in the discussions, the stories, the struggles, and the dreams that will be shared. It is hoped that scholars and teachers will also find a theological synthesis that will be useful in their classrooms or discover a springboard for deeper research into the issues treated in this book.

In working on this book over the last three years I have personally experienced the emerging process. Very often as I read and pondered the material for a section of the book, I would fall into a state of confusion, not knowing how to order all the ideas and texts that were available. My solution was to sit in my recliner and just let all the issues and questions bubble around with no effort on my part. Usually, after a period of time—sometimes fifteen minutes and other times two days—the clouds began to disperse and the multitude of my thoughts precipitated and a new order appeared. This was truly order out of chaos, a characteristic of an emerging universe. Sometime during my regular early morning meditation time, I would turn my mind and heart to the God dwelling within me. Suddenly, my attention would fly to the chapter on which I was working or the problem with which I was struggling. I could not get rid of it, so I just opened my mind and my heart and listened. Such an experience would overwhelm me by its depths and its clarity. The outcome was neither random nor determined. It was creative. It was part of the emerging process.

As you can see, I am not primarily a research theologian. I am much more a teacher, a preacher, and a seeker of wisdom. I am a provocateur who tries to stimulate people by presenting ideas that are soundly based yet invite fuller research by others. I am a storyteller who wants to serve as a guide into the mysteries of the universe and the God who unfolds in the universe. I am a reconciler who seeks to be a peacemaker looking for unity in the deepest realities of faith and reason. I am a deeply committed Christian whose life has been molded by the Christian tradition at its best; yet I am also a restless Christian, always looking for the surprising novelty of God.

One of the sections in chapter 5, "The Story of Jesus," is entitled "It Takes a Gang to Make a Messiah." Beneath what may appear to be flippancy in that subsection title, there lies a great truth: a leader is judged by those who want to follow his or her path. During the writing of this book—without having any pretenses about being in a league with Jesus—I learned that it takes a "gang" to make a book. My local Dominican community in Minneapolis as well as my extended family in the provincial community have been a gang, people who have supported me and from whom I have learned so much during the past fifty years. Another gang became indispensable in the writing of this book. We came to call ourselves the "First Friday Group," and we met each month over a period of more than three years and have continued to meet monthly. We have become both good friends and critics of one another's writing, and I want to thank each and every member of this group for their contributions. They are Christie Lord, Greg Peterson, Norrine Bohman, Mary Martin, Tom Eland, Mary Testin, Sally McGraw, Margaret McDowell, Mary Jane Steinhagen, and Bob Veitch. Bob Veitch's name will pop up at several points in the text. He is a voracious reader and commentator on things historical and current, as well as a budding novelist. "The Story of Jesus" section also shows how Jesus had some special friends such as Mary, Martha, and Lazarus, and I feel called to thank my special friend who has walked this journey with me and has supported me throughout these years. I also thank some special people who have read the entire manuscript, commented on it, and made positive suggestions. Bill Burrows and the staff at Orbis Books have walked with me from the beginning, and I thank them for their guidance in bringing this book to life. It does take a "gang" to give birth to a new vision.

THE STORY OF THE UNIVERSE

The origin moment of the universe presents us with an amazing process that we begin to appreciate as a mystery unfolding through the ages. The flaring forth of the primordial energy carried within itself all that would bring the universe into its present mode of being.[1]

For more than eight thousand years, Western culture and civilization had a story of the universe, a story of beauty and order based on information drawn from sense experience. This story was not a scientific story or a story based on history. Rather, it emerged from the efforts of people trying to discover their origins, their place in the world, and their relationship to the gods. These people were storytellers who spun their tales of the origins of creation in poetry and picture language. The following is my own brief summary of the foundational cosmology that has been at the heart of the Western world.

The ancient peoples interpreted the world as three-layered, consisting of the earth, the heavens, and the underworld. The earth was a flat surface that was home to the plants, animals, fish, birds, and humans. The firmament was an inverted bowl supported by huge pillars. The vault of heaven contained the sun, moon, and stars to give light, and it had openings through which the rain poured. Above the firmament was the place in which God resided along with the angels and good spirits. The underworld, known in Hebrew as Sheol, was a dark place of chaos, death, and evil powers. In Christian tradition, God was joined up in heaven by the saints, and Satan was joined down below by the devils and the evil spirits.

The Jewish biblical story of creation in Genesis follows this same pattern. It is not meant to tell us a scientific story, since the Hebrew people did not think in modern scientific terms. The biblical story is not intended to give us a historically accurate picture of the beginnings, since

---

1. Thomas Berry, *The Great Work: Our Way into the Future,* New York, Bell Tower, 1999, p. 27.

people in that era did not think in terms of our sense of scientific history. Rather, they dealt with stories orally passed on and reinterpreted in light of the concerns of each generation and the historical context of the people. The Jewish stories of creation were theological poetry in the sense that they used picture language to teach each generation the fundamental faith of the community and the relationship of God to the chosen people. The biblical story is very powerful and still speaks to some deeply held theological views, but it is also limited in its perspective and in its scope.

The twentieth-century explosion of information about our universe flows from an expanded sense experience made possible by scientific and technological advances. Giant telescopes scan the length and breadth of the universe and capture the birth and death of stars and galaxies. Physicists explore the deep inner workings of matter, atoms, and subatomic particles and waves. The universe that flashed forth about fifteen billion years ago is expanding, the Earth community is continually evolving, and the Earth has become conscious in the emergence of the human. The story of the universe has moved from the universe as a vast and fixed infinite space with the sun and moon, the stars and planets all moving in unchanging orbits to an expanding universe that came into existence, not all at once, but over billions of years in a time-development sequence. Truly a new universe story!

The new universe story is a foundational story that is taught in most classrooms from junior high to university, and that is now commonly shared by the scientific community worldwide. For the first time in history, there is the possibility for a creation story that is common to all cultures throughout the world. This story as told from a theological perspective can be interpreted as the unfolding presence of God within the universe, and, as we will see, it is the foundational story that underlies the whole concept of an emerging universe. This new story will deepen our images of God, challenge the structures of the church,[2] and open for us new ways of interpreting the meaning of Jesus for contemporary believers.

There are many ways of telling the story of the universe. The scientific story is told by astronomers and physicists in their efforts to chart the movements of the stars and the mutations within the galaxies and to gaze in awe at the mystery of black holes and a creative vacuum. Most scientists agree that the universe flashed forth between thirteen and fifteen billion years ago, and that the solar system emerged about five billion years ago. The scientific story can be found in great detail in almost any science textbook. At this point and for this work, an overall picture is sufficient.

---

2. Cletus Wessels, *The Holy Web: Church and the New Universe Story,* Maryknoll, N.Y., Orbis Books, 2000.

A common way of telling this story is found in "The Cosmic Walk." This is a ritual that originated with the staff of Genesis Farms in New Jersey. The story is told in words and in visual form by arranging a spiral with major moments in the universe story marked off. These moments are marked by candles placed separately according to the time line of the unfolding of the universe. A narrator walks the pathway, tells the story, and lights a candle for each event. This format provides an experiential awareness of the magnitude of the universe and the time-development sequence in which the universe unfolded.

Another profound telling of this story is found in *The Everything Seed: A Story of Beginnings,* written by Carole Martignacco and illustrated by Joy Troyer. It combines a simple, almost childlike, story with beautiful batik illustrations. I have chosen to use the text of this story to introduce the reader to the new universe story.

THE EVERYTHING SEED

A Story of Beginnings
by Carole Martignacco[1]

Have you ever watched a seed grow?
Have you ever noticed how it begins
so small,
so quietly,
like a gift wanting to be opened—
and how
slowly
it wakes up,
begins to unfold
growing into
something
larger
     and
          Larger
             and
                  LARGER?
Then you know that whatever
comes from a seed
usually ends up

---

1. "The Everything Seed" (copyright © 2000 by Carole Martignacco, all rights reserved) is reproduced with the permission of Carole Martignacco, a poet, artist, and minister in the Unitarian Universalist Church of Christ of North Hatley in the Province of Quebec, Canada. "The Everything Seed" accompanies twenty-eight original paintings by Joy Troyer, a Minneapolis artist. They are printed in a privately produced book *The Everything Seed: A Story of Beginnings,* copyright © 2000 by Carole Martignacco and Joy Troyer. Ms Troyer's website is accessible at: www.dyeingarts.com. The publisher regrets that Ms Troyer's work could not be reproduced in this book because of cost constraints.

looking very little
like the seed it comes from—
which is also true of the
    very
        first
            seed.
Once long long ago, way back before the beginning
so long ago there was no such thing as time
because there was no one there to count it . . .

Everywhere was a huge deep mysterious place
like something wanting to happen.

There were no stars, no Sun or Moon.
There was no place like Earth—
not a drop of water,
or a single tree,
or rock,
or flower—
and no living beings
anywhere.
But in that deep waiting space
    was hidden the tiniest pinpoint of something
        no bigger than a seed.
It was not a flower seed.
It was not an elm tree seed.
It was not a seed of corn . . .
although all those things were included in the seed.
        You might call it an Everything Seed
        because that is what it became.
No one knows where that first seed came from
    or how it was planted
        or how it knew how long to wait—
            in the way that only seeds seem to know—
                for just the right moment to sprout and grow.
But all at once this tiny seed
cradled and nourished
in the rich soil of space
woke up
    broke open
        and began to unfold . . .
Unfolding
    Unfolding,

and blossoming forth
into an enormous blazing ball of bright light...
like a great Grandmother Sun
and the Universe was born.
Out fluttered the galaxies, like a storm of snowflakes swirling and
gathering into the brightest most blindingly beautiful clouds of stars.

And out of those starclouds whirled our own star—the one we call the
Sun and our Earth,
and the Moon, and all the round spinning planets we have learned to
name.

And this is the secret of that tiny seed: You and I were there in the very
beginning...
like the idea for leaves on a big oak tree lie hidden inside an acorn.

We were there with all the stars and the planets, all the rocks and oceans
and plants and animals
and people—everything that is now, ever was or will be—was inside that
first tiny seed.

So whenever you hold a seed in your hand and wonder what it could
become—imagine...
How you, and all that is here once came from the tiniest speck of
an Everything Seed
before it sprouted and grew long, long ago in the way
back beginning of time.
Now if this were an ordinary story it would end right here.
But this story of the Universe keeps unfolding.
What once began in a blazing blossom of light continues every
day.

New stars sprout open in the deep soil of space.
New plants and animals appear on the Earth.
Seeds of many kinds are scattered all over the Earth to help us
remember.
And new people are born every day with the spark of that first light still
alive
and burning deep inside them—waiting...
like the Everything Seed, to shine in ways that are yet to be
known.

PART I

THE FOUNDATIONAL STORIES

1

THE HUMAN STORY IN THREE STAGES

We are in trouble just now because we do not have a good story. We are in between stories. The old story, the account of how the world came to be and how we fit into it, is no longer effective. Yet we have not learned the new story.[1]

Foundational to every tribe and people and to every human culture is a creation story. Creation stories are often very imaginative stories involving cosmic events that ground all their social norms and religious rituals. These stories seek to answer basic human questions. Where did we come from? Why are we here? What is our relationship with the gods? What is our relationship to each other? Our contemporary culture has discovered a new story, an exciting story that opens us to an unknown future. As this story matures, it will also ground in new ways our social norms and our religious rituals. Rather than imagining creation as one event with the simultaneous creation of the non-living, the living, and the human, we now see creation in an unfinished time-development sequence flowing into an unknown future. In order to have some perspective on this time-development sequence and its impact on the human story, we can imagine that the unfolding of the universe over fifteen billion years ago until today is equivalent to one year of 365 days.

Thus, after an unimaginable period of time, on the last day, the final twenty-four hours of the story of the universe, some form of human life appeared on Earth. In terms of the entire process of the divine unfolding in the universe, the appearance of the human species is a very recent development, almost like the blink of an eye relative to the vast age of our Earth. But as *we* perceive the human story from our historical perspective it does not seem like "the blink of an eye." Rather, it is a long and com-

---

1. Thomas Berry, *The Dream of the Earth,* San Francisco, Sierra Club Books, 1988, p. 123.

COSMIC CALENDAR

15 billion years ago
365 days ago   The flashing forth of the universe
January 1st

10 billion years ago
243 days ago   The giant galaxies evolve
May 1st

5 billion years ago
122 days ago   The birth of the sun
September 1st   and the solar system

4 billion years ago
98 days ago   Life begins on Earth
September 25th

700 million years ago
18 days ago   The first multi-cellular life forms emerge
December 13th   and creativity expands rapidly

2.6 million years ago
On the last day   Earliest humanoid types develop
December 31st

40 thousand years ago
Last 96 seconds   Modern *Homo sapiens* emerges,
December 31st 11:58.36   developing the earliest languages

10 thousand years ago
Last 21 seconds   The beginning of agriculture
December 31st 11:59.39   and the domestication of animals

2 thousand years ago
Last 5 seconds   Jesus lives and teaches
December 31st 11:59.55   throughout Judea

plex story rising from the mists of prehistory and gradually becoming known in the archeological ruins left by ancient peoples and finally appearing on the pages of historical records. It is difficult to chronicle this complex story within the limitations of this work, but in very broad strokes we will attempt to paint a picture of the human story in the context of the unfolding of the story of the Earth.

As we describe the human story, it is important to be forewarned about the sources of the story. Bob Veitch of the "First Friday Group" describes it well.[2]

> Our past—mankind's, the universe's—is best seen as a gigantic mosaic with billions upon billions of events, each represented as a single stone chip. We look backward and we find chips, one here and another there. We place them where we think they might go, and little by little parts of pictures emerge. We know that at best we will discover a miniscule fraction of the chips. Most are lost forever. Many are buried, only to be revealed by rare circumstances. So we must tell our story by letting our imagination fill in the missing chips. All archeologists are, at heart, story tellers. The stories they tell of our past are largely myth, wrapped around a handful of artifacts and shards.

With that caveat, we will present the story in three stages: Stage One, Childhood, from the beginning of human history two to three million years ago to the agricultural revolution, focusing on humanity's *physical development;* Stage Two, Adolescence, from ten thousand years ago until the present, focusing on humanity's *ego and mental development;* and Stage Three, Adulthood, beginning now and leading into the unknown future, focusing on humanity's *spiritual development.* Each of these stages has basic values and characteristics, and we will ultimately integrate these values and characteristics into our understanding of the life and meaning of Jesus of Nazareth. We will also explain the process of transformation as humanity moves from childhood to adolescence and from adolescence to adulthood. It is essential to remember that the words *childhood, adolescence,* and *adulthood* are used metaphorically and not literally. In terms of these metaphors, not all of our ancient ancestors are children, and not all humans during the last ten thousand years are adolescents, and

---

2. Bob is a member of the First Friday Group that meets monthly to discuss theological issues and critique my manuscripts. He frequently responds by e-mail with some deep insights.

not all humans will become adults. What follows is a brief sketch of the gradual development of the human species as it has emerged over the last two to three million years.

STAGE ONE: THE CHILDHOOD OF THE HUMAN— PHYSICAL DEVELOPMENT

> For the first time, I became aware of my spiritual continuity and solidarity with early mankind. They were no longer "those primitive creatures"; they were "my people."[3]

> In its beginning, and in its early development, the human was so frail, so unimpressive, a creature hardly worth the attention of the other animals in the forest. But these early humans were on a path that would in time explode with unexpectedly significant new power, a power of consciousness whereby Earth, and the universe as a whole, turned back and reflected on itself.[4]

Prior to the introduction of modern technology, the conception of a child was an event that took place within the dark mystery of the womb. Nothing was known clearly of its origins and its early growth. The history and life of our earliest forerunners, called hominids, who came before the birth of the human race, is also shrouded in the dark mystery of the past. We have only the merest hint of their presence based on some footprints and the earliest skull discovered in Africa. The following is a description of hominids by Brian Swimme and Thomas Berry.

> The hominids were distinguished by their increased brain size and by their capacity for walking in an upright posture, although they still spent time in trees, as is indicated by the length and muscular quality of their arms relative to their shorter legs. They lived now mostly in the savannas, the grasslands of the region.
>
> Such was the situation some four million years ago when a young female hominid, now designated as "Lucy," lived in southern Ethiopia. Her brain capacity, between four hundred and

3. Raymond J. Nogar, *The Lord of the Absurd,* New York, Herder and Herder, 1972, p. 28.

4. Brian Swimme and Thomas Berry, *The Universe Story,* HarperSanFrancisco, 1992, p. 143.

five hundred cubic centimeters, was slightly greater than that of the chimpanzee. In diet, Lucy and the other hominids apparently were vegetarians; neither Lucy nor any of the others left behind any evidence of implements for hunting or dissecting, or of bones discarded after eating.[5]

During the period of gestation, the fetus in the womb begins to develop and to take on the bodily shape of a human, with arms and legs, heartbeat, and brain functioning. Likewise, there is evidence that human evolution began about 2.6 million years ago when the African climate changed. Because of widespread drought, the lakes shrank and the forest thinned out to savannah, and our ancestors were not well adapted to such conditions. In dealing with these climactic changes *Homo habilis,* formerly a tree dweller, had to adapt to becoming a forager on the ground. Now the human appears in its species identity possessing skills in working with stone, skills that manifest not only a sense of utility but also an emerging feeling for esthetic beauty. Moreover, our earliest ancestors depended on the Earth and the community of species for food, clothing, and shelter. They developed a rapport with the natural world. Theirs was a relationship that evoked both awe in the presence of the great beauty and harmony of creation and the life-giving and nourishing gifts of the Earth as well as terror in the face of the seemingly negative power of the wind and rain and the thunder and lightning.

Perhaps the appearance some 120,000 years ago of archaic *Homo sapiens,* the human species that succeeded these other forms and from which all contemporary humans are descended, might be compared to the birth of a child. During the time of the Neanderthals there was a continuing migration into a wide area of Europe, and these newborn children exhibited an amazing ability to adapt to varied geographical terrain and environmental conditions. The Neanderthals used fire extensively and they were not only food gatherers but also hunters, as is evidenced by the remains in their living sites. They experienced the need to relate to the all-pervasive spiritual powers within the world and to seek the psychic support needed by the human mode of consciousness. "To obtain this support, to invoke that numinous presence perceived as the origin, support, and final destiny of all that exists, humans from the earliest times engaged in symbolic rituals, often with sacrificial aspects."[6] Evidence of a spiritual consciousness can be found in elaborate burial sites.

---

5. Ibid., p. 145.
6. Ibid., p. 153.

Such a burial site with its ordered arrangement of stones is a mythic, ritual mode of expression that from its beginning is the manner in which humans respond to the universe... There appears to be a psychic tendency in humans consciously to integrate their own human process with this cosmological process. From these earliest times humans experienced themselves within the encompassing order of the universe.[7]

There is a temptation to romanticize this Paleolithic culture as we tend to romanticize Native American culture. However, life was difficult and many conflicts were present. The search for food and shelter was ongoing, often resulting in a nomadic way of life. Violence and chaos were present and at times disrupted the settled life of the people. But these early cultures did have a deep sense of the sacred in their lives, along with their dependency on the community of species and their need for worship and ritual.

About forty thousand years ago, the Neanderthals disappeared from the European scene and modern *Homo sapiens* took the stage. This period was a time of continuing migration during which humans reached the Americas and Australia. With the last advance of the Ice Ages throughout the Northern hemisphere, many species that had retreated south returned to flourish in the north. Humans survived the Ice Ages because of their mental flexibility; they were able to recognize climactic changes, adapt to those changes, and develop systems of functional community living. Much as is the case with growing children, collaboration and socialization became necessary. The people had to work together and learn to anticipate and even to adopt the habits of the hunted.

Upon their arrival in the European region, these peoples, the Cro-Magnon culture, manifested an artistic and inventive genius unknown in earlier peoples.

Since these artistic abilities were associated with a new capacity for the understanding and use of spoken language, we are meeting here not simply with another change in methods of stone working or the processing of some physical material but with a transformation of human consciousness on a scale and with a dramatic impact such as we seldom encounter in this narrative of our emerging human development.[8]

---

7. Ibid., p. 152.
8. Ibid., p. 156.

The artistic and cultural dimension of the first-stage Soul can be found in the many instances of cave art "which provides the largest body of evidence helping us to understand humanity's childhood Soul."[9] This art seems to illustrate the non-violent character of these people because "in over three hundred cave 'art galleries,' presenting an extensive display of the spiritual values of this twenty-five-thousand-year period, we find no depictions of war, no celebration of warrior-priests, and no evidence of human or animal sacrifice."[10]

Throughout the Paleolithic period, hunting and gathering are the basic life-support systems of the people, implying a knowledge of and a dependence on the other species and a need to be in tune with the Earth and its creatures. More and more highly developed tools and implements, as well as the use of fire, show a specifically human mode of adaptation to a given place in the community of species. These new ways of living, as well as the continual presence of danger and the fear of the unknown, also called for new social relationships, the building of family groupings, collaborative hunting, shared housing, and communal rituals. The artistic and ritualistic genius of both early and later *Homo sapiens* is evidence of the experience of the deep mystery contained within the Earth. This was the unfolding of a spiritual consciousness and reverence for Gaia, the Earth Mother.

It is no surprise that *Homo sapiens* at this stage saw the mystery of life in terms of the feminine. The miracle of birth and the wonder of the nourishing breasts of the woman were symbolic of the overwhelming life-giving and nourishing power of Mother Earth. Robert Keck says that humanity "had a deep value system that included a celebration of and focus upon the female body's capacity for giving and nourishing life and the understandable religious consequence of worshiping a feminine image of divinity, namely, the Goddess."[11]

The values and characteristics of the Stage One Soul can be summarized as follows:

1. dependence on the Earth for food, clothing, and shelter, and an experience of harmony with nature and within community of species;

2. relatively non-violent relationships with other humans and nature in the context of a difficult nomadic way of life;

---

9. L. Robert Keck, *Sacred Quest: The Evolution and Future of the Human Soul*, West Chester, Pa., Chrysalis Books, 2000, p. 15.

10. Ibid., p. xxi.

11. Ibid., p. 30.

3. a highly developed artistic sense based on a growing spiritual consciousness; and

4. celebration of and focus on the life-giving and nourishing role of women and a worship of the Mother Earth Goddess.

The story of the Garden of Paradise in Genesis may be a romanticized expression of the collective human memory of the story of its childhood. The coming of agriculture and the domestication of animals is the beginning of a new era, a period of adolescence when the human experiences the attractiveness of the Earth and the desire to be like God, knowing good and evil. Humans become aware of their own nakedness and the need to earn their bread by the sweat of their brow.

STAGE TWO: THE ADOLESCENCE OF THE HUMAN— EGO AND MENTAL DEVELOPMENT

It is extraordinary to think that only in the last twelve thousand years has civilization, as we understand it, taken off. There must have been an extraordinary explosion about 10,000 BC—and there was.[12]

That explosion was the agricultural revolution, the domestication of animals, and the change from a Neolithic village to an horticultural-based, city-centered mode of human living. The extent of this transformation is summarized by Robert Keck.

Prior to this transformation, all of humanity, on every continent, lived as nomadic hunter-gatherers, apparently were nonviolent, and worshiped an immanent feminine image of the Divine, the Earth Goddess. After this transformational "moment," most of humanity turned to agriculture, began clustering in settled communities, grew in number, [and] began to value the masculine over the feminine and humanity over nature.[13]

The history of this ten-thousand-year revolution is beyond the scope of this work. The revolution was, in terms of ego and mental develop-

---

12. Jacob Bronowski, *The Ascent of Man,* Boston, Little Brown, 1973, p. 60.
13. Keck, *Sacred Quest,* pp. 37–38.

ment, a time of marvelous human accomplishments, cultural and artistic masterpieces, and scientific and technical developments. But hanging over all these wonders is the reality that they took place within the context of an adolescent culture. Our primary interest is not to underrate human progress but to articulate the adolescent flaw which has been exaggerated in ways that threaten even to destroy humanity itself. There are three interrelated characteristics of the adolescent stage of the human story: Separateness, Patriarchy, and "Man Becomes God."

What is the meaning of this adolescent phase? Frequently, when sharing this material with groups, I invite the participants to describe their experience of or with adolescents. The words people use are significant. Adolescents are rebels, they want to be free, they seek independence, and they like to experiment with new things. At the same time, they have to deal with raging hormones and they struggle with insecurity and ambiguity. Adolescents, as they search for identity, need to belong and want control over their lives. They are both self-centered and driven by peer pressure. They seek immediate gratification and take risks because the future is now and death is never. The mental development and personal abilities of many young people open up new worlds for them to conquer; many *do* want to conquer the great big world that opens before them.

Separateness

About ten thousand years ago, the human entered into adolescence. As the peoples of the Earth moved toward the development of an agricultural way of life and the domestication of animals, humans began to see themselves as able to till the soil and harvest its produce. They could harness the power and the endurance of their animals. They could control the Earth and its fruits. The use of fire and the power of words also helped humans establish their species identity, and, as in the case of an adolescent searching for identity, this "clarity of species identity tended toward isolating the human within itself over against the nonhuman components of the larger Earth community."[14] Robert Keck describes this process as it develops:

> With ego maturation coming to center stage, the first deep value to emerge from humanity's transformed Soul was that of a changed relationship with nature. Just as an individual develops his or her ego by distinguishing "self" from "other," humanity

---

14. Swimme and Berry, *The Universe Story,* p. 178.

distinguished itself from the rest of nature. The human/nature relationship was changed from one of cooperation to one of separation, manipulation, management, control, use, and abuse.[15]

The cosmology of the Western world, rather than affirming the inner presence of God, reinforced the idea of separation of the human and the divine. From biblical times throughout the Middle Ages both the learned and the ordinary folks shared a creation story with Heaven above separated from the Earth below. God was found in Heaven along with the spirits and the angels. The Earth was the home of the human race and all its other creatures. Sheol was the abode of the dead beneath the Earth where the dead lived a shadowy existence. This so-called triple-decker universe was the generally accepted and culturally approved way of describing "the world."

The harmony with nature and within the community of species was deeply disturbed. What had been a cooperative relationship became a competitive relationship. We wanted to conquer rather than learn from and live within the community of species, and we gradually came to view ourselves as masters of nature, ordained by God to rule over the Earth and all its creatures. This view has been reinforced by the story in Genesis where God says, "Be fertile and multiply; fill the earth and subdue it. Have dominion over the fish of the sea, the birds of the air, and all the living things that move on the earth" (Genesis 1:28). In our search for identity, which is both necessary and risky, we were led more and more to a self-centered way of life of subduing, dominating, and using nature for our own needs.

In the childhood of the human story, God was encountered in the awesome beauty and harmony of the Earth. Nature was the prism through which our earliest ancestors saw the deepest spiritual dimensions of their lives. The Earth and all that was in it were impregnated by the divine mystery and this mystery was found everywhere. Over the last ten thousand years this intimate relationship was transformed by our newly found anthropocentric self.

The mystical bonding of the human with the natural world was progressively weakened. Humans, in differing degrees, lost their capacity to hear the voices of the natural world. They no longer heard the voices of the mountains or the valleys, the rivers or the sea, the sun, moon, or stars; they no longer had a sense of the ex-

---

15. Keck, *Sacred Quest,* p. xxi.

perience communicated by the various animals, an experience that was emotional and esthetic, but even more than that. These languages of the dawn and sunset are transformations of the soul at its deepest level.[16]

During Stage Two, the separation of the human from nature also impacted the relationship of the human to the divine. As we lost our intimacy with the Earth, we lost our intimacy with the divine. We no longer heard the voices of the natural world that echoed with the voice of God within us. The transcendent God communicated with the human family not directly through nature but through the mediation of the Word, through Wisdom/Sophia, through the spirit and through messengers (angels), and later through the patriarchs, the judges, and the prophets. The Jewish biblical tradition mirrors this change.

> The biblical tradition begins with the creation narrative wherein the Earth Mother of the eastern Mediterranean is abandoned in favor of the transcendent Heaven Father. Later the relationship between the human and the divine is constituted in terms of a covenant between a chosen people and a personal transcendent creative Father deity. This becomes the context in which human-divine affairs are worked out over the succeeding centuries. The natural world is no longer the locus for the meeting of the divine and the human.[17]

But enfolded within this separation between the divine and the human there flows a stream of deep spirituality based on the presence of God. As Richard Woods says, "Whether among the patriarchs, the prophets or sages, the dominant characteristic of Jewish spirituality has centered implicitly or explicitly, as it does today, on the presence of God."[18] This special presence of God is found in the call of Abram (Genesis 12:1-3), in the powerful story of Jacob wrestling with God (Genesis 28:10-19), and especially in the theophany to Moses in the burning bush and the revealing of the divine name (Exodus 3:1-14). This divine name, which expresses the intimate presence as well as the mysterious "more than" character of God, might be paraphrased as: *I shall be with you as who I am shall I be with you.* In other words, God is always intimately

---

16. Swimme and Berry, *The Universe Story,* p. 199.

17. Berry, *The Dream of the Earth,* p. 149.

18. Richard Woods, Mysterion: *An Approach to Mystical Spirituality,* Chicago, Thomas More Press, 1981, p. 239.

present to the people, but in a numinous way that is uniquely proper to this God.[19] In the midst of the growing adolescent separation of the human and the divine, these formative experiences show both the intimacy of God with the patriarchs and the people, and the powerful guiding presence of that God.

Separateness from nature gradually affected other human relationships. In order to maintain our identity, we began to separate ourselves from the "other," whether that other was the neighbor from the next village or the tribe that worshiped a different god or the people with different customs. The necessity of defining and defending ourselves over against others kept villages, tribes, and nations separated and eventually led us into war and violence.

> In virtually every case, when a sacred relationship is fractured, when a "thou" is conceptually transformed into an "it," the rationalization for the use of violence is not far behind, particularly when combined with an adolescent ego. When the "it" doesn't obey, when "it" gets in the way, when the "it" does not conform to the controlling efforts of the ruling person or class, violence is easily rationalized and justified.[20]

As humans claimed a right to conquer and rule the Earth, they also claimed the right to conquer and rule other humans. This led to the constant waging of war with spears and arrows, with guns and cannons, and finally with the ultimate violence of nuclear warfare. This led to forms of slavery that have been endemic to the "human family" since its adolescence began. The universal existence of poverty throughout all nations and in all ages arose as power and control allowed the rich and powerful to oppress and overwhelm the poor. Religious wars continue to afflict the peoples of the Earth, and unknown millions of people are being killed in the name of the God whom we proclaim as the compassionate and merciful one.

The Psalmist in the Hebrew Scriptures gives witness to the fact that tribal and national solidarity can give birth to destruction and hatred for the "other."

> Give thanks, the Lord is good,
> "God is lasting Love!"

---

19. John Courtney Murray, S.J., *The Problem of God,* New Haven, Yale University Press, 1964, pp. 5–10.

20. Keck, *Sacred Quest,* p. 62.

Now let Israel say,
"God is lasting love!"

Let the house of Aaron say,
"God is lasting love!"
Let all who revere the Lord say,
"God is lasting love!"

The nations surrounded me:
In God's name, I will crush them!
Surrounded me completely;
In God's name, I will crush them!

Surrounded me like bees,
Blazed like brushwood fire;
In God's name, I will crush them!
(Psalm 118)

In the story of Ishmael, the Teacher describes our society and the impact of our violence on our own lives.

The people of your culture cling with fanatical tenacity to the specialness of man. They want desperately to perceive a vast gulf between man and the rest of creation. This mythology of human superiority justifies their doing whatever they please to the world, just the way Hitler's mythology of Aryan superiority justified his doing whatever he pleased with Europe. But in the end this mythology is not deeply satisfying. The Takers [our society] are a profoundly lonely people. The world for them is enemy territory, and they live in it like an army of occupation, alienated and isolated by their extraordinary specialness.[21]

A destructive separateness persists throughout the second stage of the human story. There is nothing wrong with diversity. Earth revels in its diversity, but separateness ends up pitting one against another and putting one above the other—human over nature, heaven over Earth, divine over human, supernatural over natural, soul over body, spirit over matter, master over slave, ruler over subject, and male over female. Such separateness is the source of the threat to our ongoing existence.

---

21. Daniel Quinn, *Ishmael: An Adventure of the Mind and Spirit,* New York, Bantam Turner Book, 1992, p. 146. The author often uses exclusive language, perhaps in an attempt to dramatize the assumed superiority of the human.

Patriarchy

> Perhaps the primary consequence of humanity's separating itself
> from nature, however, was the estrangement from the feminine
> side of Soul. It made the subsequent deep values of patriarchy
> and hierarchy inevitable, [and] led humanity into an immature
> and distorted expression of power.[22]

During its adolescence, the human species, at least in Western culture,
has been infected with a patriarchal poison that is a powerful obstacle to
our ability to choose life. I asked my friend Bob Veitch, who is both a father and a grandfather, to describe some of the characteristics of adolescence. His description of adolescent sexuality gives us an insight into a patriarchal culture based on "power over" and destructive of relationships.

> Awakening sexuality is a powerful force. The adolescent be-
> comes aware of a powerful need to couple. For men, this drive is
> usually quite separate from any desire to assume adulthood and
> start a family. It is an urge to spill seed. This need often is awak-
> ened before the adolescent boy discovers that girls are people
> and not just forces that awaken sexual desire. Unfortunately,
> many men never grow beyond this state.

As a result of our adolescence, humans are living in a social and an
ecological crisis of unimagined proportions. We attempt to conquer the
Earth; we squander its resources; and we dump our wastes in its oceans,
its atmosphere, and its land. In order to satisfy our own needs we continue to destroy our topsoil, our rain forests, and our water tables. Warfare
and violence stalk our Earth with nation rising against nation, tribe
against tribe, race against race, and neighbor against neighbor. Patriarchy
is a pervasive poison that is eating away our society.

It is not my intention to present a negative critique of the male sex or
of men in general. The male sex is not internally programmed to patriarchy,
and there are many men who are well aware of the dangers of patriarchy
and who are working to overcome its negative impact on our society. The
social institution of patriarchy, however, is so deeply ingrained in many cultures and in institutional religion that most of us are not even aware of it.

The etymology of the word *patriarchy* is simply "father-rule" over an extended family or tribal people. As a social reality, it most likely began very

---

22. Keck, *Sacred Quest,* p. xxii. See also Berry, *The Dream of the Earth,* ch. 11, pp.
138–162.

gradually about the same time as the agricultural revolution and the domestication of animals. In its origins, patriarchy may have met some of the social needs of the time, but it later developed into a negative force in the lives of many humans. Patriarchal culture is characterized by several features:

- The institutionalization of male privilege and power and the accompanying social mythology to account for it.

- The hierarchy of male rulers' control over slave labor, the land, and women.

- The social and cultural inequality of men and women and the assumption that this represents the appropriate (and even God-given) pattern for all social relationships.

- The formation and legitimation of vertical structures of power based on the presumed superiority and inferiority of given classes of people based on gender, race, class, ethnic origin, and sexual orientation.

This patriarchal culture became an integral dimension of the whole of Western civilization. Most of history and literature, whether biblical or cultural, was written by men from a patriarchal viewpoint. This bias deeply infected the biblical stories and the use of religious language, and once a deep value like patriarchy shapes religions, the patriarchal perspective is perceived as divinely ordained, permanently and absolutely. Moreover, traditional speech about God made use of male language and descriptions and became the predominant way to describe God. For centuries such God language was accepted as normative despite its being exclusive and oppressive. Elizabeth Johnson summarizes the negative effects of patriarchal language.

> Whether consciously, or not, sexist God language undermines the human equality of women made in the divine image and likeness. The result is broken community, human beings shaped by patterns of dominance and subordination with attendant violence and suffering...insofar as male-dominant language is honored as the only or the supremely fitting way of speaking about God, it absolutizes a single set of metaphors and obscures the height and depth and length and breadth of divine mystery.[23]

---

23. Elizabeth Johnson, *She Who Is: The Mystery of God in Feminist Theological Discourse,* New York, Crossroad, 1994, p. 18.

Patriarchy is deeply entrenched in our Western culture and in our language, and perhaps even more so in the beliefs and structures presented by the church. The stories contained in the Bible and in our living traditions emerged within the context of the Stage Two adolescent world view, and the church's interpretation of these sources flowed from that same patriarchal viewpoint. Ecclesiastical authority in the West, until very recently, has always been exercised by a male priesthood, a reality unquestioned until very recent times. As we know it ecclesiastical authority was and is the embodiment of patriarchy. That the church developed a patriarchal structure is not surprising because the church emerged in a society that was deeply rooted in patriarchy. We cannot lay blame upon our religious ancestors; they were products of the social and religious milieu in which the church emerged.

"MAN BECOMES GOD"

> Consequently, with a surge of testosterone, the desire for self-determination, the evolutionary necessity for identity, rebellion, and freedom, and with a growing self-confidence and an emboldened ego, the Prodigal Son [humanity] decided to save itself.[24]

As kids in grade school we often played a game called "King of the Mountain." In this game we sought to rule over a small hill or a large pile of snow on the playground or just a circular space designated the "mountain." The one on the hill had to fight against all comers in order to keep the title of "king." On national television, a more "adult" version of this adolescent game is called "Survivor." It is a real, live struggle played out in a wilderness, and the contestants use every trick and every deception to outwit the others and become the million-dollar "survivor." The adolescent needs to prove his or her ego and sense of self-identity, and this requires a constant search to become king of the hill, to be "number one." During Stage Two of the human story, people in our culture tried to prove their sense of independence and control not only by being the survivor but by becoming God.

> The direction and quality of [the Modern Age] character reflected a gradual but finally radical shift of psychological allegiance from God to man, from dependence to independence, from other-worldliness to this world, from the transcendent to the empirical, from myth and belief to reason and fact.[25]

---

24. Keck, *Sacred Quest,* p. 68.
25. Richard Tarnas, *The Passion of the Western Mind,* New York, Harmony Books, 1991, pp. 319–320.

Individualism begins to win out over community as the Western world seeks to establish communities based on an association of individuals. The individual is primary; community is derivative. The struggle for independence leads to a powerful impulse to gain and maintain control over the community. Nationalism and national security become the hallmark of the nations. National identity is primary and the community of nations is derivative. Beginning in the eighteenth century, nationalism leads to colonialism and political imperialism. The European countries, in the name of nationalism, carve up the globe into various spheres of influence without any respect for the ethnic, linguistic, or natural boundaries of the native lands.

> Nationalism, together with progress, democratic freedoms, and limitless rights to private property and economic gain, might be considered the pervasive mystique of the late eighteenth, the nineteenth, and the twentieth centuries... Of primary concern to the nation-state is the territory that it occupies. National boundaries are sacred. To be born within this sacred territory is to be a citizen. The territory must be defended at whatever cost... Membership in a nation community easily becomes more significant than membership in a religious or cultural tradition. The nation-state has indeed become the sacred community.[26]

During these centuries a series of major revolutions took place. They were the result of a growing sense of the human ego and its mental development. The scientific revolution challenged many traditional "truths." The empirical method of experimentation and the discovery of the telescope and microscope enabled scientists to see farther and deeper into the mysteries of universe. "Despite their personal beliefs, they [Galileo and Newton] had initiated a process that shifted power from God to man."[27] Human reason replaced dependence on divine revelation and led to the inevitable debates between science and religion. The industrial revolution challenged our way of living as the family was transformed by the man working outside the home and the woman caring for the home. This revolution, along with exploitation of the natural resources of colonized countries, provided many people with a "higher" standard of living that enabled them to purchase the products of industry. World commerce exploded, and manufacturing became central to our culture and our lives. Finally, the technological revolution with computers and instantaneous

---

26. Swimme and Berry, *The Universe Story*, pp. 212–213.
27. Gabriel Moran, *The Present Revelation: In Quest of Religious Foundations*, New York, Seabury Press, 1972, p. 49.

communications ushered in the Information Age with its vast and as yet untapped pool of knowledge.

The scientific, industrial, and technical world in which we live has produced a nation of materialist consumers with information and products at their fingertips. We live in what Swimme and Berry call "Wonderland," although it is a land of wonders only for a few and its existence can be destructive to the entire Earth. The Wonderland vision is the basis of the advertising that attracts the populace toward ever-increased consumption of products that have been taken violently from the Earth or that react violently with the Earth.[28] Man is the "King of the Mountain." Man has become God. We have reached our pinnacle.

> There was a new optimism about humanity as control over the natural world, which had once held mankind in thrall, appeared to advance in leaps and bounds. People began to believe that better education and improved laws could bring light to the human spirit. This new confidence in the natural powers of human beings meant that people came to believe that they could achieve enlightenment by means of their own exertions. They no longer needed to rely on inherited tradition, an institution, or an elite— or, even, a revelation from God—to discover the truth.[29]

The adolescence of the human race has brought about a world that is separated and divided, a culture that is patriarchal, and a global village where the villagers have become gods. The adolescence of the human race has also produced progress in learning, exploration, agriculture, science and industry, information, and technology, but at what a cost! A cost in oppression, violence, slavery, war, grinding poverty and hunger, environmental exploitation and pollution, and competitiveness always leaving more losers than winners. Yet, without our period of adolescence, perhaps, the human race could never have been able to move on to adulthood. Without the strong sense of self developed in the youth of the human race and without the mental development of the past centuries, the transformation to adulthood would not been possible. It is essential that humans *now* claim their adulthood, not by leaving all the positive dimensions of childhood and adolescence behind, but by learning from the past and moving into a spiritual revolution that can bring integration and wholeness to our lives.

---

28. Swimme and Berry, *The Universe Story,* p. 218.
29. Karen Armstrong, *A History of God,* New York, Alfred A. Knopf, 1993, p. 296.

STAGE THREE: ADULTHOOD—
SPIRITUAL DEVELOPMENT

Before describing the core characteristics of the adulthood of the human, it is important to examine the way in which the planet Earth itself is moving into a new and exciting period of transition. Humanity's future must be seen in the context of the thrilling yet risky future of the evolution not only of the human but also of the entire Earth and the Earth's community of species. This is described by Patricia Mische:

> We are entering a new and dangerous phase in human history and in the Earth's evolution. We can consciously shape the future evolution of the planet. A new maturity is demanded of us. We must become wiser than we've ever been before, for the world is far more complex than our old visions, analyses and structures can accommodate. We must become more conscious and more holistically spiritual than ever before. Our awareness and our spirituality must be attuned to the sacred presence in all life—to the inner workings of the Spirit in the Earth's processes—lest we destroy our own lifeline out of arrogance.[30]

Robert Keck tells us that "the most important thing happening in the world right now is the transformation of humanity's Soul,"[31] and that "spirituality will take center stage. Immature and out-dated notions of God and of religion, however, must die before more mature ones can be born. Old faith must be buried before new faith can be resurrected."[32] Thomas Berry even more forcefully lays out the magnitude of the change that we are already experiencing in our guts even though we are often unconscious of its powerful presence.

> The change that is taking place on the Earth and in our minds is one of the greatest changes ever to take place in human affairs, perhaps *the* greatest, since what we are talking about is not simply another historical change or cultural modification, but a change of geological and biological as well as psychological order of magnitude.[33]

---

30. Patricia Mische, "Towards a Global Spirituality," in *The Whole Earth Papers,* no. 16, 1982, p. 4.

31. Keck, *Sacred Quest,* p. 78.

32. Ibid., p. 73.

33. Berry, *The Dream of the Earth,* p. 11.

Thomas Berry calls this great change the transition from the Cenozoic Era (an era that began about fifty-five million years ago) to the Ecozoic Era. The Cenozoic was the time when the Earth decked itself with marvelous beauty, mysterious diversity, and puzzling complexity. Flowers burst forth in all their gorgeous colors and fantastic shapes, the deciduous trees covered the land, and the tropical rain forests emerged. The air was filled with birds of every size, shape, and color, with all their varied songs and mating rituals. A marvelous diversity of animals began to roam the Earth. There were rodents and bats, monkeys and apes, cats and dogs, seals and fish, gorillas and elephants, horses and cattle—possibly twenty million living species splendidly unfolding in the era.

"The late Cenozoic was a wildly creative period of inspired fantasy and extravagant play. It was a supremely lyrical moment when humans emerged on the scene, quietly, somewhere on the edge of the savanna in northeast Africa."[34] At this stage, the emergence of the human did not greatly impact the Earth or the Earth community. The early humans were not special to their neighbors; they were just one more species among the vast number making up the community of the Earth's creatures. They lived in relative harmony with their environment, learned from it, and shared in its suffering and gradual growth.

But now a distorted myth of progress has brought about a potential destruction of the beauty and marvelous diversity of this era. We will do anything for the sake of progress. There used to be an oft-repeated corporate slogan, "Progress is our most important product." According to the myth, progress will give us a life of plenty and a life of ease, it will give us health and prosperity beyond our imagining, and it will enable us to worship daily at the "Mall of America," the cathedral of conspicuous consumerism.

The myth of progress requires the ongoing conquest of the Earth in order to satisfy the thirst of a consumer society. "The problem is that man's conquest of the world has itself devastated the world. And in spite of all the mastery we've attained, we don't have enough mastery to *stop* devastating the world—or to repair the devastation we've already wrought."[35] Thus the Cenozoic Era comes to its end along with the adolescence of the human species, and our culture is faced with a choice: either to continue the mystique of our plundering industrial society and embrace an even more humanly controlled relationship to the Earth, or to challenge this mystique and awaken to a new consciousness of our mutual relationships within the community of species. A new consciousness will guide our society in transitioning into an Ecozoic Era, moving from

---

34. Berry, *The Great Work,* p. 30.
35. Quinn, *Ishmael,* pp. 80–81.

our human-centered to an Earth-centered norm of reality and value. Swimme and Berry describe the challenge and take us even deeper into the sacred dimension of our dilemma.

> Only a comprehensive commitment to the Ecozoic can effectively counter the mystical commitment of our present commercial-industrial establishments to the Technozoic. There is a special need in this transitional phase out of the Cenozoic to awaken a consciousness of the sacred dimension of the Earth. For what is at stake is not simply an economic resource, it is the meaning of existence itself. Ultimately it is the survival of the world of the sacred...We cannot change the outer world without also changing our inner world. A desolate Earth will be reflected in the depths of the human. The comprehensive objective of the Ecozoic is to assist in establishing a mutually enhancing human presence upon the Earth.[36]

The Earth can move into a new era of "a mutually enhancing human presence upon the Earth" only if the human moves out of adolescence and into the maturity of adulthood. In fact, the qualities of the Ecozoic Era are the same as the core characteristics of adulthood, and, as we look to the future of this transition, we can begin to unfold these qualities and characteristics.

RE-MEMBERING AND RE-INTEGRATING

> The deepest cause of the present devastation is found in a mode of consciousness that has established a radical discontinuity between the human and other modes of being and the bestowal of all rights on the humans. They have reality and value only through their use by the human.[37]

In their search for identity, humans separated themselves from nature, began to seek control *over* nature, and sought to conquer the Earth. Humanity distanced itself from nature and viewed other earthly species as there simply for our use and abuse. In doing so we demeaned ourselves as we have demeaned the Earth. We are alienated from the larger sacred community to which we belong. We are Earthlings, born of the Earth, nourished by the Earth, and finally return to the Earth. In our alienation we cry

---

36. Swimme and Berry, *The Universe Story,* p. 250.
37. Berry, *The Great Work,* p. 4.

out: *Sometimes I feel like a motherless child, sometimes I feel like a motherless child, a long way from home.* But we can re-member all that we have been separated from and re-integrate ourselves in the earthly womb.

> In reality there is a single integral community of the Earth that includes all its component members whether human or other than human. In this community every being has its own role to fulfill, its own dignity, its inner spontaneity. Every being has its own voice. Every being declares itself to the entire universe. Every being enters into communion with other beings. This capacity for relatedness, for presence to other beings, for spontaneity in action, is a capacity possessed by every mode of being throughout the entire universe.[38]

Once we have re-membered the split between the human and nature and have changed from a human-centered view to an Earth-centered view, we experience a new sense of the sacred within the universe community and among all its members. The human community is sacred because of its relationship to the larger planetary community.

> For we will recover our sense of wonder and our sense of the sacred only if we appreciate the universe beyond ourselves as a revelatory experience of that numinous presence whence all things come into being. Indeed, the universe is the primary sacred reality. We become sacred by our participation in this more sublime dimension of the world about us.[39]

This sense of the sacred is deepened immeasurably by the awareness of the new creation story. The flashing forth of the universe led to a process in which the latent potential present at the beginning has gradually been unfolding over billions of years in billions of galaxies, our solar system, and finally our planet Earth. The latent potential of the Earth has gradually unfolded over millions of years and led to the vast array of riches and beauty of our living Earth. In the last two to three million years, humanity has emerged and the Earth has become conscious. And this entire process is actually the unfolding presence of God within the entire universe at every moment.

To be a creature emerging from the inner presence of the Holy God is to be *holy.* The word *holy* describes the reality of goodness, truth, and

---

38. Ibid., p. 4.
39. Ibid., p. 49.

wholeness within the universe whose inner source is God. And human holiness is found in our very being as well as in our conscious awareness of this dynamic power of God within ourselves. Holiness is not something we do or practice or merit, it is something we experience as a divine dimension of the universe. The entire community of the universe is a *Holy Web*[40] because everything is holy now, and the presence of God in this community is the source of holiness to all creatures, including the human. Thomas Aquinas, along with many mystical authors, reaffirms that "the whole universe together participates in the divine goodness and represents it better than any single being whatsoever" (Thomas Aquinas, *Summa Theologica*, Q. 47, Art. 1).

In light of this new sense of the presence, power, and love of God in all things, of God as the source of all being, it is impossible to separate nature and the human from the divine because doing so reduces the human and all of nature to non-being. This does not mean that God and the whole of creation are identical or merged. The God who is the mystery behind all creation is far beyond and other than the whole community of the universe. God and creation are not identical, but they are also not separable. In Christian theology it has become common to separate the natural from the supernatural in order to determine which effects have their source in nature and which are caused directly by God. In an emerging universe, however, every being and every activity flows from the inner presence of God, and there is no way to separate the natural from the supernatural.

The process of re-membering nature and the human into one living community and re-integrating the divine with the human and with nature is the first quality and characteristic of the Ecozoic Era and the adulthood of humanity. This process leads to adulthood and will have a profound effect on the way we approach Jesus in an emerging universe. In the Gospel story Jesus says, "The Father and I are one [inseparable]," and "The Father is greater than I [beyond]" (John 10:30 and John 14:28).

WHOLENESS AND INCLUSIVITY

Now is the time for change, the time for a Soul-level reunion, reconciliation, healing, and whole making. It is the time for us to grow up and remember our innate connection with nature and to remember the essential nature of humanity.[41]

---

40. For a discussion of the Holy Web and its relationship to the church, see my book, *The Holy Web: Church and the New Universe Story.*

41. Keck, *Sacred Quest,* p. 116.

Toward the end of the twentieth century, David Bohm, a prominent physicist, presented a new theory of the dynamics of the universe. This theory is found in his classic work entitled *Wholeness and the Implicate Order.* He developed his theory of the implicate order in answer to what he saw as the "fragmentation of human consciousness," and what I have called adolescent separateness. Bohm writes:

> I would, in this connection, call attention to the general problem of fragmentation of human consciousness . . . It is proposed there that the widespread and pervasive distinctions between people (race, nation, family, profession, etc., etc.), which are now preventing mankind from working together for the common good, and indeed, even for survival, have one of the key factors of their origin in a kind of thought that treats *things* as inherently divided, disconnected, and broken up into yet smaller constituent parts. Each part is considered to be essentially independent and self-existent.
>
> When man[42] thinks of himself in this way, he will inevitably tend to defend the needs of his own "Ego" against those of the others; or if he identifies with a group of people of the same kind, he will defend this group in a similar way. He cannot seriously think of mankind as the basic reality, whose claims come first . . . If he thinks of the totality as constituted of independent fragments, then that is how his mind will tend to operate, but if he can include everything coherently and harmoniously in an overall whole that is undivided, unbroken, and without a border (for every border is a division or break) then his mind will tend to move in a similar way, and from this will flow an orderly action within the whole.[43]

Bohm is searching for a way to discover the inner wholeness within all reality in order to help people ultimately find a sense of wholeness and of holiness despite the apparent fragmentation of the world. He has more to say to us:

> Men have been aware from time immemorial of this state of apparently autonomously existent fragmentation and have often

---

42. As is the case with most authors in past years, Bohm does not use inclusive language. It is my hope that, if he were writing today, he would use language that does not exclude. I have, however, refrained from the pedantic "sic." I will refrain from using "sic" when I quote from other authors.

43. David Bohm, *Wholeness and the Implicate Order,* New York, Routledge & Kegan Paul, 1980, p. x.

projected myths of a yet earlier "golden age," before the split between man and nature and between man and man had yet taken
place. Indeed, man has always been seeking wholeness—mental,
physical, social, individual.[44]

We might ask Bohm how the study of physics and of the natural
world relates to the search for wholeness:

> All this calls attention to the relevance of a new distinction be-
> tween implicate and explicate order. Generally speaking, the
> laws of physics have thus far referred mainly to the explicate
> order. Indeed, it may be said that the principal function of Carte-
> sian coordinates is just to give a clear and precise description of
> explicate order. Now, we are proposing that in the formulation of
> the laws of physics, primary relevance is to be given to the impli-
> cate order, while the explicate order is to have a secondary kind
> of significance.[45]

In order to understand better the meaning of the implicate and explicate order, we can think in terms of the ocean or, rather, for me, Lake
Michigan. I have often camped and vacationed on the eastern shore of
Lake Michigan. In the morning as the sun rises over the sand dunes I
walk along the beach and discover what has been tossed up on the shore
line. Usually there are small pieces of driftwood, some seashells, refuse
that had been cast overboard by boaters, and some dead fish. If there has
been a storm, there are large floating logs and tree branches and occasion-
ally the wreckage of a small boat. Each morning the lake shore is different, since the lake often reclaims much of the debris, although there are
some very big logs that seem to have been there forever.

The explicate order is found in the debris that is cast up on the lake
shore. It is visible and measurable, it comes forth from the depths of the
lake and can return there, and while it is on the shore it is relatively stable. The implicate order is like the hidden depths of the lake out of which
comes the flotsam on the shore. The lake is the source of all that unfolds
on the shore and that which ultimately enfolds everything. Thus, Bohm's
contention is that the reality we perceive with our senses (the debris on
the shore) is explicated from the deeper reality that we cannot perceive
with our senses (the mysterious depths of the lake). The universal implicate order, out of which everything unfolds, gives us the underlying sense

44. Ibid., p. 3.
45. Ibid., p. 150.

of the wholeness and unity of all reality, while the explicate order manifests our diversity.

In summary, David Bohm is proposing that in the formulation of the laws of physics primary relevance is to be given to the implicate order carried by the *holomovement* (the word comes from *holo* meaning *whole* and from *movement* meaning *flux*), while the explicate order with its laws is to have a secondary kind of significance. But what is this holomovement and what are its characteristics? Bohm, here and in other places, describes the holomovement in terms reminiscent of the divine. The holomovement is undefinable and immeasurable; it is one unbroken whole, including the entire universe with all its "fields" and "particles." It is the ground for the existence of everything, including ourselves, and it is an immense ocean of cosmic energy creating a sudden wave pulse from which our "universe" was born billions of years ago. The holomovement is beyond space and time and yet contains within itself all space and time; it is infinite insofar as it goes beyond any limits.

Berry also sees the role of the implicate order and explicate order in the unfolding of the universe when he says: "The flaring forth of the primordial energy carried within itself all that would bring the universe into its present mode of being. The origin moment of the universe was the implicate form of the present as the present is the explicate form of the origin moment."[46]

This sense of wholeness within the implicate order can help to reconcile the apparent separateness of the explicate order. The sense of wholeness will heal the patriarchal separation between male and female and will call for full and equal rights, dignity, and opportunity for men and women in all areas of life, including religion. The separation between master and slave would be seen as totally unacceptable, because no human person has the right to exploit or own another, and no human person should be treated as an object to be used and abused. Violence and war resulting from the separation of nations, races, and ethnic groups would be challenged in all parts of the globe, since the differences are part of the richness of the Earth community. Competition would have to give way to collaboration and inclusivity.

Wholeness and inclusivity comprise the second quality and characteristic of the Ecozoic Era and of human adulthood. Wholeness found in God, the common womb of the universe, can bring us as humans together in a new sense of interdependence. Inclusivity can do away with the fragmentation of human consciousness and the widespread and pervasive feelings of separateness among the peoples of the Earth. The welfare of

---

46. Berry, *The Great Work*, p. 27.

the Earth community depends on welcoming all creatures to the common table and working together for the common good.

In the Gospel parable of the great feast, the master of the house says: "Go out quickly into the streets and alleys of the town and bring in here the poor and the crippled, the blind and the lame" (Luke 14:21).

POWER AND SERVICE

We will discover how essential power is not handed down from on high or conferred on us from external authorities: it is an emerging quality from within the individual and from within relationships between and coalitions of individuals.[47]

All of the adolescent versions of power developed as the inevitable result of humanity's separation from nature and the fracture of the human psyche and human society. Patriarchal and hierarchical manifestations of power began to show up in both political society and in religious communities. Power was conceived as the ability to exercise control over others—the rulers over the ruled, fathers over families, patriarchs over tribes, the clergy over the people. The source of power was found in the physical, psychological, or political strength of the ruler, the father, the patriarch, or the clergyman, and the resultant loss of power in the ruled, the family, the tribe, and the people. Power tended to be an external reality that could be passed on by birth or by law, by violence or by war, or by sheer strength of body or mind.

The movement of humanity into the Ecozoic Era and into adulthood requires a new vision of power. Power, first of all, can be understood as existing within each person and in each member of the Earth community. It flows from the very heart of the Earth and involves the three following basic characteristics of the universe: diversity, interiority or subjectivity, and communion.[48] Over a period of 4.6 billion years the living Earth has evolved with the maximum possible diversity of species and the maximum diversity of races and tribes within the human species. It is only in this diversity that the full beauty and richness of the unfolding presence and power of God can be made manifest. And each and every member of the Earth community has some aspect of interiority and a sense of subjectivity (even the most apparently solid and stubborn rock, at the quantum level, is a dynamic buzz of inner activity). A rock, a mountain, a river, a robin, a horse, all things have a right to be themselves within the larger cosmic web of relationships. Berry says that "every mode of being has in-

---

47. Keck, *Sacred Quest,* p. xxiv.
48. For a discussion of these three characteristics, see my *The Holy Web,* pp. 83–87.

herent rights to their place in this community, rights that come by existence itself."[49] And finally the Earth community has a real thirst for communion. Wherever we look, various species are forming "neighborhoods" and nature emerges as a example of collaboration and interdependence. Every creature great or small has its own inner power of being that is to be shared for the benefit of all.

As humans and as adults we seek the inner power within us and the ability to develop our gifts to the fullest. But beyond that, our power is a power to serve. Bob Veitch of the First Friday Group describes this adult power as follows:

> As children, we accept the world for what it is and ourselves as special within that world. As adolescents, we question who we are and try to resolve that question by making the world satisfy our appetites. And as adults? Do we perhaps come to realize that we are the world? And that appetites, like other natural forces, have their place, but that place is not one of control? Do we begin to understand that, like a good provider, we care for others first, then satisfy our needs? And that the order—first those in our care, then ourselves—extends to all species and all of nature?

Many would challenge Bob by saying that we must first love and care for ourselves so that we are able to help others. That is true, but once we find and love our true selves we are empowered and driven from within to care for others and all species even at the sacrifice of our talents, of our time, and of our material resources. Albert Nolan observes:

> There is no mistaking the two quite different ways in which power and authority are understood and exercised. It is the difference between *domination* and *service*. The power of this new society is not a power which has to *be* served, a power before which a person must bow down and cringe. It is the power which has an enormous influence in the lives of people by being of service to them. It is the power which is so unselfish that it will serve others even by dying for them.[50]

As a society we have the inner power to transform the Earth community and the human dimension of that community, and these questions hover over us and call us to a life of service as communities and individuals:

---

49. Berry, *The Great Work*, p. 115.

50. Albert Nolan, *Jesus before Christianity,* Maryknoll, N.Y., Orbis Books, 1992, p. 85.

- Why is there so much poverty in this world when there are more than adequate resources if only we would consume less and share more with others?

- Why are so many people killed in the name of race, religion, or ethnic background when there is so much beauty and wisdom and diversity to share?

- Why do so many people suffer and die of starvation and hunger when the Earth has superabundant resources to feed all its people?

- Why do we continue to use violence, murder, and warfare to settle our differences when there are many peaceful ways of conflict resolution?

- Why can we not provide every person on this Earth with decent shelter when many people in the first world dwell in conspicuously large and ostentatious homes?

- Why do we allow young girls and teenagers in so many countries to be raped and abused when these young lives are so precious?

- Why do we continue to destroy and pollute the air and the water and the Earth when there are renewable and clean resources that will preserve our environment?

- Why do we continue to assault the Earth and waste its rivers, its topsoil, its rain forests, and its species when we have the technology and sustainable methods of collaborating with rather than conquering our beautiful home for our own benefit?

The answer to these questions is that we lack the collective will to conserve more, consume less, and share our bounty. Humanity has not begun to understand that, having learned to love ourselves, we can care for others first, then satisfy our own needs, and that the order, first those in our care, then ourselves, extends to all species and all of nature. In that way, everybody and every species could have a sufficient abundance and all would be enabled to fulfill their own welfare as they serve others. This is the only pathway toward the Ecozoic Era and true human adulthood. In the Gospel Jesus says: "You know that the rulers of the Gentiles lord it over them, and the great ones make their authority felt. But it shall not be so among you. Rather, whoever wishes to be great among you shall be your servant; whoever wishes to be first among you shall be your slave" (Matthew 20:25-27).

THE WISDOM OF THE AGES

> We need to consider these wisdom traditions in terms of their
> distinctive functioning, in the historical periods of their fluores-
> cence, and in their common support for the emerging age when
> humans will be a mutually enhancing presence of Earth.[51]

The wisdom of the ages emerges from many different sources, and
we desperately need to mine all of these sources as the human community
makes the transition from a Cenozoic Era to an Ecozoic Era and from
adolescence to adulthood. Among these many sources are the following:
the wisdom of the indigenous peoples; the wisdom of the sacred books;
the wisdom of women; the wisdom of classical traditions; the wisdom of
the universe; the wisdom of love.

The Wisdom of the Indigenous Peoples.   The wisdom of the indigenous peoples of the world flows from their intimacy with and participation in the Earth community. Throughout their history they shared in the
lives of plants and animals as if they were neighbors; they knew the
habits and powers of their companions; they asked pardon of the oak tree
and the buffalo before taking their lives and promised to use them only
for food and shelter and warmth. These peoples were deeply immersed in
the ever-renewing sequence of sunrise and sunset, of the change of sea-
sons, and of life and death. The native wisdom was passed on generation
after generation and expressed in the lives of the people and in their elaborate rituals, customs, songs, and arts.

The native peoples had a deep experience of the spirit world and of
the benign and fearsome forces surrounding the human community. Their
stories of the Great Spirit were told in many distinctive ways by the various tribes, and the spirits were seen as personal powers immediately present and influential in human life. Woven within the ceremonial rituals of
the tribal peoples and the stories of their ancestors there is a wealth of
wisdom that is gradually becoming more evident to us. As we listen more
carefully in an honest dialogue with the wisdom of indigenous peoples
we can rediscover a more integral human presence to the Earth and the
more intimate presence of God within creation.

The Wisdom of the Sacred Books.   A deep river of wisdom flows from
the sacred books of various cultures and religions, such as the Hebrew

---

51. Berry, *The Great Work,* p. 176; see also all of ch. 16, pp. 176–195.

and Christian Scriptures, the Muslim Koran, and the Book of Mormon. These writings often describe the miraculous founding of the religion, its struggles, its triumphs, and its heroes and heroines, in a process seen to be under the guidance of God. Among the various literary forms used in the sacred books are stories with or without a historical basis, poetry, prophecies, folk tales, wisdom sayings, parables, and more.

Many of these books have been produced by believing communities whose wisdom has been handed down over generations in an oral tradition, constantly reinterpreted in the light of subsequent events, and gradually added to and weeded out. Oral traditions containing the lived experience, thoughts, and interpretations of many generations are finally distilled and put in writing. The sacred writings are seen as embodying the shared wisdom of ancestors and of God, and are treasured by the community as a guide for its ongoing life. These books are, of course, limited by their unique cultural, historical, and linguistic roots, but they are a profound source of perennial wisdom which we ignore at our own peril and in which we can find helpful guidance as we move into our twenty-first-century transition to adulthood and an Ecozoic Era.

The Wisdom of Women. In any society, civilization, religion, or organization, the voice that is most needed is the voice that has not been heard. For the most part, women's voices have not been heard during the adolescence of the human race; their voices have been stifled by the rise of patriarchy with its use of physical and psychological domination to silence women. One clear example is the astounding fact that the United States, the beacon of democracy and freedom, refused to allow women to vote in political elections until the 1920s. Now, at the beginning of a new century, women are asserting their personal dignity and natural rights in all of human affairs whether socio-economic, political, scientific, or religious. And the whole of society is challenged to listen to and rejoice in the wisdom of women so long repressed.

Women's voices must also be heard because women bring certain characteristics, such as a relational view of the world, a more personal sense of values, a cooperative spirit, a taste for beauty, and a nourishing and creative quality to life. Women have an experience of the rhythms of life in the monthly cycle of their bodies as well as the sense of bodily connectedness and maternal nurturance through the processes of gestation, birth, and nursing of a newborn. These are values that have been, by and large, lost in patriarchy. The specific wisdom of women seems to flow out of women's intimacy with and presence to the body and to Mother Earth. Rather than in any way minimizing the intellectual capacity of women, these qualities add a specific and valuable dimension to their intellectual contribution.

Women's wisdom knows well the extravagant experience of their bodily birthing and of the continual physical birthing within the Earth community. In its closeness to the Earth, women's wisdom recognizes that existence is a mutual dependence on a diversity of components. The process of journeying to adulthood in the human story is a single enterprise that brings together women and men, young people and elders, natives and newcomers of all races, farmers and business people, teachers and students, artists and performers, all sharing their particular experiences, gifts, and creativity. Nothing can become itself without the support of everything else, and at this point in the human story the wisdom of women is essential.

The Wisdom of the Classical Traditions.   The various classical traditions of the world discovered, preserved, and developed a deep well of wisdom from which our ancestors and we too could draw. So many and so complex are these sources of wisdom that we can only list some of them in order to get a sense of their depth and breadth.

Traditions such as the Hindu tradition in India focus on the unity of the deepest self of the universe with the inner self of the human. The Buddhist tradition teaches a universe revealed as transient, sorrowful, and unreal and this tradition is expressed through universal compassion. The Chinese experience the inner rhythms of the cosmos and a deep sense of the unity of the universe. These Eastern traditions have become very influential in modern Western culture.

The classical wisdom of the Western world is rooted in the biblical revelation focusing on a monotheistic personal deity and direct communication with this supreme being. The Greek humanist tradition can be found in literary and artistic accomplishments and is articulated by teachers and philosophers, especially Plato and Aristotle. In Europe in the twelfth and thirteenth centuries there emerged a new classical wisdom based on biblical writings, Greek humanist philosophy, and Roman imperial law. This Christian intellectual tradition flowered in the universities founded during the medieval period with the introduction of Aristotelian philosophy into the schools and its incorporation into the theological writings of Thomas Aquinas, among others. There was a growing confidence in the reasoning processes of the human mind and a new commitment to the search for truth. That commitment in the European world also formed a foundation for the succeeding age of science.

The Wisdom of the Universe

The universe carries in itself the norm of authenticity of every spiritual as well as physical activity within it. The spiritual and the physical are two dimensions of the single reality that is the universe itself.[52]

At its heart the universe unfolds from within and that reality is the source of its message of wisdom. From the flashing forth of the universe to the formation of galaxies and the solar system to the emergence of this great and beautiful Earth of ours we experience a vast embryogenesis from the inside out. The universe shows us a system which is self-organizing, unfolding, and emerging, resulting in a dynamic web of relationships in which every dimension has a part to play. According to the self-organizing principle, systems seem to have an innate sense of direction and guidance that enables them to change and restructure themselves from within. This dynamic is found in all aspects of the universe. Margaret Wheatley says that such a system "possesses the capacity for spontaneously emerging structures, depending on what is required. It is not locked into any one form but instead is capable of organizing information in the structure that best suits the present need."[53] As we will see later, this wisdom leads us to a deeper image of God's presence within every dimension of the universe and a deeper awareness of God's power unfolding within the universe.

Moreover, the universe is engaged in an irreversible process in which time is experienced not only as a recurring, seasonal renewal but also as an emerging cosmogenesis. There is a flow to the universe story, a directional flow that cannot be repeated and always flows on and on. The simple images of creation, fall, redemption, and a second coming are now inadequate as a human story. An emerging universe calls for a deeper metaphor that embraces a dynamic self-organizing world ripening from within over billions of years. Thomas Berry tells us that "the primary educator as well as the primary lawgiver and primary healer would be the natural world itself. The integral Earth community would be a self-educating community within the context of a self-educating universe."[54] And in this self-educating community of species we find the wisdom of the universe.

The Wisdom of Love

Our discussion of wholeness would be incomplete if we were only to look at scientific evidence and spiritual intuition from the outside. Wholeness is not fully understood without understand-

---

52. Berry, *The Great Work,* pp. 49–50.

53. Margaret J. Wheatley, *Leadership and the New Science,* San Francisco, Berrett-Koehler Publishers, 1994, p. 91.

54. Berry, *The Great Work,* p. 71.

ing and living the internal power and energy of what makes everything whole—love.[55]

The wisdom of love transforms the individual as well as the society and all of its interrelationships at the deepest level. Love is central to the entire universe and is the mutual attraction that undergirds the entire Holy Web. This transformation is so deep that Sam Keen rightly says:

> Love is not primarily something we *make* or *do*, but something we *are*. We do not define it so much as it defines us. Before it is ever manifest as an activity or behavior, love is that impulse, motivation, or energy that links us to the whole web of life. Eros is the bond in the ecological communion within which we live.[56]

Mutual love within the human community, when it is passionate, creative, and life giving, is fulfilling and nurturing of all involved in it. According to the ancient saying, "*Amor est diffusivum sui*," the aura of love spreads out in all directions. Mutual love both transforms us and calls us to the deep intimacy of a shared life and a responsible commitment for both the present and the future. The task of the lover is to be an agent of healing at every level "by becoming passionate and vowing fidelity to concrete relationships, persons, institutions, and places."[57] Love heals the wounds of our adolescence and opens us to the presence and power of God who is the inner source of our adulthood. "Beloved, let us love one another, because love is of God; everyone who loves is begotten by God and knows God" (1 John 4:7).

SUMMARY AND CONCLUSIONS

What is the source of our transition from adolescence to adulthood, from the Cenozoic Era to the Ecozoic Era? In an emerging universe this transition can only come from within. It will call for an inner change of heart flowing from the unfolding presence of God within us. Robert Keck describes this transformation.

> The transformation of humanity's Soul happens from the inside out, from the bottom up. It is happening within you and me. It is

---

55. Keck, *Sacred Quest,* p. 169.
56. Sam Keen, *The Passionate Life: Stages of Loving,* San Francisco, Harper & Row, 1983, pp. 24–25.
57. Ibid., p. 209.

a fundamental shift in humanity's collective depths, experienced in each one of us as a special-case scenario. Every one of our souls is participating in the transformation of humanity's Soul, and to be aware of it in our own lives, we need only awaken to our depths.

It is not a social program handed down from some "planner" sitting on the top of some bureaucratic ivory tower. It is not a religious program defined and described by a religious hierarchy. No leader of any kind needs to give permission to initiate these changes. This transformation of Soul is a natural and organic process within the deepest possible levels of human existence, and it works its way to the surface of our everyday lives and changes the way we experience the world...Pay attention to your depths.[58]

Despite all the ambiguity and unsureness, it is time for the human to move from adolescence into the maturity of adulthood. We now have a new story of the universe. We have gained knowledge about the universe that leaves us in awe. Our advanced technology has given us a new way of seeing both outer and inner space. It has given us the potential for a whole new relationship with the Earth and with each other through our instantaneous worldwide communication and our sense of the global village.

Adulthood also calls us to a new sense of our relationship with the whole of creation. We are no longer called to conquer the Earth or to rule over our companion creatures. The evolutionary process calls for a new stance toward the rest of creation by recognizing the dignity and rights of the whole community of species. We are called to live in harmony with the universe, and we are called to live out in new ways the web of relationships that surrounded our ancestors and surrounds us still.

Adulthood means making responsible decisions, not simply for our own benefit but for the common good of all the Earth and its community of species. The human has a significant role in the future evolution of our Earth.

The Earth that directed itself instinctively in its former phases seems now to be entering a phase of conscious decision through its human expression. This is the ultimate daring venture for the Earth, this confiding its destiny to human decision, the bestowal upon the human community of the power of life and death over its basic life systems.[59]

---

58. Keck, *Sacred Quest*, pp. 83–84.
59. Berry, *The Dream of the Earth*, p. 19.

The Earth seems to have given over its future to us and our decision-making powers, but it has not left the human without guidance.

> What is needed on our part is the capacity for listening to what the Earth is telling us. As a unique organism the Earth is self-directed. Our sense of the Earth must be sufficiently sound so that it can support the dangerous future that is calling us. It is a decisive moment. Yet we should not feel that we alone are determining the future course of events. The future shaping of the community depends on the entire Earth in the unity of its organic functioning, on its geological and biological as well as its human members.[60]

The universe continues to unfold in an irreversible time-development process that has brought us to this critical moment in the life of the Earth. The transformation ahead of the human race is well described by Thomas Berry.

> The transformation of human life indicated in this transition from the Cenozoic to the Ecozoic Era affects our sense of reality and values at such a profound level that it can be compared only to the great classical religious movements of the past. It affects our perception of the origin and meaning of existence itself. It might possibly be considered as a metareligious movement since it involves not simply a single segment of the human community but the entire human community. Even beyond the human order, the entire geobiological order of the planet is involved.[61]

In a time of such profound transition, it behooves us to look more closely at the emerging universe in which we live and which we have so recently discovered. Before we can answer the question of Jesus in this emerging universe, it is imperative that we answer the following three questions: What is the meaning of God in an emerging universe? What is the meaning of revelation in an emerging universe? What is the meaning of salvation in an emerging universe?

---

60. Ibid., p. 23.
61. Berry, *The Great Work,* pp. 84–85.

2

AN EMERGING UNIVERSE

GOD IN AN EMERGING UNIVERSE

The words "emerging universe" may sound strange to many people. It is not a common phrase in theology or in modern science or, for that matter, in the news media and everyday conversation. We might say this phrase has just "emerged" in recent years, primarily among people who are interested in the evolutionary process as found in the new universe story. It is a phrase that describes the unfolding of the universe over about fifteen billion years from the flashing forth of the universe to the formation of billions of galaxies and stars to the birth of our solar system that contains among other planets the Earth. This Earth became our mother and our home. But what does the phrase "emerging universe" really mean?

Perhaps the best way of explaining it is to compare an "emerging universe" with a "created universe." When we say that the universe was created we are often describing a process in which God creates the world out of nothing and all at once. The word "created" stresses the transcendence of God as well as the continuing presence of God; it implies a God who creates and produces his creation from the outside as the efficient cause of everything. This God rules the world through a plan called "Divine Providence," and creatures are secondary causes in carrying out God's plan. A certain separation between God and both nature and the human is found in a created universe, and the transcendence and separation of God require the use of mediators in God's actions, such as angels, the Word of God, and the Wisdom of God.

When we say that the universe is "emerging," we are describing a process in which the whole universe is emerging in a time-development sequence from within. This kind of language stresses the immanence of God; it implies a God who acts from the inside out with internal causality. Because of the immediate internal presence of the power, energy, and love of God as the source of all things, there is no need for mediators.

There are common elements in the concepts of a created universe and an emerging universe insofar as both hold that God is the source of all being and is present to all creatures. The difference lies in *how* God is the source and *how* God is present. In an emerging universe God is the source of all being, not by an external efficient causality, but by an internal causality. This is a new concept flowing from the quantum make-up of the universe, and it will be explained more clearly as we go along. In an emerging universe the inner presence of God is found in the very unfolding and emerging of the universe and not in an external divine plan. As Ivone Gebara says, "The model that leads us to look for the grounding of this world somewhere outside it—and seeks assistance from supportive divinities—would appear to be destined for oblivion."[1]

How, then, does the universe emerge and what are the dynamics of this process? The answer to this question will come from a discussion of the holon theory, the quantum nature of being, the characteristics of the emerging process, and the emergence of human consciousness.

THE THEORY OF HOLONS

Throughout the centuries philosophers have searched for the depth of reality, and, as a budding scientist and philosopher, I too was led through that search. Some thinkers proposed that all reality was made up of individual "atoms." Others suggested the four elements (earth, air, fire, and water), and still others came up with "matter" and "form" as the intrinsic meaning of reality. More recently, theorists believed that the modern discovery of the atomic elements gave us the ultimate building block of all reality. Then the atom was smashed, and the various sub-atomic particles and waves took over as the ultimate reality.

But now a new twist on this search for the ultimate meaning of reality is found in the theory of holons that describes the inner relationships fundamental to the universe. A holon is not a kind of matter or a particle or a wave or a process; a holon is a whole/part. The theory, as integrated and presented by Ken Wilber, states that whatever exists in the universe is a whole/part. Every whole is also a part, and every part is also a whole. This is true in the realms of matter, of life, and of mind. In his book entitled *Sex, Ecology, Spirituality* Wilber is a primary expounder of the theory of holons as a way of describing the web of relationships in the universe. In his introduction he says:

---

1. Ivone Gebara, *Longing for Running Water: Ecofeminism and Liberation,* Minneapolis, Minn., Fortress Press, 1999, p. 7.

This is a book about holons—about wholes that are parts of other wholes, indefinitely. Whole atoms are parts of molecules; whole molecules are parts of cells; whole cells are parts of organisms, and so on. Each *whole* is simulaneously a *part*, a whole/part, a holon. And reality is composed, not of things nor processes nor wholes nor parts, but of whole/parts, of holons. We will be looking at holons in the cosmos, in the bios, in the psyche, and in theos; and at the evolutionary thread that connects them all, unfolds them all, embraces them all, endlessly.[2]

I do not think Wilber or anyone else can actually prove the holon theory. It is too basic a premise. One of my philosophy professors once said that if he saw a bird in a bush, there was no way he could prove it. He could just point to it, and you either saw it or you didn't. It is the same with holons. We can only point to them, describe them, and discern their patterns and capacities. Then you either perceive holons or you don't. If the theory makes sense to you in terms of your experience, you will indeed see the relevance of holons in science and in an emerging universe.

Wilber contends that "holons display four fundamental capacities: self-preservation, self-adaptation, self-transcendence, and self-dissolution."[3] I will give a brief explanation of each of these four capacities using the example of hydrogen, oxygen, and water.

Self-preservation.   All holons seek to preserve their own particular wholeness or autonomy, and all holons differ in their level of stability. Oxygen is a whole with various electrons and protons as its parts, and it seeks to maintain its own individuality. But oxygen tends to be unstable and easily combines with other elements to form a new holon such as water. On the other hand, water, as a holon, maintains its wholeness and autonomy with much greater stability. Thus, holons often exist by virtue of their interlinking relationship, but they are not defined by their role as a part. Its intrinsic form, or pattern, or structure is what defines oxygen, not its relationship to hydrogen or water.

Self-adaptation.   A holon functions not only as a self-preserving whole but also as a part of a larger whole, and in its capacity as a part it must adapt or accommodate itself to other holons. Hydrogen is a whole, but it is also a part when combined with oxygen to make water. As a part, it

---

2. Ken Wilber, *Sex, Ecology, Spirituality: The Spirit of Evolution,* Boston, Shambhala, 1995, p. viii.

3. Ibid., p. 40.

needs to adapt to its relationship with oxygen and with the new holon of water. Another example is found in two autonomous people who enter marriage and thus form a new social holon. They are defined as wholes in their autonomous selves, but in their role as partners in a marriage they are called to fit into and adapt to a new environment.

Thus self-preservation and self-adaptation can set up two opposed tendencies in a holon.

> We can just as well think of these two opposed tendencies as a holon's *agency* and *communion*. Its agency—its self-asserting, self-preserving, assimilating tendencies—expresses its *wholeness*, its relative autonomy; whereas its communion—its participatory, bonding, joining tendencies—expresses its *partness*, its relationship to something larger.[4]

Self-transcendence.   When different holons come together to form a new and different holon, there is a creative twist on what has gone before. When hydrogen and oxygen come together to form water, something radically new emerges. Two gases come together to form a liquid. When two people come together in marriage, the whole is something new and creative, and the character of the new holon cannot be predicted simply on the basis of the character of the two people. Self-transcendence introduces a vertical dimension to our sense of a holon, one that cuts at a right angle to the horizontal relationship between self-preservation and self-adaptation.

> Self-transcendence is simply a system's capacity to reach beyond the given and introduce some measure of novelty, a capacity without which, it is quite certain, evolution would never, and could never, have even gotten started. Self-transcendence, which leaves no corner of the universe untouched (or evolution would have *no point* of departure), means nothing more—and nothing less—than that the universe has an intrinsic capacity to go beyond what went before.[5]

Self-dissolution.   Just as holons are capable of building up through transformation and self-transcendence, they are able to break down. Water can break down into its component parts of oxygen and hydrogen, and a marriage can break down because of various conflicts, struggles, and loss of cohesion. The general direction of evolution and of human society leads to self-transcendence, but the reality of self-dissolution is also

---

4. Ibid., p. 41.
5. Ibid., p. 44.

an integral part of nature and society. Yet even self-dissolution is ambiguous because, while it leads to the dissolution of one holon, it can also prepare the way to new life and a deeper sense of self-transcendence. Wilber concludes his discussion of the four capacities of holons by saying, "Preserve or accommodate, transcend or dissolve—the four very different pulls on each and every holon in the Kosmos."[6] (See the schema below.)

CAPACITIES OF HOLONS

SELF-TRANSCENDENCE

Self-transcendence is a transformation that results in something novel and emerging—different wholes have come together to form a new and different whole. There is an emergent twist on what has gone before.

SELF-PRESERVATION

All holons display a capacity to preserve their individuality, to preserve their own particular wholeness or autonomy.

SELF-ADAPTATION

A holon functions not only as a self-preserving whole but also as a part of a larger whole, and in its capacity as a part it must adapt or accommodate itself to other holons.

SELF-DISSOLUTION

Holons that are built up through vertical self-transcendence can also break down. Not surprisingly, when holons "dissolve" or "come unglued," they tend to do so along the same vertical sequence in which they were built up.

6. Ibid., p. 46.

Because of the self-transcendent capacity of holons, it is evident that *holons emerge*—first atoms, then molecules, and then cells. Emerging holons are always in some ways novel, surprising, and indeterminate. They possess properties that cannot be strictly and totally deduced from their components. There is no way to predict from a study of hydrogen and oxygen that when these two atoms are combined the new holon will emerge as water. We can never know what a holon will do next, but we do know that in some way the emerging holon will be of a more complex or deeper level, because the new holon is a whole containing within itself its constituent parts.

> Organisms contain cells, but not vice versa; cells contain mole-cules, but not vice versa; molecules contain atoms, but not vice versa. And it is that *not vice versa*, at *each* stage, that constitutes unavoidable asymmetry and hierarchy (holarchy). Each deeper or higher holon embraces its junior predecessors and then *adds* its own new and more encompassing pattern or wholeness.[7]

Other modern scientists describe the emergence of an unpredictable yet deeper level of holons as a hierarchical or holarchical order. I prefer the term *holarchy*, because this emergence flows from an ordering of holons and at the same time the term avoids the negative dimensions of the term *hierarchy*. The following is a typical example:

> Reality, in the modern conception, appears as a tremendous hier-archical [holarchical] order of organized entities, leading, in a su-perposition of many levels, from physical and chemical to bio-logical and sociological systems. Such hierarchical [holarchical] structure and combination into systems of ever higher order, is characteristic of reality as a whole and is of fundamental impor-tance especially in biology, psychology and sociology.[8]

Bob Veitch of the "First Friday Group" talks about the dynamism of holons.

> A property not discussed but I believe equally true is that holons are dynamic, i.e., always in the process of change and that this tendency to change increases with significance. Any social holon changes with the addition of each new member or the loss of any

---

7. Ibid., p. 49.
8. L. von Bertalanffy, *General System Theory,* New York, Braziller, 1969, p. 74.

member. Take away one whole/part and all relationships are re-defined. Add a new whole/part and the same is true. Now, we may want to say that with any change we have, in effect, a new holon—just as adding a hydrogen to H_2O creates heavy water with considerably different properties from normal water. Taking an oxygen away from CO_2 likewise creates a whole new molecule with properties that are very different and not at all hospitable to humans.

The four characteristics of holons—self-preservation, self-adaptation, self-transcendence, and self-dissolution—give to an emerging universe its inner dynamic evolutionary power and direction.

THE QUANTUM NATURE OF BEING

An even more mysterious aspect of the universe lies hidden in the quantum make-up of all things. Danah Zohar explains:

The most revolutionary, and for our purposes the most important statement that quantum physics makes about the nature of matter, and perhaps being itself, follows from its description of the wave/particle duality—the assertion that all being at the sub-atomic level can be described equally well either as solid particles, like so many minute billiard balls, or as waves, like undulations of the surface of the sea.[9]

Quanta (minute bundles of energy) can be seen as either waves or particles, and the mystery gets even more complex. According to quantum theory as explicated by Zohar, "both the wavelike and the particlelike aspects of being must be considered when trying to understand the nature of things, and . . . it is the duality itself that is most basic. Quantum 'stuff' is, essentially, *both* wavelike and particlelike, simultaneously."[10]

Quantum stuff is not *either* wavelike *or* particlelike but it is *both* wavelike *and* particlelike *simultaneously*. Moreover, there is strong evidence that the relationality and interaction among things at the quantum level are dependent on whether a system is more or less in a "particle" or a "wave" state. Particles are more like separate individuals; they are anti-social; they are the self-preservation capacity of holons. Waves are more

---

9. Danah Zohar, *The Quantum Self: Human Nature and Consciousness Defined by the New Physics,* New York, Quill/William Morrow, 1990, p. 25.
    10. Ibid.

correlated and behave more like a group; they love parties; they are the self-adaptation capacity of holons. This powerful relationality of all things flowing from the wave dimension of matter can profoundly impact our vision of reality. Quantum physics tells us that there is a dynamic web of relationships within the whole of the universe.

The quantum view of the universe also gives us a new sense of what we have called *internal causality*. When Newtonian billiard balls are bouncing around on a table, they do have a kind of relationship to each other, but it is an *external* relation. When electrons are bouncing around in a box, they relate in an entirely different way. Their wave aspects interfere with each other and overlap. They "merge, drawing the electrons into an existential relationship where their actual inner qualities—their masses, charges, and spins as well as their positions and momenta—become indistinguishable from the relationship among them."[11] This brings about a deeper relationship of *internal causality*.

This is evident in the case of the intimacy of lovers. Zohar explains that "in intimacy, I and you appear to influence *each other*; we seem to 'get inside' each other and change each other *from within* in such a way that 'I' and 'you' become a 'we.' This 'we' that we experience is not just 'I *and* you'; it is a new thing in itself, a new unity."[12] In other words, two lovers are changed internally by their love and, in a real sense, become a new being, a new holon with its own unique characteristics. Sometimes this new reality is expressed by a couple who take a new name that is different from either of their previous names. Sometimes this new holon becomes enfleshed in a child born of their intimacy, or in giving birth to a life-enhancing project or theory.

Perhaps the most powerful dimension of the theory of holons and the quantum dimension of the universe is seen when the stress between self-preservation (the particle aspect) and self-adaptation (the wave aspect) of any holon reaches a critical point and actualizes the capacity for self-transcendence. A poignant human example of this dynamic is found at times of personal crisis or loss, such as a divorce or the death of a child. This creates such a radically different external environment and such profound stress that the person's very identity is at stake. It also can be a moment of self-transcendence when a new dimension of the person's identity emerges. In self-transcendence something novel emerges, resulting in a new and different holon. This is what is meant by an emerging universe, and this internal power to renew and transcend self is found in all holons in all dimensions of the universe.

---

11. Ibid., p. 99.
12. Ibid., p. 128.

THE CHARACTERISTICS OF THE EMERGING PROCESS

According to Thomas Berry, the self-transcendence of holons that is the emerging process "is neither random nor determined but creative. Just as in the human order, creativity is neither a rational deductive process nor the irrational wandering of the undisciplined mind but the emergence of beauty as mysterious as the blossoming of a field of daisies out of the dark Earth."[13] We can experience this kind of creativity in working with clay. The artistic creation is neither random, since the artist has an inner idea of what she wants to create, nor is it determined, since the outcome will depend on the dynamic relationship between the artist and the clay. The sculpture emerges from the creativity of the artist and the limitations of the clay. Thus the emerging process is open to uncertainty and creativity based on the inner limitations found in holon theory.

Similarly, the emergence of new holons is always in some sense novel. The unlikely emergence of water as a liquid from two gases, oxygen and hydrogen, illustrates the novelty of the universe. However, the emergence of holons is not random, since there is a direction in this emergence—organisms contain cells, but not vice versa; cells contain molecules, but not vice versa; molecules contain atoms, but not vice versa. These form what can be called *nested* or *growth* holarchies in which the more complex and deeper holons enfold or nest their predecessors within themselves because an organism contains within itself cells, molecules, and atoms. On the other hand, the more simple holons are the more fundamental, because without atoms there could be no molecules, cells, or organisms. Therefore, there is a certain order or "plan" built into holons and into the universe. Each successive level transcends and embraces its more simple holons in a completely new way. The emerging process is neither random nor determined but creative, and without this process there would be no novelty and no evolution.

The ongoing emergence of the human species is likewise neither random nor determined but creative. The future of the human presence on this Earth will unfold in ways that are unpredictable, and this unfolding is likely to differ from one cultural or national or geographical environment to another. Events such as the disastrous attack on the World Trade Center and the Pentagon may move the American people and the human race toward an escalation of violence and a deeper divisiveness or toward a recognition of our interdependence and the mutual vulnerability within

---

13. Berry, *The Great Work*, p. 31.

the human community. Such events can even impact the whole ecosystem of the Earth on which the human race depends. How will different cultures, religious groups, and nations react to these events? There is no essentialist's model of the future of the human race, nor is the continuing presence of humans on the Earth inevitable.

Bob Veitch, in making an observation on this matter, said:

> The emerging process is neither planned nor random. Instead it unfolds, building on itself, gathering momentum and taking shape from what comes before but never predicting what will come next. The act of creating is not random because it has a beginning and thereafter one thing builds on another. There is a string of relationships from the first act to the last. This is not to say, "after this, therefore because of this" but rather to say, "without this, there is no after this."

The emerging process also challenges our sense of time. Throughout most of human history people perceived the movement of time as a cyclical and ever-renewing process, with season following season in a continual pattern. According to Robert Keck,

> The ancient Greeks, astrologers, as well as native and indigenous people began with assuming that time ran around in circles . . . After all we had no science back then that contradicted our primary experience of daily, monthly, and annual cycles within cycles within cycles . . . Time and change, it appeared, repeated in a timely fashion, so that the fundamental structure of the universe remained essentially timeless, stable, predictable, and dependable.[14]

The commonly held view of an "all at once" creation of the universe is shattered by the modern experience of a universe that has been emerging for about fifteen billion years. The universe is no longer perceived only as a seasonal cycle of realities that keep their basic identity, or as a fixed space with planets and stars moving in unchangeable orbits. The universe is now revealed as an irreversible emerging process, more a cosmogenesis than a cosmos. And this process has a direction as is manifested in the self-transcendent quality of holons. The novelty of the universe appears as an irreversible process, always changing and renewing the entire web of relationships as the universe moves toward an unknown future. The cosmos, especially for humans, still retains a certain stability in the ever-recurring celestial cycles of the solar system, but these now must be

---

14. Keck, *Sacred Quest,* p. 233.

understood in the deeper terms of an irreversible emerging process that guides the entire universe.

THE EMERGENCE OF HUMAN CONSCIOUSNESS

As a student in the 1950s and as a teacher in the 1960s I held the opinion that evolution was compatible with Christian theology with the exception of the transition from non-living to living beings and the transition to human life and the creation of the "soul." In both of these instances, a created universe calls for the direct intervention of God, but in an emerging universe there is no necessity for such a divine intervention. In an emerging universe everything that eventually emerges is already present in a latent stage in the presence and love of God. The beautiful Earth gradually unfolds from within with its non-living and living beings and with the emergence of the human in which the Earth becomes conscious of itself and its source in the loving presence of God.

How is it possible that human consciousness can emerge without some intervention by God? Recent developments in the field of natural science and a deeper understanding of cosmology provide some clues. Danah Zohar speaks of "the possibility that consciousness, like matter, emerges from the world of quantum events...the two though wholly different from each other, have a common 'mother' in quantum reality."[15] Evidence presented in the new story of the universe paints a picture of the radical unity of all things moving forward with an inner drive toward greater complexity and fuller expression. The planet Earth takes its place in the solar system with the gradual shaping of its lands and seas and atmosphere. Living creatures begin to emerge and swim and crawl and run and fly, and finally the Earth becomes conscious in the human.

> The law of complexity-consciousness reveals that ever more intricate physical combinations, as can be traced in the evolution of the brain, yield ever more powerful forms of spirit. Matter, alive with energy, evolves to spirit. While distinctive, human intelligence and creativity rise out of the very nature of the universe, which is itself intelligent and creative. In other words, human spirit is the cosmos come to consciousness.[16]

If human consciousness emerges from the potentiality of the universe, then there must be a way in which consciousness is latent in the whole evo-

---

15. Zohar, *The Quantum Self,* p. 23.
16. Elizabeth Johnson, *Women, Earth, and Creator Spirit,* New York, Paulist Press, 1993, p. 37.

lutionary process. We are closer to the Earth than we had ever before imagined. Just as water emerges from hydrogen and oxygen and transcends its parts, becoming a new holon, the human emerges from the Earth and transcends its parts, becoming a new holon—the conscious human person.

In discussing holons above, we noted three of the capacities of holons as self-preservation, self-adaptation, and self-transcendence. We can use these capacities to understand human emergence as well. As a deeper awareness gradually emerges within living creatures, there is a tendency toward self-preservation founded in the particle dimension of reality as well as a tendency to self-adaptation founded in the wave dimension of reality that tends toward interrelationships. At a particular point, this tension between preservation and adaptation gives rise to self-transcendence and the emergence of a new holon, human consciousness and the human person. "We must accept that unless consciousness is something that just suddenly emerges, just gets added on with no apparent cause, then it was there in some form all along as a basic property of the constituents of all matter."[17]

Having described the various characteristics of an emerging universe, what then is the ultimate source of the gradually emerging universe? From whence come the energy, power, and love that unfolded in such newness as giant galaxies, the wonderful solar system, the beautiful planet Earth with all its creatures, and very recently the emergence of the human race on Earth? For me there can be only one answer. God is the ultimate source of the whole evolutionary process. God does not act as an external cause of the universe, but as an internal cause of the unfolding of the mysterious web of relationships found everywhere and of every holon in the entire universe. And *how* does God act in this emerging universe? All the evidence leads us to a sense of a God acting and unfolding from within as the immediate inner source of all that is.

This is not to say that the universe is God. This is not a veiled version of pantheism. Our loving God is clearly other than and infinitely more than the universe, but God is also inseparable from every being in the universe. Just as matter at the quantum level is both particlelike and wavelike simultaneously, so within an emerging universe God is both immanent and transcendent simultaneously.

As noted earlier, there are common elements in the ideas of a created universe and an emerging universe insofar as both hold that God is the source of all being and is present to all creatures. However, there is a profound difference in how God acts and how God is present. This difference is illustrated in the way that the created universe sees a need for the intervention of God as an external cause, for example, in the creation of the human soul. We are not denying the creation of the soul by God. However,

---

17. Zohar, *The Quantum Self,* p. 58.

the emerging universe goes much deeper in seeing the unfolding of the entire universe as well as of the human race not as an intervention of God, but as the inner unfolding of God's immediate presence in all things as an internal cause. Thus, the emerging universe places before us the concept of a God unfolding in all of creation. In this context, the emergence of the entire human person is the result of the internal emerging presence and extravagant love of God that bring forth a creature who is able to return that love in a freely chosen way. This way of understanding creation gives us a deeper personal awareness of the intimate presence of God within us and of the internal unity between the human person and the entire human race.

An emerging universe with a deeper awareness of God's presence within the universe and within ourselves calls us to a new approach and a new understanding of revelation and salvation, which are two fundamental dimensions of the intimate presence of God unfolding within human consciousness. A created universe describes a process that is time constrained, namely, a creation that takes place all at once, and a process that flows from God as an extrinsic cause. In accord with the concept of a created universe, revelation in a created universe takes place within a definite time period. In my theological studies during the 1960s revelation was limited to the biblical times up to the death of the last apostle. No new revelation was expected, only a deeper understanding of what has been revealed, and this revelation was a gift directly from God. Likewise, salvation in a created universe has a certain time constraint. Salvation, in its objective sense, was accomplished once and for all by Jesus Christ through his death and resurrection. This salvation, which flows directly from God, is appropriated subjectively by all peoples, both those who lived before Christ and those who came after him.

How will this understanding of revelation and salvation be reinterpreted within the context of our twenty-first-century awareness of an emerging universe? An understanding of revelation and salvation in an emerging universe is essential to theology in the twenty-first century and to any discussion of Jesus in the context of a new universe story.

REVELATION IN AN EMERGING UNIVERSE

I begin with the premise that human experience is where one looks to grasp anything that can be grasped about revelation.[18]

Consequently, we are invited to move toward a new revelatory horizon. It is new in terms of recent theological reflection, but very

---

18. Moran, *The Present Revelation*, p. 77.

old in terms of our human spiritual unfolding. It suggests that the creation is the *primary* revelation, of which the various disclosures of the major religions are particular expressions offered in the specific context of certain historical and cultural milieu.[19]

All our thinking moves from the world to God, and can never move in the opposite direction. Revelation in no way suspends this law. Revelation is the experienced self-communication of God *in* human history, which thereby becomes the history of salvation.[20]

In a moment of synchronicity, while doing research for this section on revelation, I discovered a student's notes from a course I taught in the fall of 1975 entitled "God, Revelation, and Theology." It brought back memories of my struggles with the concept of revelation in terms of a culture that was rapidly changing and becoming more and more secular. During 1975 I was studying a book by Gabriel Moran entitled *The Present Revelation: In Quest of Religious Foundations.* It opened for me a new realization of the inadequacy of my language and theology to portray a useful and workable description of revelation. My sense of revelation was being broadened within the context of an emerging universe and a multicultural and religiously diverse world.

A Definition of Revelation

In the light of these various views about revelation and in the context of an emerging universe, the following definition seems to be developing: Revelation is a dynamic relationship between God and humankind who perceive the presence of God through historical and symbolic events. Revelation is dynamic on the part of God because God is actively present, unfolding in the entire story of the universe; revelation is dynamic on the part of humankind insofar as humans actively perceive the presence of God and actively interpret God's presence in symbols and rituals. Each dimension of this definition is interrelated to all other dimensions, and none of the "pieces" can be understood except in the light of the whole definition. Yet the whole will have to be discussed in terms of its different pieces in order to clarify the terms of the definition, but always keeping in mind the whole reality of revelation.

---

19. Diarmuid O'Murchu, *Quantum Theology,* New York, Crossroad, 1997, p. 74.

20. Piet Schoonenberg, "Trinity—The Consummated Covenant, Theses on the Doctrine of the Trinitarian God," in *Studies in Religion* 5 (1975–1976), p. 111.

Since revelation is a multifaceted concept embracing events, interpretations, words, saving activity, dialogue, human experience, symbols, and a communal dimension, it is essential to position the meaning of revelation at the deepest possible level. This definition of revelation finds its center in the intimate presence of God. God's presence is understood in terms of the ongoing unfolding of the power, presence, and love of God in the totality of the universe from its first flashing forth to the rising of the sun each day and to the coming of human consciousness. This divine presence is manifested in many different ways in many different times to many cultures in many different languages and symbols and in many different religions.

This diversity of manifestations of God, in whatever names used to address God, produced a great diversity of creation stories throughout human history. But now, for the first time in human history, we have a new universe story based on our human experience and the scientific evidence of an emerging universe, and it is a story that is gradually being accepted in all parts of the literate world. Hence our definition of revelation must be broad enough to embrace the universal presence of God within the whole of the universe.

In our adolescence we separated ourselves from nature and from a relationship to God in nature, and in doing so we lost a sense of the presence of God in the universe as the primary and ultimate basis for revelation. We lost our sense of wonder and awe. As we re-member and re-integrate what we have split off, and as we move toward adulthood, we must experience the universe as the most basic sacred reality. We must become sacred by our participation in this more sublime dimension of the world about us and realize that revelation is of its very nature accomplished in history.

Revelation is the presence of God, but only *as perceived through historical and symbolic events and their interpretation.* There are three elements in this dimension of revelation: first, *as perceived;* second, *through historical and symbolic events;* and third, *their interpretation.* From the human point of view, revelation is possible only insofar as the presence of God is perceived, and this perception involves a deep relationship between the presence of God and those who perceive and experience that presence.

Once I was hosting a Dominican priest from Nigeria in Minneapolis. I suggested that we go out for lunch at noon followed by a brief walk around one of the lakes. He was astounded that we would go out in the noonday sun and he said, "Our sun in Nigeria is so hot and bright that it is impossible to go out at noon." I told him that we have a different sun in Minnesota, and we *can* walk in the noonday sun. In reality, it is the same sun, but it is *perceived* differently because of the latitudes of the two areas and the clarity of the skies. Likewise, the same God is *perceived* differently by people with different cultural histories, ecological stories, and symbol systems. Thus, although the presence of God is the same throughout the universe, the various peoples of our planet experience that presence in profoundly different ways. Revelation is rooted in the presence of God, but it is always and only as perceived in the historical context of an event and a particular experience of God in the context of that event.

Revelation is God's presence as perceived *through historical and symbolic events*. These are very large categories. Throughout history, the people of the Earth have perceived God's presence in historical events, such as the liberation of the Israelites from slavery in Egypt. This event, regardless of the historical foundations of the story, was perceived by the Jewish people as the loving care and presence of God through the symbolic events of the plagues in Egypt. God was guiding the people in the desert by the cloud in the day and the fire by night. In our own historical beginnings, many of the colonists who came to the shores of the new land of the Americas perceived God's presence in the new opportunities to be freed from religious persecution in a new land of opportunity. Some even saw this new land as the kingdom of God. The native peoples of the Americas experienced the presence of God much more in the events and symbols of the Earth. The universal presence of God was found in the four geographic directions. The wisdom of God was discovered in the wise old owl, God's strength in the horse, God's speed in the deer, and God's vision in the eagle. God's self was revealed in the qualities of the animals and the symbols of the totem.

There is an ancient philosophical principle that states in Latin: *Quidquid recipitur secundum modum recipientis recipitur.* Freely translated, it means that whatever is received is received in the terms or after the manner of the recipient. In other words, the perception of God's presence is determined by the cultural, historical, and symbolic character of the people who receive and experience it. This principle is applicable to such diverse peoples as the native peoples in Africa, the Jewish people in biblical times, the Hindus in India, and peoples throughout the world who are Buddhist, or Muslim, or Christian.

Revelation is the presence of God as perceived through historical and symbolic events *and their interpretation*. The very perception of the presence of God within the context of any culture simultaneously calls for an interpretation of that presence. The story of the call of Abraham is an example. The tribe of Abraham was one of many tribes during that period of history going from what we would presently call Iraq across the Fertile Crescent into what today is the land of the Israelis and the Palestinians. It was a time of major migrations of nomadic peoples in search of more fertile lands. This foundational historical event was interpreted down through many generations by the Hebrew people as the calling of Abraham by God out of his homeland and into a new land promised to the people by their God. "Yahweh said to Abram, 'Leave your country, your family and your father's house, for the land I will show you. I will make you a great nation; I will bless you and make your name so famous that it will be used as a blessing'" (Genesis 12:1-2).

Moreover, the oral and written interpretation of God's presence in the story of a people becomes itself an event, which is reinterpreted by later generations in light of their stories and their cultural experiences. For example, the African peoples who were enslaved in America reinterpreted the exodus event in the Hebrew Scriptures in terms of their own oppression and anguish. In their song, "Go down Moses, way down in Egypt land, tell ole Pharaoh: let my people go," it was clear that the "Massa" was the Pharaoh, and that they were calling on God to free them from their slavery. The exodus was interpreted as a defining historical and symbolic event by and for both the Israelites and the Africans. It is often the voice of the prophet that calls the community to return to God by reinterpreting their history in the light of a new and deeper experience of the presence of God.

DEPTH PSYCHOLOGY AND REVELATION

How can this experience of God as the source of our interpretations of God's presence be described? Ira Progoff, a depth psychologist, describes the prophetic experience in terms of levels of awareness in the psyche. "The crucial question is neither what nor how but *where* the work [of human experience] is taking place. In this context, *where* means, at what level of depth in the psyche the personality is focused."[21]

Progoff applies a developmental model in his approach to the unconscious. The objective is to search for the principle of human potential at the depths of the person and free it to reach its fullest actualization. According to Progoff, the psyche is "the directive principle in the human being which guides its growth from the moment of conception forward."[22] The psyche is like a seed that contains within itself potentially all that the plant can be as it develops toward maturity. It is similar to the genetic coding that directs first the growth of the embryo and then the physical characteristics that gradually develop over the years. Deep within us is also a seed, a psychic coding that contains in potentiality all that the self

---

21. Ira Progoff, *The Symbolic and the Real,* New York, McGraw-Hill, 1973, p. 207.
22. Ibid., p. 73.

is and can become. The emerging of this genetic and psychic coding is a reflection of the evolutionary emerging of the whole of creation. The psyche is the driving force within us that teaches and guides us. It is the inner source of unity, directing both the conscious and unconscious, the inward and outward dimensions of the human person.

The psyche is also a connective principle. We begin to realize that the pattern of developmental unfolding in our personal existence reflects not only the unfolding of our individual life but also in some ways our connection to a larger purpose unfolding transpersonally in the universe.

> By its very nature, therefore, the functioning of the psyche tends to have a connective effect. As it brings about an experience of meaning within the person, it awakens in the finite being a sensitivity to the infinite. It leads to the realization that since this sensitivity is possible it must be that somewhere in the depths of the finite person there lies a capacity to perceive some of the meanings implicit in the infinite.[23]

We are opened to an experience of the infinite within us! Prophets and mystics participate so intensely in the dimension of depth within themselves that the psyche expresses itself for them as a person-to-person dialogue with the divine. They recognize and articulate this dialogue both symbolically and actually, because they enter into the experience with a firm awareness that this dimension of reality is one in which they, as prophets, authentically belong.

> An experience of this prophetic type indicates the deep psychological atmosphere that underlies ancient Israelite experience. With it in the background, it became possible for certain individuals to know that there was present within them and accessible to them personally a dimension of reality that is valid in ultimate terms.[24]

And who are the prophets? Within a religious context in past history, they are the Jewish prophets and patriarchs, the shamans in various cultures, Christian saints and mystics, the medicine people in the native cultures, the diviners and soothsayers, the Eastern gurus and swamis, and the imam of Islam. In modern civilization, however, the persons who become capable of reflecting the in-depth experience of God's presence often do

---

23. Ibid., p. 81.
24. Ibid., pp. 218–219.

not function directly within the domain of formal religion. They are linked to the continuity of religious experience not by a formal tie but by the common quality of sensitivity to the symbolic dimension. Along with the prophetic and mystical voices within various religious traditions there are the artists, the poets, the playwrights, and the creative scientists who reach out not merely toward a knowledge of the physical world but toward a larger contact with the mystery of reality. We can call them all "visionaries" because of their deep awareness of the mystery of God.

The interpretation of the experience of the presence of God flows, therefore, from the inner depths of the visionary. Theirs is not simply an individual experience, but rather a communal one in relationship to the specific culture and people within which their experience of historical events and symbols unfolds. Visionaries come *via* the psyche with their individuality serving as the vehicle by which a larger context of meaning can be brought into the world—the psyche as a connective principle.

> Meaning always enters the world in that way. It unfolds and extends itself in the course of history by moving in and through the lives of those sensitive psyches who reflect the cosmos at their depth and are able to translate its images into the words of the world. Reality grows and expands by means of such persons. They are the prophets and the poets who go to the highest and furthest mountain top that their culture and time in history permit.[25]

Gabriel Moran in his work entitled *The Present Revelation: In Quest of Religious Foundations* summarizes the role of a prophet or a visionary.

> A prophet does not tell people revelations; instead, he awakens the revelatory character of their own lives. Revelation is not what prophets have, it is what communities experience. Far from being isolated from the community, the prophet is the one most deeply in touch with the roots of the community's life. Like the artist he will not conveniently fit into the ordinary framework of the community. He will be strongly opposed by part of the community. This is the test of true prophets who persist in trying to awaken the whole community to its undreamt of possibilities. The only final test of the prophet is whether he does eventually succeed, that is, whether his words and actions resonate in the experience of mankind.[26]

---

25. Ibid., pp. 219–220.
26. Moran, *The Present Revelation,* p. 228.

SYMBOLS AND REVELATION

Revelation is the presence of God unfolding from within the universe as perceived through historical and symbolic events and their interpretation flowing from the cultural roots of the prophets and the people. But this interpretation and reinterpretation has to be *expressed in symbols and rituals within a community.* Revelation is a community event, and in order to have active communication within a community and to build up the community, the use of symbols and rituals is essential. The in-depth experiences of God can be expressed only in symbols, because humans cannot define or encompass the ultimate reality, which is infinite. We can approach the mountain of God only veiled in the robe of symbols.

A symbol is something perceived by the senses that draws us to a deeper level of consciousness and to an inner divine reality already present. It differs from a sign, which points to something separate from itself. A stop sign tells us to stop and a no smoking sign tells us to stop smoking. A symbol contains that which is symbolized. In the story of Moses, a symbol such as the burning bush draws Moses to a deeper experience of the presence of God found within the symbol. Moses is drawn to the burning bush and says, "I must go over to look at this remarkable sight, and see why the bush is not burned" (Exodus 3:3). In the burning bush Moses finds the divine presence both for himself and for the liberation of the people. According to Progoff, "One of the important functions of symbols is to point toward and communicate insights and wisdoms of life that cannot be otherwise disclosed. This is the representational role of symbols, but it is not their major role."[27]

What is the major role of symbols? In order to dig deeper into the meaning of symbols we have to examine ordinary thought processes. Our search for meaning often begins with external words, either written or spoken, or perhaps with some knowledge on the sense level. This may lead us to an authentic experience of the meaning of life, and we might use symbols to guide us into a deeper experience of the reality. Thus the movement is from the outer reality in words or sense knowledge to an inner experience, and from the inner experience to a symbol which then leads us to a reality transcending our ordinary experience. This is the representational mode of symbols, moving from the outside to the inner reality, since *we use the symbol to discover an inner reality.* But this process can be reversed. The inner reality within us can manifest itself in various symbolic ways, and then these symbols are used in our outer experience of the reality. For example, *the inner reality of God's presence uses the*

---

27. Progoff, *The Symbolic and the Real,* pp. 211–212.

symbol to communicate with us. Our experience of the inner reality of
God is then manifested in words and rituals. In this way, *inner symbols
use us in communicating with the outer world.* Progoff explains this role
of symbols.

> But there is an additional meaning in the symbols that transcends
> the symbols themselves. It is the dimension of reality for which
> the symbols are vehicles, not vehicles for man but for reality it-
> self, as reality manifests itself in the lives of men. *Symbols in this
> sense are not merely means of communicating truth; they are em-
> bodiments of reality itself.*[28]

In relationship to revelation this means that symbols can lead us to
the underlying presence of God or can be God's way of manifesting a
deeper divine presence to us. We can experience baptism as a symbol of
new life, and this symbol guides us to the inner reality of our own new
life in God; or God, who is present in the sacrament, uses the ritual or
symbol as a way of manifesting the divine gift of new life. It can go in either direction, but the essence of a symbol is that in some way the symbol
contains the divine reality that is symbolized.

There is a serious question that surfaces in this description of revelation: Can God reveal God's self and in some definitive form God's meaning for the cosmos if the universe is itself emerging? The answer to that
question is in the meaning of the word *definitive*. Does definitive mean
unchanging? Does definitive mean universal? If not, you may ask, how
can any past instance of revelation be privileged? Here too the answer is
in the meaning of the word *privileged*. Does privileged mean the one and
only? If not, what happens to the authority of a religious tradition? Once
again, the answer is in the meaning of *authority*. Does it mean exclusive?
Or unchanging? Or universal?

In an emerging universe, revelation is the presence of God as perceived and articulated in community over a sufficient period of time. In
the Jewish tradition, God is perceived and articulated as righteous and
compassionate. That *experience* of God's presence by the community is
definitive, privileged, and authoritative for the people who shared in the
experience of God's presence because it is an authentic word about God.
But the *statement* "God is righteous and compassionate" is not necessarily definitive, privileged, or authoritative because it has not been immediately experienced. The experience of God found in Jesus of Nazareth as
the savior sent by God to bring the good news to the poor is for me and
for those who share this experience a definitive, privileged, and authorita-

---

28. Ibid., p. 212 (italics added).

tive revelation. It is the communal experience and articulation that is central to revelation. On the other hand, people may perceive and articulate the experience of God's presence in other ways, in the strength of the buffalo, in the vision of the eagle, and in the craftiness of the snake. Such an experience of God could also be definitive, privileged, and authoritative for that community.

Any tradition based on an authentic experience of God's presence within a community over a sufficient period of time can be definitive, privileged, and authoritative for the community that shares that experience. Thus something analogous to the "word of God" is found in that tradition, but that word is not necessarily unchanging, universal, one and only, or infallible because it is articulated only in human words that are limited. As the *Catechism of the Catholic Church* says, "Since our knowledge of God is limited, our language about him is equally so. We can name God only by taking creatures as our starting point, and in accordance with our limited human ways of knowing and thinking" (#40).[29] The same document quotes Thomas Aquinas, saying that "concerning God, we cannot grasp what he is, but only what he is not, and how other beings stand in relation to him" (#43). Revelation in an emerging universe is only a grasping after an ultimate mystery that is far beyond our comprehension. Revelation is not a *thing* but a *dynamic relationship* between a human community and an inexpressible presence. In an emerging universe within which God has been unfolding for fifteen billion years in a dynamic evolutionary process, it is appropriate that the revelation of God's presence be perceived not as an unchanging doctrine but as the dynamic, ongoing reality of a deepening relationship between God and the human community.

We can now return to the definition of revelation as the presence of God perceived in historical and symbolic events as interpreted and *expressed in symbols and rituals within a community.* A great variety of cultures and religions experience the inner presence of God, interpret these experiences, and express them in symbols. Progoff comments, "The belief in the transcendent quality of the divine is ubiquitous in the history of religion."[30] Revelation is as broad and as diverse as is the presence of God. The presence of God unfolds from within us, is experienced deeply within us through historical and symbolic events, and is expressed in symbols within the context of a community. The history of the human race confirms the universal character of this inner relationship to God and

---

29. *Catechism of the Catholic Church,* Mission Hills, Calif., Benziger Publishing Company, 1994. The texts taken from this book will be identified by their paragraph number. This official translation of the original Latin text makes no effort to use inclusive gender language.

30. Progoff, *The Symbolic and the Real,* p. 225.

the necessity of relationships within a community in order to guarantee the authenticity of the foundational experiences.

And what is the role of rituals in this communal experience of God's presence? Rituals are embodied symbols with strong connections to the human psyche and human history. They have become a way of articulating and celebrating the presence of God within the community. At the same time, rituals call us to conversion and transformation.[31] Rituals make God's presence more real and even tangible.

> The quality of the sacred will then become part of our existence … as an endless truth ever unfolding in our lives. With it we shall open a path by which fresh and continuing experiences of spirit breaking through the psyche will become increasingly familiar to modern man. Increasingly the modern person will feel at home on the dimension of the spirit having found his way there integrally via the depth of his psyche.[32]

In this view of revelation, what is the meaning of faith? The simplicity of the response to this question should not mask its depth. Faith is often described in phrases such as "the truths of faith" or "the deposit of faith." People sometimes say the "faith teaches us," or we are afraid that we will "lose the faith." The impression given is that somehow the faith is out there, an objective reality that we either accept or reject. In an emerging universe, however, faith is the spirit-driven human response to the presence of God as perceived through historical and symbolic events and their interpretation expressed in symbols and rituals within a community.

The source of faith, just as the source of all being and activity, is our loving God calling us to respond to our experience of God's presence as perceived in the various events and symbols in our lives. Only by an actively engaged participation can the human person touch the deeper meaning of life, and this participation on the part of the person involves a loving response to the perceived presence of God. Moreover, our response to the presence of God is always mediated through other people, because our perception of God comes from our interaction with others. It is impossible for us to respond to the God who created us, who dwells within us, whose fidelity is written on our hearts, except in terms of symbols. We need others so that we can find a way to express our response, and in expressing that response we deepen it and make it more and more an integral part of our lives. "Our unknown inner world invites exploration and discovery. The mystery lying at the heart of creation is present

---

31. See my *The Holy Web*, pp. 117–122.
32. Progoff, *The Symbolic and the Real*, pp. 225–226.

within our depths continually surprising and challenging us. The God at the core of our being acts as an inexhaustible spring flowing into our lives."[33] Faith is our loving acceptance of God's invitation based on our experience of God's presence in our individual and communal lives.

What is the role of theology in revelation? The answer to that question will differ in different cultures and religious traditions. In the Christian tradition, the role of theology is to reflect on the various interpretations of God's presence as well as on the symbols that have emerged in the biblical and historical traditions of Christianity. It is the role of theologians in responsibility to the community to articulate the meaning of Christianity in the light of the cultural and philosophical traditions in which Christianity emerged and in the light of contemporary scientific, cultural, and philosophical circumstances. Thus, theology is the servant to the believing community in order to help the community reflect on, purify, clarify, and articulate the meaning of its contemporary experience of the presence of God as it is manifested in historical and symbolic events. Theology is not a dialogue between the past and the present; dialogue is what living people do. But if there is any depth and sensitivity in theologians' interactions, if there is open and honest searching and discipline in their discussions, then in our theology the past will function in the present, and the past and present awareness of God's presence will be illuminated and celebrated in our lives as we move into the future.

The God-given and multifaceted reality of faith and revelation calls forth our human engagement in a dialectical process within the many diverse relationships that emerge from the depths of our selfhood. There is an *active* listening to the voice of God emerging from the sacred Earth with all its glory as well as the voice of God in our loving human relationships. There is an *active* participative engagement with the symbols that lead us to God's presence. We discover an inner world of mystery and love and life, and we clarify our experiences of the divine within the context of a community of believers. We celebrate the extravagant love of God in symbolic rituals, music, and dance. The dialectic between faith and revelation is a dynamic and always ongoing search for the inner source of our being and our continuing call to new life.

And after reading this section, Bob Veitch sang out a hymn that captures well this aspect of revelation:

God Speaks

God speaks
With full voice

---

33. John Welch, O. Carm., *Spiritual Pilgrims,* New York, Paulist Press, 1982, p. 59.

Singing creation
In continuous chorus
Booming the bass of Ocean against shore
Tripping the light soprano of the mountain stream.

A rich and varied voice
Seen in the brilliant red of fall's dying
And the timid green of spring's first growth
Heard in the rattle of a last breath
And the lusty howl of a first.

A voice with the power of volcanoes
And the feather touch of a spring breeze
A voice as big as the universe
And as tiny as the parts of an atom's parts
As mysterious as northern lights on a frosty evening
And as plain as the booming crack of ice, shifting under its own
weight.
A voice that is always there.
Always speaking, telling the story
Of how it began and how
It continues to begin
And now and again someone listens.
That's Revelation.

In an emerging universe, revelation is not some *thing* outside us. "I
am asserting that the demand for a divine revelation outside or above
human experience is a search for idols."[34] Rather, revelation is the presence of God unfolding through the cosmos and within us as individuals
and as communities. It is God's way of sharing divine life with the human
family. Revelation is human consciousness entering into God's dynamic
emerging process within the universe, and, as we will see, this process is
salvific as well as revelatory.

SALVATION IN AN EMERGING UNIVERSE

We may note in passing that the religious traditions usually speak
of healing, saving or redeeming as central to the religious process.
Often, however, there is little intrinsic connection between the

---

34. Moran, *The Present Revelation,* p. 82.

healing element and revelation. In fact, in Christian theology they have usually emerged as quite separate processes. One of the indications that revelation was inadequately understood is shown by the fact that revelation was not of itself a healing process.[35]

The belief in salvation has had many different meanings over time. The official church has never formulated a doctrine of salvation; it has been left to theologians to interpret salvation in many ways to meet the various needs of different times and places.[36]

In this section we will use the word *salvation* in a very broad sense meaning the many ways in which chaos and darkness, suffering and evil can be transformed by rescue and deliverance, renewal and restoration. Thus, salvation will be taken in a generic sense without regard to the many different theories that have been proposed over the centuries. We will first describe the ways in which salvation can be found within the universe itself, and then we will describe the concrete ways in which salvation can be understood in the context of the social, political, and religious dimensions of an emerging universe. As this chapter unfolds, we will also look at the intimate relationship between salvation and revelation.

Within the new universe story, it is clear that there is a self-healing power within the universe. There are many instances of the Earth, after a major calamity, healing itself and even emerging with a powerful new sense of life from within. Lawrence Joseph describes one case of the inner salvific potential of the Earth.

Judging from the progression of the fossil record and confirmed by the extraordinary diversity of natural development today, anywhere from 10 to 50 percent of the visible biota survives and eventually thrives from even the worst cataclysms. The global ecosystem invariably regenerates quickly and to a higher level of complexity, usually in less time than a hundred thousand years.[37]

A recent example can be found in Yellowstone National Park. Some years ago, a disastrous fire burned through large sections of the park, and people feared for its future. In fact, the residual ash acted as a fertilizer, producing new plant life, including some species that had not been seen in years. The restoration of the plant life also brought about an increase in

---

35. Ibid., pp. 90–91.

36. Brennan Hill, *Jesus the Christ: Contemporary Perspectives,* Mystic, Conn., Twenty-Third Publications, 1991, p. 230.

37. Lawrence E. Joseph, *Gaia: The Growth of an Idea,* New York, St. Martin's Press, 1990, pp. 203–204.

the population of various animal species. There are many examples of this inner restorative, healing, and even transforming power of the Earth and the universe.

Ilya Prigogine in his work entitled *Order Out of Chaos* presents a new model of the way restoration and transformation take place.

> In far-from-equilibrium conditions we may have transformation from disorder, from thermal chaos, into order. New dynamic states of matter may originate, states that reflect the interaction of a given system with its surroundings. We have called these new structures *dissipative structures* to emphasize the constructive role of dissipative processes in their formation.[38]

This rather abstract description is exemplified in the following story. Some years ago I was attending a major conference in the East. For one of the presentations, about two hundred people assembled in a large, narrow room. As the people gathered, it became clear that they were uneasy about the configuration of the room. The speaker's lectern was at the far end of the space, quite a distance from many participants, and all the chairs were turned to face that end. When the speaker and the introducer arrived, uneasiness gave way to some grumbling. Someone called out to the introducer, "The arrangement in this room is not satisfactory." He responded by soothing the questioner. As he started to make his introduction, someone from another section of the audience shouted, "This set-up won't work!" Some heads nodded in agreement, and other people agreed verbally. Things were getting unruly. As the speaker stepped up to the lectern, another person interrupted him and said, "We can't see, we're too far away and dispersed!" Another person took the microphone and said, "Let's each one turn our chairs sideways and re-shape this room!" Someone grabbed the lectern and took it to the side of the room, all those present turned their chairs, the speaker followed with the microphone, and the whole group settled down for an excellent presentation.

This experience illustrates clearly the constructive dynamics of a dissipative process. At first there was uneasiness in the room—the system needed an adjustment. The situation gradually became more serious as people began to grumble and negative feelings in the room increased. The introducer tried to smooth out the fluctuations in the system. When someone verbally articulated the problem, it perturbed the entire room. More people became agitated as the system tried to hold itself together. Then suddenly the entire shape of the room was transformed, and the participants entered into the process with new energy and new life returned to the group!

---

38. Ilya Prigogine, *Order Out of Chaos,* New York, Bantam Books, 1984, p. 12.

Compare this experience with the following description of a dissipative structure:

> The continuous movement of energy through the system results in fluctuations; if they are minor, the system damps them and they do not alter its structural integrity. But if the fluctuations reach a critical size, they "perturb" the system. They increase the number of novel interactions within it. They shake it up. The elements of the old pattern come into contact with each other in new ways and make new connections. *The parts reorganize into a new whole. The system escapes into a higher order.*[39]

The constructive dynamics of a dissipative process can be applied to society and to politics. Alvin Toffler makes this clear in his foreword to Ilya Prigogine's book:

> [Prigogine's] sweeping synthesis...has strong social and even political overtones. Just as the Newtonian model gave rise to analogies in politics, diplomacy, and other spheres seemingly remote from science, so, too, does the Prigoginian model lend itself to analogical extension.[40]

In an emerging universe, salvation can now be described in new terms such as restoration, transformation, and self-restoring, and it is possible to transfer these new ideas to the social, political, and religious spheres. If, as is the case in an emerging universe, God works within the universe, then this same God works in a comparable way within the personal, social, political, and religious spheres. God's salvific presence is made manifest in the self-healing, self-organizing, and self-renewing processes in the universe. In an emerging universe salvation is seen as coming from a God who dwells within the entire universe, and this salvific presence of God in found equivalently within the human race in all its manifestations. Salvation, as we will see, is directly related to the journey of the human race toward adulthood as described in chapter 1.

The more specific meaning of human salvation will emerge in various historical times and cultural settings. The description of salvation in the time and culture of Isaiah is different from that in the time and culture of the Council of Chalcedon, and the language of the Chalcedonian time

---

39. Marilyn Ferguson, *The Aquarian Conspiracy,* New York, St. Martin's Press, 1980, pp. 164–165.

40. Alvin Toffler, "Science and Change," foreword to *Order Out of Chaos,* by Ilya Prigogine, p. xxiii.

and culture differs profoundly from the language of the time and culture of the third millennium.

> Today's world is generally not seen as populated by evil spirits, or "powers and principalities." It is not so much a battlefield where God wages war with the devil, or a fallen world looking for restoration. Rather, for many it is a world often plagued with addictions, a world with social and political structures that oppress and destroy. Often contemporary experience calls for salvation in terms of healing and the struggle for justice. Any theories of salvation today will have to be relevant somehow to these contemporary experiences or they will find little response.[41]

The question that we pose is the following: What do we as twenty-first-century Americans in a secular age perceive as the meaning and necessity of salvation in our own lives? I suggest that in the context of contemporary culture there are three dimensions of salvation: (1) reconciliation, (2) healing, and (3) liberation. These are not three different kinds of salvation, but three dimensions of a single salvific process, and there will be overlapping concerns among these dimensions.

RECONCILIATION

At the heart of the secular age in America there is division and alienation, strife and loneliness. The horror of war in Viet Nam and in the Gulf and the internal divisions that result from war and terrorism have been ripping up the fabric of the global village. The disaster of terrorism grips the world as a result of the September 11th attacks on the World Trade Center and the Pentagon. Tribal, ethnic, and religious divisions within the world community as well as in places like the Middle East and Northern Ireland seem almost unresolvable. Racial divisions and violence erupt in our streets. We are often a nation of strangers who have lost our roots and become alienated from one another. Newspapers recently carried a story of a woman who was threatening to jump from a high bridge. The angry motorists who were delayed and eager to get home began to taunt her and shout, "Go ahead, jump!"

On a personal level, the fragmentation and alienation within individuals and neighborhoods lead to emotional distress and personal breakdowns. The record sales of Valium and many new comfort drugs testify to the inner chaos in people's lives. Many people have lost a sense of intimacy with nature, and very often the Earth is experienced either as a

---

41. Hill, *Jesus the Christ*, p. 248.

threat or as an object to control and to manipulate. Alienation from God, even the "death of God," leaves people with no evident source for hope and transformation. The church itself is often racked with divisions, oppression, and alienation as is evident in the number of people either marginalized or rejecting and leaving the church. There is a deep need for reconciliation within our own selves, with our neighbors, with the Earth, and with our God.

Reconciliation is possible only with a transformation of our lives from within, which will enable us to live as adults in an adult society. This transformation requires a reconciliation that will re-member the fragmentation within our psyche and will shape a deeper sense of wholeness within our personality. Such a transformation makes possible the breaking down of the barriers that divide us. The racial divisions and wars that pit one race and nation against another will come only when the injustices and oppression among us are wiped out. Terrorism will not be destroyed by counter-terrorism and more violence, but by a demand for justice for the convicted perpetrators along with a movement toward respect, mutuality, and true peace among nations. Various movements, such as the Initiative for Violence-Free Families, call for families and neighborhoods to find new ways to deal with conflict and provide an environment conducive to reconciliation. Reconciliation will blossom when societies recognize and celebrate the interdependence of the whole community of species and the interdependence of the whole human community. The heart of reconciliation is found in the sacredness of the whole universe and the extravagant love of God, which is present and unfolding within us and within the universe.

There is a danger when people in denial smooth over and hide from obvious fragmentation and oppression. The presence of conflicts and diversity does not mean that there can be no reconciliation. In fact, conflict is often essential to reconciliation because, without conflict, serious, honest, and open communication is difficult, if not impossible. Without serious, honest, and open communication, there can be no real reconciliation. Moreover, reconciliation, whether personal or social, is possible only in the context of communities with mutual respect and love for one another. Real communication and an inner transformation flowing from trust and love form the foundation of true reconciliation both within individuals and within societies.

HEALING

The need for healing is very broad and deep in our society. The number of new medicines and drugs coming on the market along with the constant commercials on television are indicators of our "addiction" to drugs and our need for healing. And as we find new cures, either new illnesses or new strains of old illnesses break out. The spiraling cost of health care and health insurance bears witness to the avid demand for healing despite the costs, and this results in a health care system facing bankruptcy. Because the health system ignores or rejects the uninsured and marginal groups, many of the poor struggle to find affordable health care. In some parts of our society, seeing a psychiatrist is viewed as almost a normal part of life. The physical and emotional illnesses of so many people indicate the need for healing in our selves, in our neighborhoods, and in our planet. The church itself needs healing from the wounds of power politics, clergy sexual abuse, and the oppression of women. Healing is an essential dimension of salvation.

Salvation involves the healing of the total person; this healing must take place in the depths of one's being and include the physical, personal, and social aspects of one's life. The need for physical healing is often interwoven with the need for an inner spiritual healing. At times addictive behavior is a symptom of a family or social situation, and healing for the individual will come only with the healing of the family or society. Once again, it is important to recall that healing flows from within through the presence of an inner healing power. This healing center within is founded on the very physical make-up of the person and in the DNA itself. "DNA has learned to repair itself. It can sense exactly which kind of damage has occurred and via special enzymes the appropriate missing links are spliced back into space."[42]

In a similar way, the psyche functions as the deep source of growth and healing in both the unconscious and conscious faculties of our minds. More and more efforts have been made to tap these alternative sources of healing in conjunction with the more traditional medical procedures. The inner healing power of the individual gains real strength from the loving presence of a family community, the health care community, and a prayer community. In my pastoral experience, the anointing of the sick, while it does not always cure a physical sickness, will usually bring healing to the individual and hence to the family. Deep personal and spiritual healing leads to a transformation of institutions and relationships, and often the healing of institutions and relationships will lead to personal and spiritual healing.

Sometimes people say that holiness is wholeness. There is a basic truth to this saying, but it also contains the possibility of a serious misunderstanding. Does that mean that someone who is schizophrenic, whose inner life is seriously disjointed, is not holy? Does that mean that someone living with AIDS cannot be healed spiritually? Does that mean that

---

42. Deepak Chopra, *Ageless Body, Timeless Mind: The Quantum Alternative to Growing Old,* New York, Harmony Books, 1993, p. 117.

where there is physical illness there is no salvation? On the other hand, does it mean that one who is spiritually healed does not need physical healing? There is a deep mystery here. The presence of God and the healing center within the person are always focused on wholeness and a healing of the whole person, and all possible and appropriate means of healing should be used. But limitations are woven into all of creation. The acceptance of our limitations is part of the healing process. The universe story tells us that chaos, darkness, and the shadow side are an integral part of all things, and the acceptance of ugliness may lead to a deeper inner healing that will reveal God's loving presence within us.

LIBERATION

Liberation movements are found throughout our global society, from ethnic groups seeking freedom from oppression to tribal struggles in the former Soviet Union, from the call for black power among African Americans to liberation theology in Latin America to the American Indian Movement. The feminist movement is calling for an abolition of the social and religious oppression of women; there is a need to recognize the dignity as well as the personal and social rights of women in the culture and in the church. A growing climate of oppressive fear has emerged in the Catholic Church as the Pope and Vatican officials have attempted to silence dissent by placing unnecessary limits on freedom of expression and the exchange of information. The United States continues its destructive sanctions on Iraq; these measures are causing the death of many children and destroying the infrastructure of the nation. Those with power, whether political, military, or religious, tend to use fear of guilt or of physical harm, economic sanctions, and social oppression as ways of maintaining control. In the process they take away people's God-given freedom.

How is it that one person can oppress another and take away that person's freedom? There are two foundations supporting oppression: fear of guilt or sin and fear of bodily harm or death. The fear of guilt is frequently used by religious leaders to control and oppress people. When a preacher uses guilt to motivate the actions of parishioners, he is subtly controlling the congregation. When a bishop or religious authorities threaten an individual or a group with excommunication, they are using guilt in an effort to bring dissidents in line. The fear of harm or death is a much more obvious way of oppressing an individual or a group. This kind of violence has been perpetrated on many people in Central America, where torture, assassination, and "disappearance" have often been used to oppress and take away the freedom of the people. Terrorism, such as that experienced in the September 11th attacks, is a worldwide method of using violence and fear for political and economic goals. Refugees the world over face rejection and the loss of their homelands and even death. It is clear that persons or groups can hold other persons or groups in bondage through fear of guilt or harm.

How can we break down the chains of fear, oppression, and violence that bind so many people on the Earth? Ultimately, liberation must come from within. The oppressor never sets the oppressed free. Freedom that is given to another is no freedom at all. Such freedom can be taken back at the will of the oppressor. The only liberation that is true salvation is the liberation that comes from within.

I grew up as a culturally deprived young man because I had no experience with African American people or with other minorities who are an integral part of our culture. Later, as I began to work and interact with black people, my attitude was very "Uncle Tom." I was kind and generous to *them,* and I bent over backwards not to offend *them.* I was trying, in my bungling way, to set them free. One day, while watching the Olympic Games in Mexico City on television, I saw two black athletes standing on the podium to receive their medals. As they sang the Star Spangled Banner, these two winners stood with clenched fist held high over their heads. I was deeply moved by that sight. It changed me deep inside. I said to myself, "I can't give those two winners anything. Their freedom will come from within themselves and their communities."

The lesson contained in this experience is crucial for an adequate understanding of liberation. Our freedom as human beings comes from God and not from any human person or institution. The only limitation on our inner freedom is the necessity to use it in an adult way, namely, to use it first for others and then for ourselves. Liberation is for the sake of service, but a service that comes from within. Women will be free when they find their voice, and choose to benefit from that voice to claim their God-given freedom. Then they must use that freedom to transform their societies and institutions. Racial oppression will be wiped out when the people find their voice, and choose to benefit from that voice to claim their God-given freedom. Then they must use that freedom to transform their societies and institutions. The formation and transformation of personal and social communities from within are an essential part of the maintenance of freedom. We must learn to respect the different cultures and religions in our human community, and we must help enable them to live out their own sense of dignity. The most that any outsider can do is to help remove some of the obstacles that block the voices of the oppressed. We do not set anyone free. Only the God within us sets us free.

Reconciliation, healing, and liberation are essential dimensions of salvation in American and global culture. These three dimensions of salvation emerge from within by means of a personal transformation within community. Within us at the deepest level is a desire to be reconciled with each other and to find a new sense of wholeness, a desire to be healed by the inner healing center within us, and a desire to discover our inner freedom and use it in service to the whole of society. Moreover, wherever and whenever reconciliation, healing, and liberation are found, there is salvation. This salvation unfolds from the loving presence of God within us. Reconciliation, healing, and liberation are also the manifestations of the reign of God in our human lives, a concept that will be treated in greater detail in what follows.

SUMMARY

In these two chapters on the universe story and the emerging universe the foundational stories have been laid out. They describe a vision of the universe that is becoming more and more common among not only educated Christians but also people worldwide. Children in junior high school are familiar with the general outline of the universe story. The vision of an emerging universe does not have the same broad consensus, but the universe story itself will lead many to a new way of envisioning the unfolding of the presence of God within an emerging universe. Revelation is the presence of God emerging within the universe and in a special way in the human family. Salvation is the transforming presence of God emerging within the universe and in a special way within the human family. Revelation and salvation are the two sides of the presence of God unfolding in the universe, and you can't have one without the other. If revelation is not salvific, it is not true revelation. If salvation is not revelatory, it is not true salvation. Revelation and salvation are intimately bound up with and emerge from our experience of the human community and the entire community of species.

This vision of an emerging universe is foundational for all that follows as we begin to search deeply in the biblical stories that open up the life of Jesus of Nazareth. We will describe the ways in which his disciples in the first century C.E. articulated their experience of his life, death, and resurrection. The question then arises: Given the profound cosmological, cultural, and religious differences between the first century and the twenty-first century, is it possible to articulate the meaning of Jesus of Nazareth in language and symbols that will touch the hearts and minds of contemporary Christians? Are we able to provide a foundation for the mission of the Christian church throughout our multi-cultural and multi-religious family on Earth? Will the foundational stories deepen our sense of the extravagant love of God in Jesus, and will they broaden our willingness to respond to his call, "Come, follow me"?

PART II

THE BIBLICAL STORIES

WORLD VIEWS AND INTERPRETATION

Following Jesus is never a simple repetition or imitation, but an engagement in early Christian faith perspectives. It means not only sharing the vision of Jesus but also entering into Jesus' commitment and praxis as we know it from the remembrance of his first disciples. The Gospels are not transcripts but invitations to discipleship.[1]

Having discussed the foundational story of an emerging universe, we can now turn to the unfolding of the biblical stories as they relate to Jesus of Nazareth. It is not possible within the scope of this work to do anything like a comprehensive study of these stories. Rather, we will focus on some of the central biblical stories and what they tell us about the meaning of Jesus in the social and religious context of the first century of the Christian era. It is our hope to probe deeply into the meaning of Jesus and how he is portrayed in these stories and search for ways in which this Jesus can be interpreted in terms of an emerging universe.

This is not the first time that the Christian community has reinterpreted the meaning of Jesus of Nazareth. In the patristic period of the history of the church, the meaning of Jesus was articulated in terms of the philosophical constructs of that time as people struggled with the various viewpoints on the personhood of Jesus and his relationship to God. Later, in the thirteenth century, the scholastic theologians reinterpreted the

---

1. Elisabeth Schüssler Fiorenza, *In Memory of Her,* New York, Crossroad, 1983, p. 103.

meaning of Jesus in terms of Aristotelian philosophy; the result was the classical synthesis of Thomas Aquinas. Now, in the twenty-first century, it is incumbent upon us to look back on these same biblical stories, to search out the deeper dimensions of these stories, and to reinterpret them in the context of the new universe story and an emerging universe.

My first assumption is that the Bible is truly a book of stories and that these stories contain many deep truths about the presence of God within us. There are many literary forms in the Jewish and Christian writings, but at the heart of these writings is the story of a people and their relationship to God. The major threads running through the Bible are concerned with events in the history of the people and the interpretation of those events by the people and by their leaders, judges, and prophets. It is in these stories that the ongoing revelation of the mystery of God is found.

As noted in the previous chapter, the story of the call of Abraham is an example. Abraham's tribe was one of many nomadic tribes that, during the second millennium B.C.E, migrated in search of more fertile lands. The migration of Abraham and his tribe became the foundational historical event in the lives of the Hebrew people. Down through many generations they interpreted this event as the divine calling of Abraham and his people out of their homeland and into a new land promised by God.

Gerhard von Rad describes this tradition of interpretation and reinterpretation of ancient events:

> These stories of the patriarchs are not retold in that exclusively historical sense whose sole concern is merely to reproduce what happened at the time: instead, experiences and insights of succeeding ages also found expression in them. The narrators often digest in but a single story of only a few verses the yield of a divine story which in fact stretches from the events spoken of down into their own time.[2]

Another example is the exodus of a rag-tag group of slaves from Egypt. This was a historical event that was later interpreted as a marvelous manifestation of the power of God in freeing the people from oppression. With this interpretation, the major theme of liberation entered into the Jewish tradition. The call of Moses was seen as the reaffirmation of the call of Abraham, and the Sinai Covenant was seen as a reaffirmation of the Abrahamic Covenant.

---

2. Gerhard von Rad, *Old Testament Theology,* Volume I, The Theology of Israel's Historical Traditions, New York, Harper and Row, 1962, p. 167.

Thus, the Hebrew Scriptures contain a developing story of events and their interpretation, and of the continuing reinterpretation of these events in the light of later historical developments. The people saw their God as intimately present in all these events, as a pillar of cloud by day and a pillar of fire by night (Exodus 13:21), and the Spirit of Yahweh guided the prophetic voices among the people in the interpretation of these events.

This same unfolding process is present in the Christian Scriptures. The events in the life of Jesus of Nazareth, an itinerant peasant preacher and healer, were interpreted by his disciples and immediate followers whom I call the Jesus community. This community is described in Acts as those men and women "who accompanied us the whole time the Lord Jesus came and went among us, beginning from the baptism of John until the day on which he was taken up from us" (Acts 1:21-22). Those men and women lived intimately with Jesus and became his disciples, and it was the same Jesus community that first interpreted the events of his life, including his crucifixion and resurrection. They began to interpret these events in the light of the Hebrew Scriptures and they saw the presence of the living God manifested in these events. The new stories began to unfold in the reading of the scriptures and the remembering of the old stories.

Over the next seventy or eighty years, the various Christian writings and especially the Gospels emerged within the Christian community. It is my view that these new stories followed the emerging process of the universe, a process that is neither random nor determined, but creative. Following the crucifixion of Jesus, the stories did not randomly emerge simply by chance, nor did they emerge in a determined way. Rather, in a way similar to the way in which the universe itself emerges, they were creative stories formed by the Jewish tradition of the ancestors, by the interaction of the Jesus community with the contemporary Jewish environment, and by the cultures within which the various Christian communities preached. These dynamics are similar to the way in which holons function. In the early Christian community there was a constant tension between self-preservation and self-adaptation, and out of this tension came self-transcendence and a new sense of identity.

The resurrection story emerged in the midst of these dynamics. First, in personal experiences and in the oral traditions and interpretations of the Jesus community, we find the *history remembered* dimension of the stories. Second, there is a gradual movement toward a written tradition within the Christian community; this is the *prophecy historicized* dimension of the stories. As was the case with the Jewish writings, it is precisely the presence of the living God in these historically and culturally disparate events and their interpretation that enables us to see them as paradigmatic and gives a deeper unity to the biblical tradition. There is progress in revelation. Part of the Old Testament was outgrown before the

Old Testament was itself complete, and more of it was superseded in the New Testament. Yet amid the diversity runs a unity, and in the whole process there is a thread of true continuity that derives from the God who speaks through it all. This is what we mean when we say the scriptures are inspired. In chapter 3 we will fill in the spaces and, as far as possible, describe the emerging process of the resurrection stories and their meaning within the Christian community.

The validity of this process can be understood more readily in the terms of depth psychology. Ultimately the human mind cannot know reality in its fullness, nor can the mind encompass it intellectually or articulate it completely. In order to do so, individual human consciousness would have to be greater than reality, and that is simply not possible. Rather, the primary role of the human mind as it draws meaning from its experience of reality is to mirror that deep experience in symbols and to articulate it in symbolic language. Thus, any human understanding of or interpretation of the biblical stories of Jesus today is an effort to recover the early Christian experience of the life, ministry, and personhood of Jesus and to articulate that experience in the symbols and language of the twenty-first century. The biblical stories always contain within themselves a surplus meaning that opens up the possibility of a new interpretation in a new social and religious context.

In this way, despite the different symbols and cosmological stories which are rooted in ancient and modern cultures, we are really searching out the meaning of the same ultimate reality. As Ira Progoff notes, "When their common ground is understood, we can see that the ancient and the modern ways are two aspects of the symbolic unfoldment of a single abiding reality."[3] The common ground is our experience of "God within us and acting in history" and how this is manifested in the life and ministry of Jesus of Nazareth. Our ultimate purpose is to reinterpret the in-depth meaning of the stories of Jesus within the contemporary context of an emerging universe.

---

3. Progoff, *The Symbolic and the Real*, p. 217.

3

THE RESURRECTION OF JESUS

In the *popular and pastoral approach* the focus on the resurrection of Jesus has remained more or less physical, historical, and even fundamentalist. In this view, people actually saw Jesus after the resurrection, touched him, heard, watched him eat—all in the way in which ordinarily people see others, touch others, hear others, and watch others eat. This physical approach to the resurrection guarantees that Jesus had truly risen from the dead...The renewed theological scholarship on the resurrection understands the seeing, hearing, and touching of Jesus' risen body to be secondary issues; even the empty tomb is a secondary issue. Because of this difference in approach and this difference in what is primary and what is secondary, there seems to be a widening divergence between the popular and pastoral approach to the resurrection of Jesus and the theological developments of the past eight decades.[1]

When teaching or lecturing on the subject of Jesus in a secular culture, I would often ask the question: Where does the story of Jesus begin? Some begin the story of Jesus with the message of the angel to Mary about Jesus, because this is truly the beginning of his human life. Others say that the story of Jesus started at the time of his baptism when he began his public mission, because this was the beginning of his ministry. Others push the story back to the pre-existence of Jesus with God as the Wisdom and Word of God. At this point in my own journey I believe the story of Jesus begins with the resurrection, primarily because all we know about Jesus comes to us through the lens of the resurrection and because the experience of the resurrection colors everything that has been written concerning the life, the

---

1. Kenan B. Osborne, *The Resurrection of Jesus: New Considerations for Its Theological Interpretation,* New York, Paulist Press, 1997, p. 105.

public ministry, and the death of Jesus. Following this brief general description we begin to apply these principles to the story of the resurrection of Jesus with all of its ambiguities and diverse interpretations.

THE GENESIS OF THE STORY

The most fundamental debate about the passion-resurrection story is not about the problem of *sources* (or how our versions relate to one another) but about the problem of *origins* (or how that story was first created). The problem is not about the *brute facts* of Jesus' crucifixion outside Jerusalem around Passover but about the *specific details* of that consecutive story, blow by blow and word for word, hour by hour and day by day. There are two major disjunctive options that I summarize as prophecy historicized versus history remembered.[2]

The origins are important because the experience of the Jesus community is foundational to our understanding of the story of the resurrection. Were these stories *history remembered,* that is, emerging from what Jesus' companions knew or found out, or *prophecy historicized,* that is, narratives built up from biblical models, precedents, and prophecies? John Dominic Crossan says that these are two disjunctive options, that is, we must choose either one or the other. As I have studied the biblical stories and the history of the Jesus community during the first twenty to thirty years after the crucifixion, I have reached the conclusion that the genesis of the story involves both history remembered *and* prophecy historicized. Using *both* of these options I will outline the genesis of the biblical stories, that is, how the Jesus community actually experienced the resurrection and how they began to develop the stories about the risen Jesus. No one really knows how this came about, but we can work from our sense of the dynamics of human interactions, the history of the times, and hints from the Gospels themselves. Using both history remembered and prophecy historicized, we will trace the earliest resurrection experience from the women in Jerusalem to the disciples in Galilee and then to certain scribal followers of Jesus.

THE WOMEN IN JERUSALEM

Before their Easter experience, as far as the disciples were concerned, Jesus remained dead. What they had hoped for, whatever

---

2. John Dominic Crossan, *The Birth of Christianity: Discovering What Happened in the Years Immediately after the Execution of Jesus,* HarperSanFrancisco, 1999, p. 520.

their confused religious expectations might have been, seemed to be shattered by the sudden and sheerly definitive power of death. The Easter experience reverses this despair and fills an empty void.[3]

The role of women in the Easter event belongs to the Easter event itself. It is not a tangential issue added at a later time for whatever reason.[4]

Jesus had died. Where was he buried? Was he left on the cross for wild beasts, or was his body placed in a shallow common grave? The Gospel stories tell of a burial by influential friends in a tomb hewn out of rock and closed by a large stone. This seems unlikely, because the Jesus community was not made up of people having the political power to provide such a tomb. Crossan takes the minimalist position that "his body [was] left on the cross or in a shallow grave barely covered with dirt and stones."[5] When I first read Crossan's opinion I was shocked by much of it. It offended some of my cherished beliefs. Moreover, a friend of mine got angry at me for even mentioning it. How could there be a resurrection without an empty tomb? However, as I studied and meditated on this question of the burial of Jesus, I began to realize that, wherever and however Jesus was buried, it would not in any fundamental way weaken the reality of the resurrection. It was God who raised Jesus from the dead, and that is the essential message of Easter.

The resurrection of Jesus, many writers have said, does not depend on an empty tomb, because the resurrection of Jesus is an act of God, which is neither visible nor tangible in any simple, empirical sense, and because it involves not merely the transformation of Jesus but also the transformation and conversion of the earliest Christians. The two events are entwined in the biblical accounts we now have available. Extricating them by the crude means we have at our disposal in historical studies is a task beyond our capacities twenty centuries after the events recounted by the biblical narratives occurred. And yet the story of the empty tomb is a marvelous symbol or icon of the resurrection, one that gives us a visual memory of the transformation of Jesus and of our transformation from death to new life. No one knows just how Jesus was buried, nor exactly how he rose, but we must begin with the assumption of an ordinary burial

---

3. Roger Haight, *Jesus Symbol of God,* Maryknoll, N.Y., Orbis Books, 1999, p. 348.

4. Osborne, *The Resurrection of Jesus,* p. 37.

5. John Dominic Crossan, *Jesus: A Revolutionary Biography,* New York, Harper-Collins, 1995, p. 154.

site and then seek to unfold the likely process that led to the writing of the biblical stories in the middle seventies of the first century.

Jesus has died. Jesus has been buried in a shallow, common grave. The male disciples have seemingly scattered and returned to Galilee. The women of the Jesus community stayed behind to mourn the death of Jesus (all four Gospels testify to this), and their ongoing grief would have been expected in the Jewish and Middle East tradition. Indeed, in many parts of the world, both in the past and today, women keen and publicly mourn the dead.

Before me as I write is *The Way of the Cross*, a series of oil paintings by Ted De Grazia. The fourteenth station, "Jesus is laid in the tomb," depicts a circle of women obviously in deep mourning around a shrouded body. The shrouded body is filmy white and lies on the ground or on a slightly raised platform. When I first saw this painting, I thought it portrayed the history remembered of these women companions of Jesus who gathered, as women always do, at the grave site. But then something happened! In the midst of their mourning, the women became aware of the presence of the living Jesus around them and within them. Was this a trance, that altered state of consciousness, which was, and is, a common experience among many cultures? Was it a dream, or was it a visual appearance of the living Jesus? No one knows! But whatever this experience of the risen Jesus involved, it had a profound impact on these women and on the entire Jesus community.

The fifteenth station by De Grazia, "Jesus rises from the dead," shows an upright Jesus still shrouded in white. His head is surrounded by a golden glow, and the women are joyfully dancing around him in a native dance. He is risen. He has been raised. They must have hurried off to share this joyful news with the Jesus community. To me, this is history remembered, even though it is already history interpreted.

THE DISCIPLES IN GALILEE

> With the arrest and trial of Jesus, and especially with his death, there is reason to believe that the male disciples left Jerusalem and retreated to their well-known and therefore more secure environs in Galilee.[6]

Jesus was dead. The Galilean disciples had returned to their homeland, the location of both their travels and their experiences of Jesus' preaching and healing ministry among the people. Jesus was dead. Was

---

6. Osborne, *The Resurrection of Jesus,* p. 116.

their commitment to the ministry of Jesus also dead? They began to tell stories about how the Jesus community had formed and gradually found its self-identity. Was it possible that their hopes for a transformation of both the ordinary people and the leaders of the nation would be crushed? While the disciples talked and grieved on the shores of the lake, they experienced the presence of the living Jesus around and within themselves. They were confused. Was this a trance, or a dream, or was it a visual appearance of the living Jesus? Was it faith newly transformed and renewed? No one knows! What was clear was that Jesus was alive and the mission of Jesus was alive. Somehow God had raised up Jesus from the dead, and the power of God found in Jesus was still with them.

The people who gathered on the shore sat around and shared a meal of bread and the fish they had caught during the night. They continued to discuss their memories of Jesus and their conviction that he was alive. As they talked, the community began to ask themselves, "Just who is this Jesus?" Once again they felt the deep presence of Jesus as if he were asking them the question, "Who do *you* say that I am?" There were different opinions among the group, but they began to realize that Jesus was more than another prophet, more than the Baptist. Was it possible that the risen Jesus was the Messiah, the anointed one? Was he the just one, the son of God? Jesus was certainly the beloved of God, and the disciples experienced the great love of God in his message and his deeds. They wondered and marveled at their awareness that Jesus was alive and that Jesus had been raised, but who was this Messiah who had transformed their lives and called them to share in his message and his mission?

The Jesus community began to preach this message of good news to the poor, the displaced, the homeless peasants, and broken families. Many people began to follow the disciples and to commit themselves to the way of Jesus. One day the disciples went up a mountain to pray and to discuss the growth of the community and what this meant to their mission. As they prayed and talked, once again they experienced the presence of the risen Jesus. It was a powerful and awesome moment! They sensed Jesus as clothed in dazzling white, speaking to them about Moses and Elijah. The Jesus community was not rejecting Moses and Elijah, but rather it was reinterpreting the Jewish tradition in a new way; it was a different way to live out the promises of the Hebrew Scriptures. What did it all mean? Was it a trance, was it a dream, or was it a visual appearance of the living Jesus? No one knows! The growing Jesus community emerged from its Jewish roots and, with the ongoing presence of the risen Jesus, this community continued to preach the good news of God's extravagant love found in Jesus. This is history remembered, even though it is already history interpreted.

Scripture portrays the experiences of the women in Jerusalem and the disciples in Galilee taking place over a few weeks after the death of Jesus, but some interpreters suggest that the total process of realizing what had occurred in the resurrection may have taken many months or even years. Crossan, for example, says that "what we have here is not an event from Easter Sunday but a process that happened over many years."[7] He also notes that "what happened historically is that those who believed in Jesus before his execution *continued* to do so afterward. Easter is not about the start of a new faith but about the continuation of an old one."[8]

Was the resurrection *real*? Of course, but that does not mean we have a scientific explanation for it. Instead, narratives tell the tale of something very different from the mere resuscitation of a dead man, and the question of *how* the resurrection is real is ultimately not resolvable in ordinary human categories. My suggestion is that people persuaded by contemporary cosmology and astrophysics need to interpret what happened at the resurrection in the light of our new world view. Arriving at a consensus in the church about the adequacy of what I am saying here and what other authors have written and will write will not be easy to achieve.

CERTAIN LEARNED DISCIPLES

> If there is any truth to the various hints in the Gospels that Jesus claimed at various points to be a fulfiller of, or one who brought about the fulfillment of, Old Testament prophecies and ideas, then it would have been natural for the earliest followers of Jesus to turn to the Old Testament to help them express their new faith in Jesus...It was this sort of imaginative rereading of the Old Testament that characterized various of the earliest Jewish Christian interpreters of Jesus and explains some of the remarkable christological developments we find in the New Testament.[9]

Having imagined how the early disciples experienced the resurrection and began to share their memories within the growing Jesus community (history remembered), another group of learned disciples, equally deflated by the death of Jesus, began to search for meaning in the Hebrew Scriptures (prophecy historicized). Usually we think of the disciples of Jesus as uneducated peasants, and this is for the most part true, but some of them, such as Matthew, were literate and all were well versed in the

---

7. Crossan, *Jesus: A Revolutionary Biography,* p. 172.
8. Ibid., p. 190.
9. Ben Witherington, *The Many Faces of the Christ: The Christologies of the New Testament and Beyond,* New York, Crossroad, 1998, p. 6.

scriptures. Some may have been part of the more learned and scribal class and, as Crossan says, "all the evidence is that there were such people among Jesus' followers, probably at Jerusalem and probably at a very early stage."[10] What does it mean for prophecy to be historicized?

One way of interpreting the prophetic texts in the Old Testament is to proceed as if the prophetic literature in Hebrew Scriptures foresaw, at least in broad general categories, certain things about the life of Jesus, and Jesus then fulfilled those prophecies. This suggests a linear and historical continuity between prophecy and fulfillment. However, there is another way of looking at the Jewish prophetic literature. In this view, the early Jesus community had a deep experience of the person, life, and work of Jesus, and it was an experience they felt compelled to express in language and symbols. They looked back to the religious and social background of their Jewish ancestors and then used the language and concepts of the Hebrew Scriptures, such as the "Suffering Servant" from Isaiah and the "Son of Man" in Daniel, to express their experience of Jesus. They reinterpreted, idealized, and applied these ideas to the life, death, and resurrection of Jesus. The early Christians used the prophetic language of the ancient literature to express their contemporary experience. Their methodology was more proleptic than linear.

There is a scene in Franco Zefferelli's movie *Jesus of Nazareth* in which Jesus hangs on the cross in his final agony. Slightly in the background stands someone who is clearly a Jewish scholar reading from the book of the prophets. The scene illustrates the fact that the death and resurrection were early on interpreted in the light of the Jewish traditions. One generic pattern in the Jewish texts used to search for meaning in the death and resurrection of Jesus involves the persecution and vindication of righteous or innocent people. "In the two centuries before Jesus Christ as well as during the first century C.E., there was a major concern with the question of the vindication of the righteous. It is in this context that the notion of resurrection appears and develops."[11] Examples of this pattern are found in the texts about the Suffering Servant in Isaiah and the "Just One" in Wisdom.

The four Servant Songs of Isaiah are dispersed among chapters 49–53. The songs begin by the Servant speaking of the righteousness he has received from the Lord:

> The Lord called me from birth, from my mother's womb he gave
> me my name.

---

10. Crossan, *Jesus: A Revolutionary Biography,* p. 146.

11. Donald Goergen, *The Death and Resurrection of Jesus,* Wilmington, Del., Michael Glazier, 1988, p. 80.

The Lord made of me a sharp-edged sword and concealed me in
the shadow of his arm.
The Lord made me a polished arrow, in his quiver he hid me.
You are my servant, he said to me, Israel, through whom I show
my glory. (Isaiah 49:1-3)

The Servant is a righteous one, called by God, gifted with a well-
trained tongue, and refusing to turn back in the face of persecution. But
the suffering of the Servant does not let up. The persecution grows
stronger even unto the threat of death.

He was spurned and avoided by men, a man of suffering, accus-
tomed to infirmity,
One of those from whom men hide their faces, spurned, and we
held him in no esteem.
But he was pierced for our offenses, crushed for our sins,
Upon him was the chastisement that makes us whole, by his
stripes we were healed.
A grave was assigned him among the wicked and a burial place
with evildoers,
Though he had done no wrong nor spoken any falsehood.
(Isaiah 53:3, 5, 9)

The Jesus community could certainly see Jesus in these words. Their
own grief and disappointment at the death of Jesus, who had done no
wrong nor spoken any falsehood, opened up this passage for them. But
the passage includes not only vindication for the Just One, but also a mission to the nations:

And I am made glorious in the sight of the Lord, and my God is
now my strength!
It is too little, he says, for you to be my servant, to raise up the
tribes of Jacob, and restore the survivors of Israel;
I will make you a light of the nations, that my salvation may
reach the ends of the earth. (Isaiah 49:5-6)

In the Jewish tradition, the Servant is seen as both a symbol of the
Righteous One and a symbol of the nation Israel. In both of these symbols
the theme of vindication is clearly found, because both the Righteous One
and the nation were called and gifted by God, both were persecuted by individual and national enemies, both were vindicated, and both were called to
be emissaries of God's compassion and healing. The Jesus community used
this language to begin to understand the meaning of the life, death, and res-

urrection of Jesus. Jesus as the Suffering Servant became one of the earliest and most important images in the development of the Gospel stories.

> One can see why Christians came to interpret Jesus and espe-
> cially Jesus' death and exaltation through the images of servant-
> hood. The many facets of that image helped them to understand
> the ministry, mission and death of Jesus: obedience, suffering, re-
> jection, suffering on behalf of others, the ideal Israelite, a mes-
> sianic figure, a prophetic figure, one sent to the Gentiles.[12]

The second example is found in the book of Wisdom in which the voice of the ungodly persecutors taunts the Just One.

> Let us see whether his words be true; let us find out what will
> happen to him. For if the just one be the son of God, he will de-
> fend him and deliver him from the hand of his foes. With revile-
> ment and torture let us put him to the test that we may have proof
> of his gentleness and try his patience. Let us condemn him to a
> shameful death; for according to his own words, God will take
> care of him. (Wisdom 2:17-20)

Will God always provide protection for those unjustly accused, as God did in the case of Joseph accused by Potiphar's wife in Genesis 39-41, or in the case of Susanna accused by the elders in Daniel 13? Not necessarily. God does not always protect the just in this life. Vindication can and will always come, but sometimes only after death.

> But the souls of the just are in the hand of God, and no torment
> shall touch them. They seemed, in the view of the foolish, to be
> dead; and their passing away was thought an affliction and their
> going forth from us, utter destruction. But they are in peace. For
> if before men, indeed, they be punished, yet is their hope full of
> immortality. (Wisdom 3:1-4)

The use of these and other Jewish traditions in order to explicate the meaning of Jesus and his death and resurrection is made clear in the story of the appearance of Jesus on the road to Emmaus. The two disciples on their journey were unknowingly joined by Jesus. They tell this stranger that Jesus, who was a mighty prophet, was handed over to a sentence of death and crucifixion. They had hoped that Jesus would be the one to re-

---

12. Ibid., p. 62.

deem Israel. Then some women went to the tomb and did not find his body, and an angel announced that Jesus was alive. The stranger answered them and said, "'Oh, how foolish you are! How slow of heart to believe all that the prophets spoke! Was it not necessary that the Messiah should suffer these things and enter into his glory?' Then, beginning with Moses and all the prophets, the stranger interpreted to the two disciples what referred to the Messiah in all the scriptures" (Luke 24:25-26). After they ate with him, and he took bread, said the blessing, broke it, and gave it to them, their eyes were opened and they recognized Jesus. After he vanished, they said to each other, "Were not our hearts burning within us while he spoke to us on the way and opened the scriptures to us?" (Luke 24:32). This Emmaus story embodies the whole process of prophecy historicized. The life, death, and resurrection of Jesus opened up for the disciples a new way of interpreting the Hebrew Scriptures. New interpretations of "history remembered" described above provided the basis for the genesis of the canonical Gospels.

Jesus died and was raised. Driven by the power of his Spirit, the Jesus community took up the mission and message of Jesus. The story and the new way of life of an itinerant peasant preacher and healer in Galilee with a few disciples grew and developed into a major religious movement. Although it was predominantly a Jewish movement, the apostles and preachers, especially Paul of Tarsus, reached out to the gentiles. By about the year 70 C.E. the synoptic Gospels had emerged from various communities as they told the story of Jesus in various ways and from different perspectives. These stories were developed by a process of filtering out the unimportant details, filling in new interpretations, and using new picture language to make the stories more available to the whole Christian community, which had by 50 C.E. spread out from Jerusalem as far as Rome.

THE STORIES—RESURRECTION NARRATIVES

> The New Testament was written and Christianity came into existence on the presupposition of what was called the resurrection. The documents of the New Testament are written in the light of that belief by people who believed that Jesus had "risen."[13]

THE CONVERSION OF PAUL

As the stories of the resurrection unfolded in the scriptures, the experience of Paul of Tarsus holds a very important place. The fact that the

---

13. Moran, *The Present Revelation,* p. 284.

story of his conversion is found in three places in the Acts of the Apostles (Acts 9:1-19, 22:3-21, 26:2-18) is one indication of its importance. Moreover, Paul was one of the most significant personalities in the early Christian community, and the story of his conversion, which resulted from an encounter with the risen Christ, was central to his understanding of the resurrection. We will begin with the story of the conversion of Saul (as he was called before the appearance of the light from the sky).

> Now Saul, still breathing murderous threats against the disciples of the Lord, went to the high priest and asked him for letters to the synagogues in Damascus, that, if he should find any men or women who belonged to the Way, he might bring them back to Jerusalem in chains. On his journey, as he was nearing Damascus, *a light from the sky suddenly flashed around him. He fell to the ground and heard a voice saying to him,* "Saul, Saul, why are you persecuting me?" He said, "Who are you, sir?" The reply came, "*I am Jesus, whom you are persecuting.* Now get up and go into the city and you will be told what you must do." The men who were traveling with him stood speechless, for they heard the voice but could see no one. *Saul got up from the ground, but when he opened his eyes he could see nothing; so they led him by the hand and brought him to Damascus.* For three days he was unable to see, and he neither ate nor drank. (Acts 9:1-9; italics added)

This conversion story contains many of the symbolic events found in typical developmental crises as well as in trance experiences. A developmental crisis usually begins with a trigger event, such as the death of a spouse or the loss of a job or even the birth of a child. In such a crisis, ordinary ways of thinking or operating are challenged, and we find ourselves unable to deal with the situation and overwhelmed with anxiety and fear. We become disoriented and unable to cope with the new situation. We experience a deep sense of the loss of our selfhood, and we don't know what to do or where to go. Often in the midst of a deep crisis we come face to face with our own limits and with the profound mystery of the divine within us. We feel like we need to be guided and even led by the hand.

Entering into the heightened mental and spiritual states known as "trances" is common in many ancient and also many modern societies. As Crossan says, "Trance and ecstasy, vision and apparition are perfectly normal and natural phenomena."[14] Robert Keck observes that "shamans

---

14. Crossan, *The Birth of Christianity,* p. xviii.

go into a trance, either passive or frenzied, to heal the sick, obtain a special relationship with the animal world, converse with spirits, etc."[15] Trances involve images and light as well as possible spiritual transformation. After one of the descriptions of Paul's conversion in the Acts of the Apostles he says, "After I had returned to Jerusalem and while I was praying in the temple, I fell into a trance and saw the Lord saying to me..." (Acts 22:17-18). It seems likely that the profound religious experience of Paul had the characteristics of a trance as well as of a religious crisis.

The transformation of Saul described in picture language contains the symbolic dimensions of both a crisis and a trance. There is, first of all, the sign of a divine presence in the light from the sky flashing around him and the voice speaking to him. The persecutor of the Christian Way meets the Jesus whom he is persecuting. His whole life is turned inside out, and he becomes disoriented and fearful. The light from the sky is the symbol of his meeting with God, and the voice is the symbolic presence of Jesus. This overwhelming presence blinds Saul, and for three days he is unable to see, and he neither eats nor drinks. The whole of his life is challenged, and his very identity seems destroyed.

The story continues with a description of the resolution of the crisis. Saul's healing involves moving from the blinding loss of sight to a new vision from God.

> There was a disciple in Damascus named Ananias, and the Lord said to him in a vision, "Ananias." He answered, "Here I am, Lord." The Lord said to him, "Get up and go to the street called Straight and ask at the house of Judas for a man from Tarsus named Saul. He is there praying."... But Ananias replied, "Lord, I have heard from many sources about this man, what evil things he has done to your holy ones in Jerusalem. And here he has authority from the chief priests to imprison all who call upon your name." But the Lord said to him, "*Go, for this man is a chosen instrument of mine to carry my name before Gentiles, kings and Israelites*, and I will show him what he will have to suffer for my name." So Ananias went and entered the house; laying his hands on him, he said, "Saul, my brother, the Lord has sent me, *Jesus who appeared to you* on the way by which you came, that you may regain your sight and be filled with the Holy Spirit." (Acts 9:10-17; italics added)

---

15. Keck, *Sacred Quest,* p. 15.

In terms of the resurrection, this story has a number of significant elements. The words of Ananias tell of Saul's experience by describing it as an *appearance*. This is an example of a resurrection appearance that was not a visual experience as found in the Gospels but a trance experience of a light from the sky and the voice of Jesus. It indicates that there are various kinds of appearances in varying situations. There is no single experience of the risen Christ. Second, the central reality of the appearance of Jesus is the conversion or transformation of Saul. Those who experience the presence of the risen Christ are transformed by that experience and, like Saul, take on a new personhood. Third, one of the purposes of this story is to establish Saul's position in the community: "This man is a chosen instrument of mine to carry my name before Gentiles, kings and Israelites" (Acts 9:15).

Crossan says that in most, if not all, of the apparition stories the underlying purpose is to reinforce the position of the existing leadership in the church. "Those [apparition] stories, then, are primarily interested not in trance and apparition but in power and authority. They presume rather than create the Christian community; they are about how it will continue, not how it began. They detail the origins of Christian leadership, not the origins of Christian faith."[16] On the other hand, it is equally possible to interpret the apparition stories as true religious experiences, which confer or bring with them an authority. This is likely because these appearances were foundational stories within the early Christian community.

While Saul's experience of the ongoing presence of Jesus presumably took place within ten years after the resurrection, about the year 40 C.E., the written account of the experience in the Acts of the Apostles dates from 80–90 C.E. Paul's own description of the meaning of the resurrection is found earlier in 1 Corinthians 15:1-58, which dates from about 56 C.E. This passage from First Corinthians is a very significant testimony to the resurrection in the early Christian community by one who was himself a witness. The passage begins with the gospel that Paul preaches.

> Now I am reminding you brothers and sisters, of the gospel I preached to you, which you indeed received and in which you also stand. Through it you are also being saved, if you hold fast to the word I preached to you, unless you believed in vain. For I handed on to you as of first importance what I also received: that Christ died for our sins in accordance with the scriptures; that *he appeared to Cephas, then to the twelve. After that he appeared to more than five hundred brothers and sisters at once, most of*

---

16. Crossan, *Jesus: A Revolutionary Biography,* pp. 169–170.

whom are still living, though some have fallen asleep. After that he appeared to James, and then to all the apostles. Last of all, as to one born out of due time, he appeared to me. For I am the least of the apostles, not fit to be called an apostle, because I persecuted the church of God. *But by the grace of God I am what I am, and his grace to me has not been ineffective. Indeed, I have toiled harder than all of them; not I, however, but the grace of God that is with me. Therefore, whether it be I or they, so we preach and so you believed.* (1 Corinthians 15:1-11; italics added)

Paul gives a very brief confession of faith: Christ died for our sins and he was raised on the third day. Interestingly enough, the rest of the passage, while affirming the appearances of Christ, primarily deals with authority and leadership. First of all, Christ appeared to Cephas and then to the Twelve, giving a priority to Peter and the Twelve. Then he appeared to more than five hundred, and after that to James and the apostles. Notice the sequence of the appearances: Cephas and the Twelve, five hundred, James and the apostles. Paul recognizes the authority of Peter and of James, but he makes a distinction between the Twelve and the apostles. Paul, as one who was born into the faith out of due time, could not claim to be one of the Twelve who shared in the birthing of the early Jesus community. However, he could claim to be an apostle because Jesus appeared to him. Not only that, but Paul *toiled even harder than all of them.* Thus Paul in this passage restates the basic gospel of the early Christian community and also reiterates his authority within that community.

Paul discusses the relationship between the resurrection of Christ and general resurrection at the end times which Paul, as a Pharisee, believed was the destiny of all the faithful.

But if Christ is preached as raised from the dead, how can some among you say there is no resurrection of the dead? *If there is no resurrection of the dead, then neither has Christ been raised.* And if Christ has not been raised, then empty is our preaching; empty too your faith. Then we are also false witnesses to God, because we testified against God that he raised Christ, whom he did not raise if in fact the dead are not raised. *For if the dead are not raised neither has Christ been raised, and if Christ has not be raised, your faith is in vain*; you are still in your sins. Then those who have fallen asleep in Christ have perished. If for this life only we have hoped in Christ, we are the most pitiable people of all. But now Christ *has* been raised from the dead, *the firstfruits of those who have fallen asleep.* (1 Corinthians 15:12-20; italics added)

The early Christian community commonly believed in a general resurrection of all the faithful at the end times. In this passage from Paul he clearly says that the raising of Christ from the dead is the inauguration of the end times. He teaches that there is an intimate relationship between the raising of Christ and the raising of the dead because, if there is no resurrection from the dead, then neither has Christ been raised. If Christ has not been raised, by implication neither is there the general resurrection and our faith is in vain. Paul sees the raising of Christ as being the first-fruits of all who have fallen asleep. Because Christ *has* been raised and the end times have begun, all the faithful will share in the hoped for resurrection of the dead. As Crossan comments, "Notice, by the way, that as Paul continues in 1 Corinthians 15, it never occurs to him that Jesus' resurrection might be an absolutely unique and personal privilege, like Elijah taken up to God long ago. Jesus' resurrection takes place only *within* the general resurrection."[17]

Paul uses the same language, *being raised from the dead*, for both Christ and for the faithful. Our resurrection depends on Christ being raised and our resurrection is the same as that of Christ. Christ is the first-fruits and we will be like Christ. There is not only an intimate relationship between the raising of Christ and the raising of the faithful, but Paul seems to be saying that the raising of Christ and the raising of the faithful are substantially the same and follow the same pattern.

This description of the resurrection written about 56 C.E. antedates the resurrection stories of the synoptic Gospels and shows that there were a variety of oral and written traditions present within the various Christian communities. It is out of the history remembered and the prophecy historicized as well as these early traditions that the interpretations of the synoptic canonical Gospels emerged.

THE EMERGENCE OF THE SYNOPTIC GOSPELS

The three synoptic Gospels of Mark, Matthew, and Luke emerged from the Christian community of the first century. After the death and resurrection of Jesus in about 30 C.E., the memories and stories of his life and ministry were passed along in what developed as oral traditions in the various early communities. Between 30 and 60 C.E. certain memories and stories were gradually put down in writing. Some of these written sources, such as Q, from the German word *Quelle,* meaning source, have been reconstructed by biblical scholars. Some written sources, such as the Gospel of Thomas, were independent of the four Gospels of Matthew,

---

17. Crossan, *The Birth of Christianity,* p. 549.

Mark, Luke, and John. These last four were canonically approved by the church. According to Crossan, "Three successive levels—involving *reten- tion* of original Jesus materials, *development* of those retained materials, and *creation* of totally new materials—are found alike in gospels both in- side and outside the New Testament."[18] Thus, the canonical writings at- tributed to Mark, Matthew, and Luke emerged within the first-century church and were the product of over forty to fifty years of oral and writ- ten traditions; Mark is dated as having been written prior to 70 C.E. and Matthew and Luke were probably written about 80–90 C.E. It is also clear that Matthew and Luke are dependent on Mark.

We will begin our examination of the resurrection narratives with the brief description of the burial of Jesus as found in Mark.

> When it was already evening, since it was the day of preparation, the day before the sabbath, Joseph of Arimathea, a distinguished member of the council, who was himself awaiting the kingdom of God, came and courageously went to Pilate, and asked for the body of Jesus. Pilate was amazed that he was already dead. He summoned the centurion and asked him if Jesus had already died. And when he learned of it from the centurion, he gave the body to Joseph. Having bought a linen cloth, he took him down, wrapped him in the linen cloth and laid him in a tomb that had been hewn out of the rock. Then he rolled a stone against the en- trance to the tomb. Mary Magdalene and Mary the mother of Joses watched where he was laid. (Mark 15:42-47)

The tragedy of death was over. The disciples were nowhere to be seen. Joseph of Arimathea (a member of the council and, according to Matthew, a rich man) saw to the burial. The women who followed Jesus looked on. All was quiet for the sabbath.

> When the sabbath was over, Mary Magdalene, Mary, the mother of James, and Salome bought spices so that they might go and anoint him. Very early when the sun had risen, on the first day of the week, they came to the tomb. They were saying to one an- other, "Who will roll back the stone for us from the entrance to the tomb?" When they looked up, they saw that the stone had been rolled back; it was very large. On entering the tomb they saw a young man sitting on the right side, clothed in a white robe, and they were utterly amazed. He said to them, "Do not be

---

18. Crossan, *Jesus: A Revolutionary Biography,* p. xiii.

amazed! You seek Jesus of Nazareth, the crucified. He has been raised; he is not here. Behold, the place where they laid him. But go and tell his disciples and Peter, 'He is going before you to Galilee; there you will see him, as he told you.'" Then they went out and fled from the tomb, seized with trembling and bewilderment. They said nothing to anyone, for they were afraid. (Mark 16:1-8)

With this scene the Gospel according to Mark ends. The women were at the tomb. The stone was rolled back. An angel was there. The tomb was apparently empty. The women fled. There were no appearances of Jesus—only the message, "He has been raised, he is not here," and a promise that the disciples and Peter will see him. This is the end of the Gospel according to Mark. What is the reader supposed to think? Is the reader to be left in suspense, or was it presumed by Mark that everybody knew what had happened? That this was not a satisfactory conclusion is seen in the fact that later, in the second century, a longer ending was added to Mark, an ending that contained an appearance to Mary Magdalene, to two disciples on their way to the country, and finally to the eleven. The postscript to this Gospel now concludes with Jesus being taken up into heaven. It seems clear that the longer ending was based on the stories in Luke, but the question remains: Why did Mark end his Gospel as he did?

Who knows? Maybe there is a hint hidden within the text of Mark. In the beginning of the passion narrative, Mark 14:3-9, there is the story of a woman who comes while Jesus is reclining at table. When she anoints him with perfumed oil, some are indignant, but Jesus says, "She has anticipated the anointing of my body for burial." Now, at the end of the passion narrative, Mark 16:1, the women "brought spices so that they might go and anoint him." Neither anointing is quite complete. "In 14:3-9, the action is premature, since Jesus is still alive. In 16:1, it is too late; his body is no longer present to them."[19] What is to happen next is found in the statement of the angel, "He is going before you to Galilee; there you will see him, as he told you." Perhaps the incompleteness of the story is intentional on the part of the biblical author. Perhaps he is addressing the reader and saying, "This is your story, too, and you must go to Galilee and see him as he told you." It calls the reader to become a participant in the completion of the story and not a spectator; each of us is called to go to Galilee and see once again the risen Christ. We all need to see Jesus and decide whether to accept or reject his message and his mission.

---

19. Robert Beck, *Nonviolent Story: Narrative Conflict Resolution in the Gospel of Mark,* Maryknoll, N.Y., Orbis Books, 1996, p. 128.

We turn next to the Gospel of Matthew. The evangelist tells of the women coming to the tomb, but now the presence of the angel and the rolling back of the stone take on a more dramatic tone.

> After the sabbath, as the first day of the week was dawning, Mary Magdalene and the other Mary came to see the tomb. And behold, there was a great earthquake; for an angel of the Lord descended from heaven, approached, rolled back the stone and sat on it. His appearance was like lightning and his clothing was white as snow. (Matthew 28:1-3)

Mark's simple description of the stone already rolled away and a young man sitting on the right side now becomes, in Matthew's version, a great earthquake, with an angel whose appearance is like lightning rolling back the stone. This is an example of an embroidering of the details in picture language, which should warn us about any attempt to literalize these biblical stories. According to Matthew, the angel then tells the women that Jesus has been raised and is going before them to Galilee. Matthew's description of the way the women react to this message is quite different from Mark's description of the women fleeing from the tomb with trembling and astonishment and saying nothing to anyone.

> Then they [the women] went away quickly from the tomb, fearful yet overjoyed, and ran to announce this to his disciples. And behold, Jesus met them on their way and greeted them. They approached, embraced his feet, and did him homage. (Matthew 28:8-9)

In our brief survey, this is the first description of an appearance. It is simple in its tone and clear in its message. Jesus is alive; the women experience his presence and do him homage. Matthew then tells the story about the rumor that the disciples stole the body while the guards were sleeping. This account tells us that the dispute between the early Christians and the Jews about the empty tomb was not about whether the tomb was empty but why. The evangelist concludes his story with the commissioning of the disciples, but there is no mention here of the return of Jesus to heaven.

> The eleven disciples went to Galilee, to the mountain to which Jesus had ordered them. When they saw him, they worshiped, but they doubted. Then Jesus approached and said to them, "All power in heaven and on earth has been given to me. Go, therefore, and make disciples of all nations, baptizing them in the name of the Father, and of the Son, and of the Holy Spirit, teaching them to ob-

serve all that I have commanded you. And behold, I am with you always, until the end of the age." (Matthew 28:16-20)

This is, indeed, a powerful mandate, and it tells us clearly that the Christian community, over its first fifty years, perceived its role as one of using the power and presence of Jesus as the basis of its preaching. The inclusion of this now familiar baptismal formula shows that some form of trinitarian language was emerging within the community.

The Gospel of Luke reiterates some dimensions of the story in a way similar to that of the other Gospels, but Luke also has some significant additions. The story begins with the women going to the tomb where they find the stone rolled away from the tomb but not Jesus' body. Then they see two men standing by them in dazzling apparel, and they are frightened.

> They [the two men] said to them, "Why do you seek the living one among the dead? He is not here, but he has been raised. Remember what he said to you while he was still in Galilee, that the Son of Man must be handed over to sinners and be crucified, and rise on the third day." And they remembered his words. Then they returned from the tomb and announced all these things to the eleven and to all the others... but their story seemed like nonsense and they did not believe them. But Peter got up and ran to the tomb, bent down, and saw the burial cloths alone; then he went home amazed at what had happened. (Luke 24:5-9, 11)

This is clearly a message similar to that found in the other Gospels, but there is an addition. The disaster of the crucifixion is now seen as part of a plan: "The Son of Man must be handed over to sinners and be crucified, and rise on the third day." The early Christians began to realize as they looked at the scriptures that the death of Jesus, even though it was a crushing blow, was part of the salvific plan of God. This realization was even more clearly expressed in the story of the appearance of Jesus on the road to Emmaus.

This story, which is inserted into the text and is found in none of the other Gospels, tells us that two of the disciples were going to a village called Emmaus and were talking about all the things that had happened. Jesus appeared to the disciples incognito and later opened the meaning of the resurrection in the words of the prophets. The story concludes with this explanation of the death and resurrection.

> And he said to them, "Oh how foolish you are! How slow of heart to believe all that the prophets spoke! Was it not necessary the Messiah should suffer these things and enter into his glory?" Then

beginning with Moses and all the prophets, he interpreted to them what referred to him in all the scriptures. As they approached the village to which they were going, he gave the impression that he was going on farther. But they urged him, "Stay with us, for it is nearly evening and the day is almost over." So he went in to stay with them. And it happened that, while he was with them at table, he took bread, said the blessing, broke it, and gave it to them. With that their eyes were opened and they recognized him. But he vanished from their sight. Then they said to each other, "Were not our hearts burning within us while he spoke to us on the way and opened the scriptures to us?" (Luke 24:25-32)

The Emmaus story traces the gradual opening of the scriptures to an understanding of the necessity of the suffering and death of Jesus. It also deals with the significance of the shared reading of the scriptures in the context of the eucharistic celebration. The hidden presence of Jesus among us is discovered in the sharing of the scriptures and the breaking of the bread.

This is followed by another story of the appearance of Jesus to the disciples gathered in Jerusalem. This appearance is an important moment in the emerging story of the resurrection. In Mark there are no appearances of the risen Christ, only a promise that the disciples will see him in Galilee. In Matthew, Jesus appeared to the women, and then to the eleven on the mountain in Galilee and some doubted. They were commissioned to go and make disciples of all nations, but there was no ascension. Now, in Luke's description of the appearance of Jesus in Jerusalem, the disciples are troubled and seem to be questioning the resurrection of Jesus.

Jesus stood in their midst and said to them, "Peace be with you." But they were startled and terrified and thought that they were seeing a ghost. Then he said to them, "Why are you troubled? And why do questions arise in your hearts? Look at my hands and my feet, that it is I myself. Touch me and see, because a ghost does not have flesh and bones as you can see I have." And as he said this, he showed them his hands and his feet. While they were still incredulous for joy and were amazed, he asked them, "Have you anything here to eat?" They gave him a piece of baked fish; and he took it and ate it in front of them. (Luke 24:36-43)

Clearly, the question of the physical reality of the resurrection was an ongoing issue within the early Christian community, as it is to this day. Writing within the context of these different viewpoints, Luke posed some of the questions arising in the community and used picture language to reinforce the reality of the physical resurrection of Jesus. In the Gospel of John this struggle over the meaning of the resurrection was to remain a disputed question, as evidenced by the story of the doubting Thomas in John 20:24-29.

Luke then for the third time in his resurrection narrative repeats the admonition in the words of Jesus, "Thus it is written that the Messiah would suffer and rise from the dead on the third day and that repentance, for the forgiveness of sins, would be preached in his name to all nations, beginning from Jerusalem" (Luke 24:46-47). The Gospel closes with the story of the ascension.

> Then he [Jesus] led them out as far as Bethany, raised his hands, and blessed them. As he blessed them he parted from them and was taken up to heaven. They did him homage and then returned to Jerusalem with great joy, and they were continually in the temple praising God. (Luke 24:50-53)

The ascension portrays in a symbolic way the reality that the physical presence of the risen Christ is no longer found in the Christian community as it was in his public ministry. He has parted from them and has returned to heaven, and, as later creeds professed, he sits at the right hand of the Father. There still remains the question of the second coming of Jesus in the eschaton. How did our Jewish and Christian ancestors deal with the end times and how did the resurrection of Jesus impact the meaning of their faith in the general resurrection?

ESCHATOLOGY—THE END TIMES

In the culture and historical period of the early Christian church there was a common expectation for an immanent coming of the end of the world. Apocalyptic writing described in some detail the events related to the end times and Paul refers to this in both First Thessalonians and First Corinthians. The earliest text is that from the First Letter to the Thessalonians which was written about 51 C.E. It tries to bring hope to the members of the Christian community who were facing persecution for their faith.

> We do not want you to be unaware, brothers and sisters, about those who have fallen asleep, so that you may not grieve like the rest, who have no hope. *For if we believe that Jesus died and rose, so too will God, through Jesus, bring with him those who have fallen asleep.* Indeed, we tell you this, on the word of the Lord, that we who are alive, who are left until the coming of the Lord, will surely not precede those who have fallen asleep. For the Lord himself, with a word of command, with the voice of an

archangel and with the trumpet of God, will come down from heaven, and the dead in Christ will rise first. Then we who are alive, who are left, will be caught up together with them in the clouds to meet the Lord in the air. *Thus we shall always be with the Lord.* Therefore, console one another with these words. (1 Thessalonians 4:13-18; italics added)

Notice Paul's use of apocalyptic and metaphorical language to open up the meaning of this great mystery of the second coming of Jesus, often called the parousia, which is a Greek word meaning presence or arrival. Jesus died and was raised and is now in heaven. The Thessalonians were concerned about their friends and neighbors who had died. Within first-century culture there was a general belief that an apocalyptic event was coming in the very near future, and the Thessalonians were concerned about what would happen to the dead when that event arrived.

In his letter, Paul first of all assures them that those who have died in Christ will rise with Christ. Second, within Paul's lifetime Jesus will return in the parousia, and Paul reassures those who are alive at the coming of the Lord that they will not go ahead of those who have already fallen asleep. Finally, Paul describes the events of the parousia. The voice of an archangel and the trumpet of God will sound, and Jesus will come down from heaven. The dead will rise and then those who are alive will join them in the clouds. The Christian community will reside with Jesus, the Lord. Interestingly enough, there is no mention of Sheol or the descent of Jesus into Sheol as there is in a passage such as 1 Peter 3:18-19, nor is there any hint of an immortal soul.

Marie-Emile Boismard briefly summarizes this passage in 1 Thessalonians:

Here is, therefore, how we must understand this passage in Paul's letter: in a relatively near future, Christ will come down from heaven (where he has been residing since his resurrection) in order to make his solemn entrance, his parousia, into the city of which he is the "Lord." At that time, the Christians who are already dead will rise, and all, those who still are alive and those who have just risen from the dead, will be carried "into the air" to meet him, not to go with him into heaven, but to return with him to earth as a solemn escort.[20]

---

20. Marie-Emile Boismard, *Our Victory over Death: Resurrection?* Collegeville, Minn., The Liturgical Press, 1999, p. 27.

Paul also provides a very significant treatment of the meaning of the end times in the First Letter to the Corinthians, chapter 15, written about 57 C.E. Before discussing Paul's text, Boismard says:

> It is important to clarify the perspective in which he [Paul] places himself: it is the same as in 1 Thessalonians, the Semitic perspective he had drawn from Daniel. At the time of death, when God withdraws the vital breath, the whole human being falls asleep in the dust of earth and waits for the day when Christ will recall him or her to life. There is no question of an immortal soul being reunited with a body.[21]

In this Semitic perspective, Paul outlines his teaching about the eschaton.

> *But now Christ has been raised from the dead, the firstfruits of those who have fallen asleep.* For since death came through a human being, the resurrection of the dead came also through a human being. For just as in Adam all die, so too in Christ shall all be brought to life, but each one in proper order: Christ the firstfruits, then, *at his coming, those who belong to Christ; then comes the end when he hands over the kingdom to his God and Father, when he has destroyed every sovereignty and every authority and power.* (1 Corinthians 15:20-24; italics added)

The sequence of events in this passage is: first of all, the resurrection of Christ as the firstfruits; second, the resurrection of all who belong to Christ and the coming of the reign of Christ in which he has put all his enemies under his feet; third, the emerging of the end times when the last enemy, death, is overcome and Christ hands over the kingdom to God the Father. There are similarities and differences between 1 Thessalonians and this passage from 1 Corinthians. Both speak of the resurrection of Christ and those who belong to him, and both speak of the parousia, the coming of Christ back to earth. But First Corinthians explicitly adds the idea of an interval between the resurrection of Jesus and the end time when Christ will reign on Earth and when he will give over the kingdom to his Father.

And then Paul searches for some way to describe *how* the dead will be raised.

---

21. Ibid., p. 38.

This I declare, brothers and sisters: flesh and blood cannot inherit the kingdom of God, nor does corruption inherit incorruption. Behold, I tell you a mystery. *We shall not all fall asleep, but we will all be changed, and in an instant, in the blink of an eye, at the last trumpet. For the trumpet will sound, the dead will be raised incorruptible, and we shall be changed.* For this which is corruptible must clothe itself with incorruptibility, and this which is mortal must clothe itself with immortality. And when this which is corruptible clothes itself with incorruptibility and this which is mortal clothes itself with immortality, then the word that is written shall come about: "Death is swallowed up in victory. Where, O death is your victory? Where, O death is your sting? (1 Corinthians 15:50-55; italics added)

The mystery of the general resurrection and the immanent coming of the end times, most likely before the death of Paul's readers, implies that those who are still alive will not die but will be changed in an instant. Then the sound of the trumpet will announce the end times, and all the dead will be raised incorruptible and immortal. The final enemy, which is death, will be "swallowed up in victory." The apocalyptic and metaphorical language Paul uses to enable his readers to grasp something of this mystery was certainly difficult for his contemporaries, and these biblical stories of the end times have raised many questions and disagreements throughout the history of Christianity. For twenty-first-century Christians, these ideas are almost impossible to comprehend. Paul's description of the end times seems like a fable.

For the Lord himself, with a word of command, with the voice of an archangel and with the trumpet of God, will come down from heaven, and the dead in Christ will rise first. Then we who are alive, who are left, will be caught up together with them in the clouds to meet the Lord in the air. (1 Thessalonians 4:17-18)

Those of us who have become aware of an emerging universe over a time span of billions of years find it hard to accept these ideas of imminent end times with the second coming of Christ. Knowing the story of an Earth that has existed for over four billion years and of an evolving community of species on the Earth, the eschaton found in Paul's letter makes no sense if it is taken literally. So the question that surfaces for us is: What is the meaning of the parousia, or the second coming of Christ and the end times, for contemporary Christians? The early Christians expected that the parousia would take place in their lifetime, but in fact Jesus did not come in their lifetime, and so the second coming was projected forward into the unknown future. As we study the solar system, it is true that eventually the energy of the sun will fade and our mother sun and the solar system will die, but a second coming of Christ at that time seems fruitless.

A better interpretation of this story is that the resurrection should not be seen in terms of a time sequence but rather in terms of a transformation sequence. Goergen talks about death and resurrection as a transformation, and then raises the following question: "Are we not talking about the same event? When we die, we are raised to a new mode of life. Death and resurrection are two aspects of the same event."[22] The traditional three-day wait for the resurrection is a metaphorical way of speaking. Since after death there is no time, death and resurrection are simultaneous. Moreover, as Osborne points out, "resurrection and ascension are simply two sides of the same coin. There was no intermediary stage, that is, a time when Jesus was 'only' risen but 'not yet' ascended. If Jesus rose, he ascended. The two are synonymous."[23] According to Roger Haight:

> In sum, what is the nature of the resurrection? It is the assumption of Jesus of Nazareth into the life of God. It is Jesus being exalted and glorified within God's reality. This occurred through and at the moment of Jesus' death, so that there was no time between his death and his resurrection and exaltation.[24]

In summary, the biblical meaning of the resurrection is a transformation from death to new life. With the crucifixion and death of Jesus he was simultaneously raised up to new life. The disciples experienced a presence of Jesus who is alive. Resurrection is not just a return to life as it was, not just the resuscitation of a corpse. It is not just the ongoing existence of an immortal soul. Resurrection is new life beyond time and space but, as we see in Jesus, with a continuity of personhood. Resurrection is also the symbol of a transformation of the disciples who experienced new life flowing from the presence of God in the risen Christ. Paul is transformed from a persecutor to an apostle; the disciples are transformed into men and women imbued with the Spirit of Jesus and ready to share the message and mission of Jesus.

Jesus lives as the firstfruits of a resurrection which is promised to all those who belong to him. New life is now the reality for all believers, as

---

22. Goergen, *The Death and Resurrection of Jesus*, p. 146.
23. Osborne, *The Resurrection of Jesus*, p. 57.
24. Haight, *Jesus Symbol of God*, p. 126.

Paul seems to indicate when he says in 1 Corinthians 15:12-19 that there is a direct relationship between the resurrection of Jesus and our resurrection. In an emerging universe, the resurrection of Jesus is the presence of God unfolding from within Jesus and giving him a new depth of life with God. Resurrection is the extravagant love of God which transforms the whole individual person of Jesus of Nazareth as well as ourselves with the final blossoming of a new depth of consciousness. Resurrection is the presence of God unfolding within each and every individual person, and therefore it is also a new inner relationship with God.

Resurrection is a revelatory symbol insofar as we experience a new dimension of God's unfolding presence within us. Resurrection is also salvific insofar as we experience a new depth of life manifested in reconciliation, healing, and liberation within the whole Earth community. Resurrection provides a deeper, more loving web of relationships within the entire human community as we enter into and return to the fullness of life.

> The resurrection of Jesus and human reception of the revelation of this resurrection together make up an integral and essential part of God's salvation as understood by Christians...What God did in Jesus, God always does and has always done. For the salvation accomplished in Jesus Christ consists in revealing the true nature and action of God. Therefore, what God did in Jesus, God has been doing from the beginning, because to save is of the very nature of God. God is one whose concern about the life of what God creates never fails; God's power of life, then, is never finally defeated by death.[25]

---

25. Ibid., p. 147.

4

RESURRECTION:
A NEW DEPTH OF CONSCIOUSNESS

The mystery of the resurrection of Jesus the Christ calls us deeply into the mystery of God who raised Jesus from the dead. Such mysteries will never be fully comprehended by the human mind and heart, but the human mind and heart always search for the meaning of the mystery of God's presence and loving kindness. The new cosmology and an emerging universe call us to probe the meaning of resurrection, to analyze its various dimensions, and to pull the threads together into some reasonable whole. In doing this we will first revisit the concept of dissipative structures and the crucifixion. Next we will discuss the more contemporary idea of near-death experiences. Third, we will use the theory of implicate matter and the quantum self to situate the resurrection in terms of contemporary physics. Finally, we will develop the idea of the resurrection experience as a new depth of human consciousness.

DISSIPATIVE STRUCTURES: DEATH AND RESURRECTION

> The continuous movement of energy through the system results in fluctuations; if they are minor, the system damps them and they do not alter its structural integrity. But if the fluctuations reach a critical size, they "perturb" the system. They increase the number of novel interactions within it. They shake it up. The elements of the old pattern come into contact with each other in new ways and make new connections. *The parts reorganize into a new whole. The system escapes into a higher order.*[1]

---

1. Ferguson, *The Aquarian Conspiracy,* pp. 164–165.

The description of the formation of a dissipative structure, given above, tells us that in the realm of physics and chemistry, any open system, when it is disturbed by outer forces or inner disequilibrium, will try to damp those fluctuations. If the turbulence reaches a critical state, the system dissipates its energy in trying to maintain itself while still possessing the innate properties to reconfigure itself into new forms of organization. There are three characteristics of an open system that make it susceptible to transformation:

First, complexity or nonlinearity. A linear system is simple because the number of connections on something like a straight line is minimal. But a living system is more like a web of interrelationships with multiple links and a large variety of interactions. The more complex the system, according to Marilyn Ferguson, "the more energy is needed to maintain all those connections. Therefore, it is more vulnerable to internal fluctuations."[2]

Second, instability. The increased coherence and connectedness in any system lead to instability because of the energy necessary to maintain equilibrium in such a system. *"This very instability is the key to transformation. The dissipation of energy . . . creates the potential for sudden re-ordering."*[3]

Third, fluctuations. Instability opens the system to increased fluctuations both from within and from without. "In Prigoginian terms, all systems contain subsystems which are continually 'fluctuating.' At times, a single fluctuation or a combination of them may become so powerful, as a result of positive feedback, that it shatters the preexisting organization."[4]

The powerful disturbances in the system flowing from its complexity, instability, and fluctuations overwhelm the system, and it will either self-destruct into chaos or completely reorganize itself into a new sense of order. Toffler describes this as a revolutionary moment, and he says that "it is inherently impossible to determine in advance which direction change will take: whether the system will disintegrate into 'chaos' or leap to a new, more differentiated, higher level or 'order' or organization which they call a 'dissipative structure.'"[5] Nevertheless, as always happens in an emerging universe, this process is not random or determined, but creative. As we have already seen in the discussion of holons, there is no way to predict the outcome of a dissipative structure, and thus the process is not determined. Yet there are certain limitations on the emergence of a new system based on the extent of its renewed energy and the

---

2. Ibid., p. 164.
3. Ibid.
4. Toffler, "Science and Change," p. xv.
5. Ibid.

environment in which it emerges, and thus the process is not random. The idea of bringing about creativity, novelty, and a new order through chaos seems outrageous, but it is an integral part of the entire universe.

One example of the formation of a dissipative structure is found in our own solar system with its origins in the dynamics of a supernova. In the early stages of the evolution of our mother star, the energy generation within it came from the conversion of hydrogen into helium. After a certain amount of time, all the hydrogen in its center was exhausted and hydrogen "burning" could continue only in a shell around the helium core. Gradually there was no more radiation pressure to balance the force of gravity. The core collapsed in on itself and an explosion occurred through the outer layers of the star, causing a fusion reaction that formed the heavy metals (which are necessary for all the life forms that would eventually emerge on Earth). As our mother star became a supernova, it exploded and formed a disk-like cloud floating in the Orion arm of the Milky Way Galaxy. Out of this cloud of stellar dust emerged our sun and the planets that form our solar system. It was truly a dissipative structure, the result of an explosion leading to stellar chaos followed by the marvelous order of the solar system and the possibility of human life on Earth.

The mathematical principles of order out of chaos can also be applied to individual people and to human society. The experience of order arising from chaos is found throughout human history, in our ordinary lives, and even in the many breakthroughs in the arts and sciences. The experience of the terrorist attack on the World Trade Center and the Pentagon can be seen and perhaps understood in terms of a dissipative structure.

Over the last fifty years our global society has experienced increased complexity, greater instability, and larger fluctuations. There are many examples: the breakup of the Soviet Union in 1991; the continuation of tribal and national warfare in both Arab and African countries; the struggle to end apartheid in South Africa; the civil unrest in Northern Ireland and in Israel and Palestine; the Gulf War and the sanctions against Iraq; the violent demonstrations against the World Trade Organization and the globalization of the economy; the possibility of bio-terrorism or germ warfare. In the midst of this political, ethnic, economic, religious, and cultural turmoil, most of us in the United States went on with life as usual, taking for granted our security and our role as the greatest military power on Earth. But all the elements leading to a dissipative structure were in place.

Then on September 11, 2001, came the terrorist attack on the World Trade Center and the Pentagon, and for the world community as well as the American people it was the equivalent of a supernova explosion. There is chaos in our hearts, on our streets, in our airports, and in our cultural relationships. As if awaking from a dream we asked, "Why do they hate us?" Global politics changed, the political and economic balance was destroyed, and the future became insecure. It was almost as if our Earth in its human dimension had been ripped apart, and the entire Earth community shuddered in the face of catastrophe. It was truly a dissipative structure, but there is no way, at this time, of knowing what the outcome will be. Will it be new life or will it be destruction? Will nations continue to use violence in resolving conflicts or will they finally realize that only true peace and justice for all peoples will bring an end to violence? The only certainty is that the order that will come out of this chaos will be radically different from the world order that has existed over the last thousand years.

There is another dimension to the theory of dissipative structures in the social, political, and religious spheres that will be helpful as we apply these principles to the resurrection of Jesus. Experience with dissipative structures seems to indicate that sometimes a minor turbulence in a system can bring about a major change in the environment. Prigogine says: "A small fluctuation may start an entirely new evolution that will drastically change the whole behavior of the macroscopic system. The analogy with social phenomena, even with history, is inescapable."[6] The catalyst for our political chaos was not a powerful-nation state but an almost unknown handful of dedicated dissidents.

Can we use the model of a dissipative structure as a way of understanding the explosive growth of the early Christian community out of the chaos of the crucifixion? Can we look at the research that is available in order to explain the dynamics of peasant communities in the time of Jesus? Marilyn Ferguson seems to be describing what happened both in twenty-first-century New York City and in first-century Jewish religious society when she says that "the theory of dissipative structures offers a scientific model for the transformation of society by a dissident minority."[7] In his major study of the years immediately after the crucifixion, John Dominic Crossan describes the situation.

The basic stratum of cross-cultural anthropology from the Lenski-Kautsky model[8] emphasized how commercialization provoked peasant resistance in agrarian empires. It also considered Rome as an example of such commercialized agrarian empires. The

---

6. Prigogine, *Order Out of Chaos,* p. 14.

7. Ferguson, *The Aquarian Conspiracy,* p. 166.

8. See Gerhard E. Lenski, *Power and Privilege: A Theory of Social Stratification,* New York, McGraw-Hill, 1966, p. 210, and John H. Kautsky, *The Politics of Aristocratic Empires,* Chapel Hill, N.C., University of North Carolina Press, 1982, pp. 20–21.

next step is to establish a hard lock between anthropology and history within my method's interdisciplinary design. That hard lock is *rural commercialization*, which the Roman Empire accepted as manifest imperial destiny and much of the Jewish tradition rejected as divinely forbidden injustice.[9]

At the deepest level, the resistance was based on the people's sense of the sacredness of their land, which many of the peasants had lost in the urbanization process. For a people who firmly believed that the land belonged to God, commercialization struck at the root of God's justice and righteousness. "That very ancient Jewish tradition was destined to clash profoundly and fiercely with Roman commercialization, urbanization, and monetization in the first-century Jewish homeland."[10]

It seems clear that the political, economic, and religious dynamics in Galilee during the late 20s of the first century were very complex and unstable. The Roman occupation was constantly in conflict with Jewish tradition and, because of this, there were divided powers with Roman procurators, such as Pilate, and petty local kings, such as Herod. The high priests, while being religious leaders, often exercised political power in the Jewish community. Within the religious community there were different factions such as the high priests, the Sadducees, and the Pharisees. The instability of the society was exacerbated by rural commercialization that led to systemic social dislocations, creating an environment conducive to peasant resistance or rebellion. Crossan tells us:

> Anthropology, history, and archeology came together to form a picture of rural commercialization and Roman urbanization against Jewish tradition and peasant resistance in Lower Galilee during the 20s of the first common-era century. What that process meant was not just taxation or even *heavy* taxation... What that process meant was a complete dislocation of peasant life, family support and village security.[11]

Many peasant revolts developed within this unstable and complex situation, and they were frequently put down with severe violence. In the late 20s of the first century, two movements arose in two separate regions of Antipas's territory: John's baptism movement in Perea and Jesus' kingdom of God movement in Galilee. Crossan explains the reason for these move-

---

9. Crossan, *The Birth of Christianity,* p. 178.
10. Ibid., p. 182.
11. Ibid., p. 330.

ments by noting that "anthropology, history, and archeology combine to predict some form of peasant resistance in Lower Galilee by the late 20s. It came with John and Jesus."[12]

Beyond that political resistance, the life and mission of Jesus disturbed in a very profound way the Jewish religious system. His message turned its holiness code inside out. The Jesus community challenged the Jewish leadership by preaching the good news to the poor and the outcasts and by calling for a powerful but non-violent response to the political, economic, and religious leaders of their time. The religious authorities tried to silence and destroy this Jesus movement, and the religious and political chaos reached its climax in the crucifixion of Jesus.

> I think it quite possible that Jesus went to Jerusalem only once and that the spiritual and economic egalitarianism he preached in Galilee exploded in indignation at the Temple as the seat and symbol of all that was nonegalitarian, patronal, and even oppressive on both the religious and the political level. Jesus' symbolic destruction simply actualized what he had already said in his teachings, effected in his healings, and realized in his mission of open commensality. But the confined and tinderbox atmosphere of the Temple at Passover, especially under Pilate, was not the same as the atmosphere in the rural reaches of Galilee, even under Antipas, and the soldiers moved in immediately to arrest him.[13]

The crucifixion of Jesus was like the supernova experience of our mother star. It was like the terrorist attack on September 11, 2001, that has shaken the world community and brought us to the edge of an unknown future. The passion, crucifixion, and death of Jesus, as well as the destruction of Jerusalem in 70 C.E., emerged as the culmination of the chaos in the Jewish homeland flowing from the strong arm of Roman occupation and commercialization and the internal struggles within the Jewish community itself. The instability of a dissipative system is embodied in all these situations. Out of the presence and love of God within the chaos of the supernova explosion the beauty of the solar system emerged; the presence and love of God will hopefully bring forth out of the chaos of the September 11th attack a new and transformed world community. In a similar way, the presence and love of God brought forth out of the chaos of the crucifixion a new life for the Jesus community in the resur-

---

12. Ibid., p. 231.
13. Crossan, *Jesus: A Revolutionary Biography,* p. 133.

rection of Jesus, a new life that has transformed the Western world. More-over, the resurrection, as we will see, becomes a new depth of conscious-ness for the human community.

Remember what Marilyn Ferguson writes, "The theory of dissipative structures offers a scientific model for the transformation of society by a dissident minority," and what Ilya Prigogine writes, "A small fluctuation may start an entirely new evolution that will drastically change the whole behavior of the macroscopic system." The resurrection of Jesus had this kind of profound effect on Western culture and on the lives of millions of people. It is the central drama of two thousand years of Christian history, and it has been a source of new life throughout the world. The theory of dissipative structures opens up a new horizon to the meaning of the resur-rection. Chaos leads to creativity, and the death of Jesus was transformed into new life in the resurrection. The impact of the resurrection on not only the early disciples but also the contemporary Christian community contin-ues to enlighten our world, just as our sun lights up the solar system.

In order to understand the deeper meaning of resurrection, we will now look more closely at some modern experiences of life after death.

LIFE AFTER DEATH

Life after death is a deep mystery that is very difficult to understand and impossible to describe. The early Hebrew tradition imagined a dark shad-owy existence somewhere under the Earth. Later Jewish speculations fo-cused on an after-death vindication of the martyrs and the just ones as well as on the idea of immortality found in the Wisdom tradition. Follow-ing the resurrection of Jesus, Paul in the letters to the Thessalonians and the Corinthians developed a growing vision of the resurrection of the dead and the second coming of Jesus. Today a new way of interpreting life after death is found in the experiences of dying persons and near-death experiences as articulated in the experience of Elisabeth Kubler-Ross and in various developments relating to quantum physics.

DYING AND NEAR-DEATH EXPERIENCES

In a period of ten years over twenty-five thousand cases of such experiences have been collected from all over the world, and they have been examined and integrated into an organic vision.[14]

---

14. Elisabeth Kubler-Ross, *On Life after Death,* Berkeley, Calif., Celestial Arts, 1991, p. 47.

An analysis of this material and an attempt to reach some hard and fast conclusions are almost impossible. Most of the evidence for life after death is anecdotal, there is little scientific proof of the authenticity of these experiences, and most of the language used is symbolic and metaphoric. And yet the number of cases and the similarity of the content from many different cultures gives some credibility to the case for near-death experiences and for life after death. Moreover, as we will see later in this section, there is some interesting grounding in theoretical physics for these experiences.

I shared in an experience of this type during the dying process of a colleague of mine. Mary, a Dominican Sister and a trained musician, was dying of cancer, and she had a very difficult time accepting the reality of this disease and the imminence of her death. One evening while I was sitting at her bedside with her mother, she asked her mother, "Is it all right if I go?" Her mother looked confused and undecided, but finally she said, "Yes." Mary closed her eyes and remained silent for a few minutes. Then she said, "Oh! Daddy is here (he had died some years before) and Betty is too, and she's got her tools with her (Betty was her best friend who had died one year earlier). Oh! The light is so bright and beautiful." She smiled and opened her eyes and said, "Let's have a party." She asked to have all her close friends gathered, and she wanted us to get some refreshments. When we had all gathered, she asked us to sing all the songs she loved. She died about one week later.

There are also near-death experiences in which a person is apparently medically dead, and later returns to life after "seeing" the actions of people around her. She is met by her loved ones, and is overwhelmed by a bright light. Kubler-Ross posits three stages to the moment of death. She describes the first stage in this manner:

> If you can accept the language used in my conversations with dying children, ... then you will accept that the death of the human body is identical to what happens when the butterfly emerges from its cocoon. The cocoon can be compared to the human body, but it is not identical with your real self for it is only a house to live in for a while. Dying is only moving from one house into a more beautiful one—if I may make a symbolic comparison.[15]

Kubler-Ross uses the cocoon as a symbol to express the fact that, when the human body is no longer able to support life, the person unfolds into a new life in a process that is almost identical to the experience of

---

15. Ibid., p. 10.

birth, a birth into a new way of existing. In the second stage, the patient will realize that she can perceive all that is happening around her, either in a hospital room or at the site of an accident. She may have a very clear sense of the details of the room or the site, even if she is unconscious at the time. "In this second stage, the 'dead' one will realize that he is whole again. People who were blind can see again. People who couldn't hear or speak can hear and speak again."[16] When one leaves the physical body that person is never alone. People testify, as my friend Mary did, to the presence of family and friends who have died. Many Christians report the presence of religious figures such as Jesus or Mary or the saints. Space and time seem to have no meaning. Existence is such that time, which is a human measure, and space, which is a physical measure, are no longer limiting.

Then begins the third stage, in which the transition is symbolized as a tunnel or bridge or mountain pass that a person passes through or over. Once again in symbolic language Kubler-Ross tells us that people experience a sense of judgment and a review of their whole life.

> What we hear from our friends who have passed over, people who came back to share with us, is that every human being, after this transition, is going to have to face something that looks very much like a television screen. You will be given an opportunity —not to be judged by a judgmental God—but to judge yourself, by having to review every single action, every word and every thought of your life.[17]

In summary, the first stage begins with the moment when the body can no longer support life and we are reborn like a butterfly from a cocoon. Then in the second stage we can perceive what is happening around our "dead" body with great accuracy and a new awareness. We realize that we are whole again and have a psychic energy within ourselves. We are not alone but greeted by our loved ones who have gone before us. As we pass through the tunnel we begin a complete review of our life with all its goodness and evil. Kubler-Ross describes at some length the final dimension of her vision of life after death.

> After we pass through this visually very beautiful and individually appropriate form of transition, say the tunnel, we are approaching a source of light that many of our patients describe

---

16. Ibid., p. 13.
17. Ibid., p. 37.

and that I myself experienced in the form of an incredibly beautiful and unforgettable life changing experience. This is called cosmic awareness. In the presence of this light, which most people in our western hemisphere called Christ or God, or love, or light, we are surrounded by total and absolute unconditional love, understanding and compassion. This light is a source of pure spiritual energy and no longer physical or psychic energy... It is an energy in the realm of existence, where negativity is impossible. This means that no matter how bad we have been in our life, or how guilty we feel, we are unable to experience any negative emotions. It is also totally impossible to be condemned in this presence, which many people call Christ or God, since He is a being of total and absolute unconditional love.[18]

Once again the symbol of light, which is the source of pure spiritual energy, brings forth a new cosmic awareness that I have called a deeper consciousness. In this light we are surrounded by unconditional love, a love that is not only unconditional but absolute.

What can we say about these stories that have been witnessed to by many thousands of people and that have been analyzed and interpreted by many researchers, physicians, and psychologists? I am aware that, as noted earlier, most of the evidence is anecdotal and not subject to controlled scientific proof and a symbolic style of language is used in describing the experience. But I am also aware that at least some of the stories of death, dying, and near death have great credibility and can be supported by the evidence of both professionals and families. Moreover, some of the symbols and language patterns can be found in other cultural and religious experiences, such as the symbol of light in the transfiguration of Jesus as found in the synoptic Gospels and the trance-like conversion experience of Paul of Tarsus. Most human cultures have some form of belief in life after death. The Native American people talk about going to their ancestors, and they often bury food for the journey with the deceased. Other cultures speak of re-incarnation as a way of returning to new life. I personally have no certitude about the authenticity of these experiences and their interpretation, but I am inclined to take them seriously and use them prudently.

This quantum universe of ours reaches beyond our grasp and leads us into mystery. Some sense of that mystery is exemplified both in David Bohm's theory of the implicate order and in Danah Zohar's explanation of the quantum self.

---

18. Ibid, pp. 60–61.

THE IMPLICATE ORDER AND THE QUANTUM SELF

As discussed in chapter 1, our society and our world are afflicted with adolescent fragmentation. This fragmentation threatens both the make-up of our society and the integrity of our Earth. We continue to deplete our resources and destroy our ecosystem. We treat our world as inherently divided, disconnected, and broken into yet smaller parts with each part considered essentially independent and self-existent. It is within this context that physicist David Bohm has developed his theory of the implicate order.

He begins by saying, "The classical idea of the separability of the world into distinct but interacting parts is no longer valid or relevant. Rather, we have to regard the universe as an undivided and unbroken whole."[19] He posits an implicate order that underlies and is the source of all that we can perceive with our senses. He writes, "We have seen that in the 'quantum' context, the order in every immediately perceptible aspect of the world is to be regarded as coming out of a more comprehensive implicate order, in which all aspects ultimately merge in the undefinable and immeasurable holomovement."[20]

Remember the metaphor of the lake that was used in chapter 1? The explicate order is found in the debris that is cast up on the lake shore during a storm. It is visible and measurable, it comes forth from the depths of the lake and can return there, and while it is on the shore it is relatively stable. The implicate order is like the hidden depths of the lake out of which come all the things on the shore. The lake is the source of all that unfolds on the shore and that into which everything is enfolded. Bohm proposes that in the formulation of the laws of physics, primary relevance is to be given to the implicate order, the depths of the lake, while the explicate order, made up of those things we can see and touch, is to have a secondary kind of significance. Thus, it is Bohm's contention that the reality that we perceive with our senses is explicated from the deeper reality that we cannot perceive with our senses. The universal implicate order, out of which everything unfolds, gives us the underlying sense of the wholeness and unity of all reality. This sense of wholeness is an integral part of the adulthood of the human race.

Bohm's theory also has ramifications for the discussion of resurrection and life after death. As we have seen, the human person and human consciousness unfold from the Earth and ultimately from the implicate

---

19. Bohm, *Wholeness and the Implicate Order*, pp. 124–125.
20. Ibid., pp. 156–157.

order that is the source of all things in the explicate order. With death, the human person and human consciousness return to the earth and are enfolded into the implicate order. To use another metaphor, just as an idea emerges from the stream of consciousness that is its source, then enfolds back into the stream of consciousness, it can, in certain circumstances, re-emerge from the stream. Does it not seem possible that the human person and human consciousness, which in death or near death are enfolded back into the implicate order, can, in certain circumstances, re-emerge into the explicate order? I am beginning to realize that the membrane between life and death is much more permeable than I have ever thought. The witness of near-death and dying experiences and now the theory of the implicate order give us a new sense of the mystery of the afterlife.

Another way of looking at this comes from Barbara Kingsolver in her novel entitled *Animal Dreams*. She relates a conversation between the heroine, Codi, and her Native American lover, Loyd, dealing with the issues of life and death.

> "Where do you think people go when they die?" Loyd asked.
> "Nowhere," I said. "I think when people die they're just dead."
> "Not heaven?"
> I looked up at the sky. It looked quite empty. "No."
> "The Pueblo story is that everybody started out underground. People and animals, everything. And then the badger dug a hole and let everybody out. They climbed out of the hole and from then on they lived on top of the ground. When they die they go back under." Loyd thought about his twin brother who had died. "I always try to think of it that way," he said. "He had a big adventure up here, and then went home."[21]

The quantum view of the universe can also provide a new way of thinking about life after death. In quantum terms, the self is seen as an internal web of relationships and an entity capable of intimate relations with others. This intimacy can be described as *relational holism*. In order to understand relational holism, it is essential to distinguish between *external* and *internal* relations. External relations are like the movement of Newtonian billiard balls on a pool table, bumping into each other but remaining external to each other. Internal relations, on the other hand, are like electrons in a box; their interaction is not external but existential and

---

21. Barbara Kingsolver, *Animal Dreams,* New York, Harper Perennial, 1991, p. 308.

involves their actual inner qualities. Internal relations cannot be adequately explained by Newtonian physics, nor by Aristotelian-Thomistic philosophy, both of which require an external cause for every change or movement.

Relational holism as an internal relationship calls for a whole new mentality, a new way of thinking, and a new paradigm. Because internal relationships are based on a quantum reality in which quanta are both waves and particles simultaneously, these waves and particles are able to have internal relations and internal causality. In order to get a personal sense of the overlapping wave patterns, it is necessary to look at our own experience of intimacy with one another. Danah Zohar uses the experience of her pregnancy with her first child.

> At first the boundaries of my body extended inwards to embrace and become one with the new life growing inside me. I felt complete and self-contained, a microcosm within which *all* life was enfolded. Later the boundaries extended outwards to include the baby's own infant form. My body and my self existed to be a source of life and nurture; my rhythms were those of another; my senses became one with hers, and through her, with those of others around me.[22]

Imagine your own relationship with a spouse, a parent, a soul friend or partner, or a life-long intimate friend from childhood. Do not the boundaries of the self extend outward to embrace the other? Is there not a mutual source of life and nurture? Do not one's rhythms and senses combine with the other's? There are many examples of soul friends who at times can anticipate the other's feelings and responses. I decide to call my friend, and the phone rings with a call from her. There is a bonding so deep that the relationship becomes a new holon, something more than its parts. This kind of relationship is not just the result of memory or imagination, but has its basis in the overlapping of brain waves which at the quantum level brings about a physical change within us.

> Through the process of quantum memory, where the wave patterns created by past experiences merge in the brain's quantum system with wave patterns created by present experience, my past is always with me. It exists not as a "memory," a finished and closed fact that I can recall, but as a living presence that partially defines what I am now. The wave patterns of the past are taken up

---

22. Zohar, *The Quantum Self,* p. 141.

and woven into now, relived afresh at each moment as something that has been but also as something that is now being.[23]

There is a deep web of relationships within our human lives, a web that bonds us both to all those people who have impacted our lives in a variety of ways and to the whole of creation. The atoms that make up our selves have existed for more than fifteen billion years. My atoms were, perhaps at one point, stars before they later became part of the planet Earth. My atoms were perhaps part of the mountains and the seas or a bird or a tree, and later may have been part of a rose or another human. In a way I am everything. And, as a conscious self, my web of relationships embraces all, especially all those other conscious selves who have most deeply impacted my life. This requires a mental shifting of gears and calls for new ways of thinking and speaking.

As we experience consciousness within ourselves and a web of relationships with all of creation and other conscious selves, there is an intimacy that has a real physical basis in relational wholeness. My father and I were very close. As the youngest of eight children, I was loved deeply by my father and early on we became close friends. He was a role model for me during adolescence and as a young adult. We shared more deeply as he grew older, until he suffered a stroke and died. As I sit here today I can remember these events clearly, but something more than memory is involved. Our bonding in an intimate relationship changed both of us and we are in many ways one like a holon, in a unity that reaches beyond the grave.

Of this kind of fundamental relationship and its power to create, Bob Veitch of the "First Friday Group" observed that the resurrection is not merely physical.

> The message [of resurrection] transcends history...It matters only that the spirit of Jesus survived the crucifixion. Who among us hasn't looked in the mirror and seen his father looking back? Or had a deceased mother or close relative appear in a dream with a message of some sort—so realistic that you would swear it was not a dream...Quite possibly the appearance of Jesus to his disciples was similarly an expression of the deep impression he had made on their lives. It matters not. The power of the resurrection is that it freed humankind to believe in joyous life after death and thus allowed humans to raise their vision and begin to embrace the unfolding universe story from a different perspective. The charac-

---

23. Ibid., p. 145.

teristic of the Christian age is hope—belief that there is an eternal reward.

Because of the overlapping of brain waves, it seems that the bonds between the living and the dead continue after death, but does one's individual consciousness continue after death? Zohar seems to say no. "If I die, it is true that there will be no more ongoing dialogue within myself—within that inimitable pattern that arises from the combination of all my past, all my awareness and experiences, all my relationships, all my genetic material, all my bodily idiosyncracies."[24]

This may be true, but it is my vision that life after death does involve the individual consciousness. I believe that the relationship between my father and myself continues. He is aware of me and is following my life path with interest and concern. We will continue to share life when I die. But how is this possible?

When I die, I will return to Mother Earth and re-enter more deeply into the Consciousness of the Earth out of which I emerged, and this Consciousness of the Earth is God. I will retain all the relationships that were part of my human existence. My self as a human is a holon made up of many parts, including my self-consciousness. My bodily actions often manifest and even ritualize my inner consciousness in an external way. My inner consciousness of love for another is often expressed externally as a touch or a kiss. In an analogous way, the return of my bodily dimension to the Earth can manifest and even ritualize the return of the conscious self to the Consciousness of the Earth and thus to the implicate order. The web of relationships that constitutes my individual conscious self does not cease to exist. It becomes part of a larger whole, the larger web of relationships, a new holon that embraces all of space and time and the whole of creation within the infinite love of the Creator God.

While writing these paragraphs I began to think about the images of the Body of Christ and the Communion of Saints. Many of the words and phrases used here ("our bonding changes us and we are one"; "the web of relationships that is my individual conscious self becomes part of a larger whole") strikingly illustrate the deeper meaning of the Body of Christ and the Communion of Saints as a dynamic web of relationships that goes beyond the grave. This web of relationships also goes beyond the Christian community to embrace all peoples, all of space and time, and the whole of creation within the extravagant love of God.

Various authors have attempted to define the indefinable mystery of the love of God who is the source of the universe and the womb of our

---

24. Ibid., p. 149.

life after death. O'Murchu calls it the *creative vacuum*: "The primary and overwhelming data of creation is the creative vacuum, a seething conundrum of spiritual energy birthing forth life in the vast array of life-forms, from galaxies to human beings."[25] Zohar explains it in terms of a *quantum vacuum*:

> The quantum vacuum is very inappropriately named because it is not empty. Rather, it is the basic, fundamental, and underlying reality of which everything in this universe—including ourselves— is an expression...The vacuum itself can be conceived as a "field of fields" or, more poetically, as a sea of potential. It contains no particles, and yet all particles come about as excitations (energy fluctuations) within it. The vacuum is the *substrate* of all that is.[26]

This idea of a quantum vacuum as the substrate of all that exists suggests Bohm's concept of holomovement. Bohm says that "the implicate order has its ground in the holomovement which is, as we have seen, vast, rich, and in a state of unending flux of enfoldment and unfoldment, with laws most of which are only vaguely known, and which may even be ultimately unknowable in their totality."[27] It is interesting to note the difference in terminology. What O'Murchu and Zohar call a *vacuum* Bohm calls *holomovement*, and yet these authors seem to be talking about the same reality. Brian Swimme uses the phrase *all-nourishing abyss* "as a way of pointing to this mystery at the base of being. One advantage of this designation is its dual emphasis: The universe's generative potentiality is indicated with the phrase 'all-nourishing,' but the universe's power of infinite absorption is indicated with 'abyss.'"[28] He explains this concept in words reminiscent of Bohm's implicate order.

> All-nourishing abyss is acting ceaselessly throughout the universe. It is not possible to find any place in the universe that is outside this activity. Even in the darkest region beyond the Great Wall of galaxies, even in the void between the superclusters, even in the gaps between the synapses of the neurons in the brain, there occurs an incessant foaming, a flashing flame, a shining-forth-from and a dissolving-back-into.[29]

25. Diarmuid O'Murchu, *Reclaiming Spirituality,* New York, Crossroad, 1998, p. 43.

26. Zohar, *The Quantum Self,* p. 225.

27. Bohm, *Wholeness and the Implicate Order,* p. 186.

28. Swimme, *The Hidden Heart of the Cosmos,* p. 100.

29. Ibid., p. 101.

Zohar goes beyond this general description and raises the possibility that the quantum vacuum might be "conscious" and could be conceived of as God.

The physics which gives us human consciousness is one of the basic potentialities within the quantum vacuum, the fundament of all reality. It might even give us some grounds to speculate that the vacuum itself (and hence the universe) is "conscious"— that is, that it is poised towards a basic sense of direction, towards a further and greater ordered coherence. If we were looking for something that we could conceive of as God within the universe of the new physics, this ground-state coherent quantum vacuum might be a good place to start.[30]

Bohm, as well, in his search for wholeness finds the footprints of one often given the name of God.

In any discussion of this sort, people often are led to speak of the totality, of a wholeness which is both immanent and transcendent, and which, in a religious context, is often given the name of God. The immanence means that the totality of what is, is immanent in matter; the transcendence means that this wholeness is also beyond matter.[31]

We are all grasping after the ungraspable which for me is the extravagant love of God who is the Source of All Being, the Eternal Word, and the Creator Spirit. Our personal experience of the extravagant love of God and our communal experience of the resurrection of Jesus give us the foundation for a belief in the fullness of life forever with God. We can now deal directly with a new depth of consciousness found in the resurrection.

RESURRECTION: A NEW DEPTH OF CONSCIOUSNESS

In the resurrection event, God acts; men and women respond. This response of the disciples was not primarily that they could "see" Jesus; that they could "hear" Jesus; that they could "touch" Jesus; that they could "see him eat"; or any other physical, sen-

---

30. Zohar, *The Quantum Self,* p. 226.
31. Renee Weber, "The Physicist and the Mystic—Is a Dialogue between Them Possible? A Conversation with David Bohm," in *The Holographic Paradigm and Other Paradoxes,* ed. Ken Wilber, The New Science Library, 1982, pp. 187–188.

sate response. The major response of these men and women was a response of faith. This cannot be stressed enough...For the men and women disciples who eventually believed, this faith element was *a religious experience.*[32]

THE RESURRECTION OF JESUS

The biblical stories of the resurrection focus on transformation and new life. Jesus is raised from the dead. Jesus still lives. Jesus is still the same person, yet somehow transformed as he appears through locked doors and is not recognized by Mary Magdalene or by the disciples on the road to Emmaus. Two symbols that capture the various coexistent patterns within the transformation of Jesus are *resurrection* and *exaltation.* Roger Haight explains the difference between these two terms.

> Comparing the two symbols [resurrection and exaltation], both affirm or express that Jesus did not remain in the power of death but is alive. But they do so with different emphases. Resurrection, to be awakened, emphasizes the continuance of life; exaltation emphasizes being lifted up out of this empirical world. Resurrection tends to locate Jesus restored to life in this world where he appeared. Exaltation carries Jesus out of this world where there are no longer appearances nor a succession of events in time; Jesus' being glorified is a single mystery.[33]

Down through history there have always been various opinions about the meaning of the bodily resurrection of Jesus. Most authors would agree that bodily resurrection does not involve the resuscitation of a corpse or a return to normal bodily life. But there have been differences of opinion about the characteristics of the resurrection from the dead. One early tradition believed in a risen Jesus without a resurrected physical body, while other traditions believed in a truly physical resurrection. Gregory Riley deals at length with this question in his book, *Resurrection Reconsidered: Thomas and John in Controversy.* The following is his general conclusion:

> So one branch of the early Christian movement could follow a non-physical risen Jesus, while others began to contend, not only for the body, but for the flesh, of the risen Christ. This development is visible in the Gospel literature: Mark has no appearances

---

32. Osborne, *The Resurrection of Jesus,* p. 117.
33. Haight, *Jesus Symbol of God,* p. 123.

or physical demonstrations of the risen Jesus; Matthew has doubters at the final appearance, but no demonstrations; Luke ...has one demonstration; and John has two. By the time of the writing of the Thomas pericope [in John], divisions in the Christian movement were clearly visible. The original community and proclamation were far closer to a "spiritual" Jesus than to a Jesus raised in the flesh.[34]

It is not possible in this work to trace the dispute through the early Christian traditions, but it is essential to maintain that "the resurrection was the exaltation and glorification of the whole individual person, Jesus of Nazareth. The one who was resurrected is no one else than Jesus, so that there is continuity and personal identity between Jesus during his lifetime and his being with God."[35] Jesus is transformed by an act of God, and at the same time the Jesus community is transformed. Their experience of the risen Jesus confirms for them his mission and message, and it gives them new life and the impetus to make Jesus' mission and message their own. This transformation of the Jesus community is verified in history, but the way it emerged is more difficult to discern. In the resurrection, as seen above, God acts and men and women respond. The response is one of faith. But, as was discussed in chapter 2, in an emerging universe faith is the spirit-driven human response to the presence of God as perceived through historical and symbolic events. The presence of God as well as the historical and symbolic events are then articulated in symbols and rituals within a community. What were the historical and symbolic events that triggered this human response to God's presence in the risen Jesus? Donald Goergen says:

However one may interpret the historical or non-historical character of the resurrection of Jesus itself, I would suggest that there is an historical dimension underlying the appearances of Jesus. We can point to a change in the disciples and to the emergence of their faith in Jesus as raised from the dead. This is an historical fact. Jesus' disciples came to believe in Jesus as raised, began to proclaim his resurrection from the dead, all as a result of an experience of conversion which led to faith. The documents themselves attribute the source or cause of this conversion of faith to the appearances of Jesus, to personal encounters with the risen Lord.[36]

---

34. Gregory J. Riley, *Resurrection Reconsidered: Thomas and John in Controversy,* Minneapolis, Minn., Fortress Press, 1995, pp. 106–107.

35. Haight, *Jesus Symbol of God,* p. 124.

36. Goergen, *The Death and Resurrection of Jesus,* p. 127.

The Jesus community found its source of faith in personal religious experiences of God's presence in the risen Jesus and it was this faith that determined the way that appearances were described in the Christian Scriptures. The community moved from experience to faith, and as the appearance stories emerged they were always connected to the mission of the community and the formation of its leadership. All of the appearances have a social or communal dimension, and all of them provide guidance for the future growth of the community. In the Acts of the Apostles there is a story that is not about an appearance of Jesus himself, but which describes the coming of the Spirit as the driving force for the faith of the community and its call to mission.

> When the time for Pentecost was fulfilled, they were all in one place together. And suddenly there came from the sky a noise like a strong driving wind, and it filled the entire house in which they were. Then there appeared to them tongues as of fire, which parted and came to rest on each one of them. And they were all filled with the holy Spirit and began to speak in different tongues, as the Spirit enabled them to proclaim. (Acts 2:1-4)

This scene summarizes the experience of the Christian community during the middle decades of the first century. They experienced the powerful presence of the Spirit of the risen Christ which came to rest on each of them and they were all filled with the holy Spirit. The Spirit then enabled them to proclaim the message of Jesus. And what was the message of Jesus? It is found in Peter's speech and it is a quote from the prophet.

> "It will come to pass in the last days," God says, "that I will pour out a portion of my spirit upon all flesh. Your sons and daughters shall prophesy, your young men shall see visions, your old men shall dream dreams. Indeed, upon my servants and handmaids I will pour out a portion of my spirit in those days, and they shall prophesy." (Acts 2:17-18)

The message of Jesus is that the Spirit will be poured out on all flesh and all will prophesy. This is true today. The resurrection is not only something that happened to Jesus; it is not only an experience that happened to the Jesus community or to the early Christian community; it is an event that is happening to us today. We are all called to transformation, to a personal experience of resurrection life, to a dynamic response of faith, and to a mission to all people. There is a universality to resurrection, to faith, and to mission. In a deep sense, Pentecost is the resurrection in action.

A New Depth of Consciousness

> However, in all of these variants [in the Jewish tradition], the res-
> urrection is seen in a collective form. Jesus' resurrection, from
> this Jewish background, cannot be understood as an isolated, per-
> sonal, individual, unique situation. If Jesus did rise bodily from
> the dead, then his resurrection is at the same time related to the
> bodily resurrection of others . . . and the opposite is true as well—
> the resurrection of others is related to the resurrection of Jesus.[37]

Jesus is raised. So shall we be raised. But this resurrection is not only
an event experienced by Jesus and his followers. Resurrection has become a universal symbol of new life. In an emerging universe, resurrection can be seen as a new depth of consciousness that has the potential of
transforming humanity from adolescence into adulthood at a moment
when the adolescence of the human race is so apparent. This adolescence
is manifested in our global village by our reliance on violence, both on
the part of terrorists and on the part of those who oppose terrorism. But
let us begin at the beginning with a personal anecdote.

> As a child I imagined that the soul was like a little white round
> disk near my heart which I had to keep clean, and, if I committed
> sin, I could wash my soul clean by going to confession. Later I
> perceived my soul as the spiritual part of me that would, when I
> died, go to heaven and enable me to see God face to face while
> awaiting the resurrection. In high school I thought a great deal
> about the resurrection. I came up with the theory that the end of
> the world would take place when the bodies of all the people that
> had ever lived equaled the total "matter" of the earth. Then when
> all these people got their bodies back, there would be no earth,
> and we would all live in eternal bliss. I actually shared this the-
> ory with the local Rotary group over lunch on one occasion. I
> have always wondered how they reacted inside.

This story can be seen as a parable of the common beliefs of our
Western society. In our childhood, many of us were taught about the soul
and the necessity to do good and avoid evil or we would go to Hell. The
concern was not particularly about helping others but about avoiding punishment. In our adolescence we began to recognize that there is a spiritual

---

37. Osborne, *The Resurrection of Jesus,* pp. 91–92.

"part" of the self, the soul, and that that "part" of us is immortal. We knew that after death came a particular judgment that determined whether we went to Heaven or Hell (or possibly Purgatory). Our soul waited patiently for the end of the world, for the resurrection of our bodies, and for the final general judgment. Typically, adult Christians believed in immortality as the continuing, separate existence of the human soul after the death of the body to be followed by the final judgment and the resurrection of the body. Our view of resurrection was primarily individualistic rather than communal, focused on Heaven rather than Earth.

In an emerging universe, however, the resurrection of Jesus is symbolic of a qualitatively new moment or a deeper level of human consciousness flowing from the chaos of the crucifixion. This deeper level of consciousness enabled the Jesus community to experience the meaning of death as new life, a re-entry into the consciousness of God, and a communal call to new life for all peoples. But they could articulate this experience only in the cosmic story and the human words available to them. Their cosmology of a triple-decker universe with a Heaven above, the Earth below, and the place of the dead under the Earth was simply not adequate to express the new depth of experience. Remnants of this cosmology remain. In a discussion with one of my friends, a thoughtful and educated man, he told me that Heaven had to be a physical "place," because the "bodies" of both Jesus and Mary are there. Limited in their ability to talk about and share their experience of the resurrection, the early Christians could describe it only in terms of the picture language of visions, appearances, and empty tombs, and later an eschatological second coming of Jesus. The Jewish-Christian cosmology was too narrow to embrace the reality of the new life of the risen Christ and it tended to limit the fullness of resurrection to Jesus alone and to the final parousia. We are now able to articulate the realization of a new sense of resurrection life for all humans and a new level of consciousness.

What triggered the emergence of human life and consciousness between two and three million years ago? Was there some climactic crisis or change in the environment or a moment of chaos that demanded and resulted in the appearance of human consciousness? Perhaps there have been many moments of new consciousness in two to three million years of human history, all of these moments flowing from external or internal chaos and change. The following are some examples:

500,000 years ago: Clothing, shelter, and fire

100,000 years ago: Ritual burials

40,000 years ago: First languages

20,000 years ago:	Spears, bows, and arrows
10,000 years ago:	Agriculture and the domestication of animals
3,500 B.C.E.:	Sumerian civilization, the wheel and cuneiform writing
1,200 B.C.E.:	Exodus of Israel from Egypt, monotheism
560 B.C.E.:	Confucius in China; Buddha in India

These are all moments when the human family, in whole or in part, seemed to reach a new level of consciousness and community life. Then came Jesus of Nazareth, a powerful peasant preacher and healer, who challenged the current Jewish holiness code and the leaders of the nation in the midst of a social crisis of Roman commercialization. Because of his call for change and transformation he was finally crucified outside the city of Jerusalem. As we have seen above, his preaching and his crucifixion became the catalyst out of which emerged a new level of consciousness and a deeper sense of faith. And now, in the twenty-first century, there is an opportunity for us to make a quantum leap into a new depth of consciousness. The chaos currently being experienced by many peoples and nations is indicative of a dissipative process about to transform our world. We have a new story of an emerging universe with which to integrate this transformation. Finally, we are experiencing a movement from a Cenozoic Era to an Ecozoic Era; this movement is indicative of a global resurrection. I will discuss the new level of consciousness first in terms of the dying and rising of the individual and second in terms of the dying and rising of the global human society, both of which are inseparable.

In an emerging universe, the individual at the moment of death re-enters the Earth from which he or she emerged. The physical body decays, as is the case with all members of the Earth's living community, but the individual, the personhood, the conscious self enters into the Consciousness of the Earth. Just as the conscious self during its lifetime manifests itself in the physical body, so in death the burial of the body symbolizes the return of the conscious self to the Consciousness of the Earth. Many people still see the Earth as a dead and lifeless thing and the heavens as the abode of God. But God is as much present in the living Earth as in the heavens. The Consciousness of the Earth is really the presence of God, and the re-entry of the self into the Earth is a re-entry into the life of God. In terms of the theory of the implicate order, dying is the process of moving from the external, explicate order to the internal, implicate order. In other words, we die to the explicate order and rise or return to the implicate order of what Bohm calls "wholeness," Zohar calls the "quantum vacuum," Swimme calls the "all-nourishing abyss," and I call the "unconditional love of God."

After death there is no time; death and resurrection are simultaneous, and death and resurrection are simply two aspects of one event. With death and through resurrection the human person enters into the life of God where space and time no longer exist. Those who have died do not have to wait to be raised from the dead; they do not have to wait for a second coming of Christ. With death comes the fullness of life in God. What happens to the conscious self at the moment of new life that we call resurrection? This is a very difficult question, and one with many different answers. We cannot speak with any certainty on these matters, but we can speculate in terms of the concept of an emerging universe. I believe that the conscious self retains its individuality and receives a new form of life with a "body" free from its limitations. We often think of matter as the basic quality of a body, but we also know that matter can be transformed into energy and energy into light. It seems clear to me that, just as the make-up of the human body recycles completely about every seven years and yet the person remains the same, the make-up of the body may be composed of matter, energy, or light while retaining its identity. Just as the implicate order transcends space and time, so the resurrected person transcends space and time.

Paul in his letter to the Corinthians also describes a vision of the resurrected self.

> But someone may say, "How are the dead raised? With what kind of body will they come back?" You fool! What you sow is not brought to life unless it dies. And *what you sow is not the body that is to be* but a bare kernel of wheat, perhaps, or of some other kind; but God gives it a body as he chooses, and to each of the seeds its own body... So also is the resurrection of the dead. It is sown corruptible; it is raised incorruptible. It is sown dishonorable; it is raised glorious. It is sown weak; it is raised powerful. It is sown a natural body; it is raised a spiritual body. If there is a natural body, there is also a spiritual one. (1 Corinthians 15:36-38, 42-44; italics added)

Is there a moment of judgment after death? This is certainly a common view in Christianity as well as the later Jewish tradition. The need for an afterlife is described in the vindication of the martyrs in Maccabees and in the reward of the just is the book of Wisdom. Jesus, in the parable of the sheep and the goats, seems to visualize a great moment of public judgment for all people. Once again we walk very cautiously in this matter, but I believe that there will be some form of judgment after death, not a judgment by God, but a self-judgment, when we are all brought face-to-face with the good and the evil in our lives.

There seem to be four options for this final judgment. The first, the traditional and most common opinion, is that in the resurrection the judgment will result in eternal life for the righteous and eternal punishment for the unrighteous. All will receive the reward or punishment that they deserve in terms of their goodness or sinfulness.

The second opinion is articulated by Marie-Emile Boismard in his book, *Our Victory over Death: Resurrection?* He begins by looking at the New Testament texts concerning hell fire and he says, "Today, all agree that this 'fire' must be understood in the metaphorical, not the literal, sense. It would symbolize the moral suffering to which sinners are subjected, and especially the pain cause by their separation from God."[38] He goes on to point out that this symbolic interpretation is not the only one possible. After citing a number of texts, he concludes that fire is the symbol, not of prolonged suffering, but of complete destruction. This is found in both the Jewish and Christian scriptural traditions. Then he concludes:

> In this case, one can think that perhaps Edward Schillebeeckx is right when he rejects the idea of eternal suffering for sinners, but visualizes their fate as a return to nothingness, as a definitive annihilation. God would take back from the wicked the existence "lent" to them and they would cease to exist, despite their souls' being "immortal by nature."[39]

A third option is transmigration of souls, sometimes known as reincarnation. Themes of rebirth are both ancient and profound. The most fully articulated doctrine of transmigration is found in Hinduism. Central to the concept of human destiny after death is the belief that human beings are born and die many times. Reincarnation is a sort of cosmic recycling, like water into ice into fog into water. There is a new personality with each incarnation, but our individuality is immortal. Thus, transmigration is closely interwoven with the concept of karma, which involves the inevitable working out, for good or ill, of all action in a future existence. The cycle of karma and transmigration may extend through innumerable lives; the ultimate goal is the reabsorption of the soul into the ocean of divinity from whence it came. Union occurs when the individual

---

38. Boismard, *Our Victory over Death: Resurrection?* p. 140.

39. Ibid., p. 141. See Edward Schillebeeckx, *Church: The Human Story of God,* New York, Crossroad, 1991, pp. 136–139.

realizes the truth about the soul and the Absolute. This stage can be called enlightenment, which brings freedom from the cycle of reincarnation. The theory of transmigration is ordinarily found more often in cultures in which nature and history are considered to be cyclical, while the theory of an eternal afterlife is usually found in cultures more in tune with a linear sense of nature and history.

Judgment in the first case results in eternal punishment for the un-righteous and in the second case in definitive annihilation. The third case involves reincarnation with a goal of enlightenment. Yet there is a fourth possibility based on the unconditional love of God. Both the righteous and the unrighteous will be faced with a moment of self-judgment in which they recognize the good and evil they have done, and this judg-ment will be a communal event, since all those touched and impacted by their lives will be present. Then, in the light of the unconditional love and the extravagant compassion of God, all will be transformed and will be given new life. This transformation would probably involve an internal, but not a temporal, journey in working through the ignorant or willful harm done on earth. The source of this transformation will be the realiza-tion among those who rejected God on Earth of the total goodness of God, leading to a free choice to embrace this unconditional love.

One time when I was sharing the death watch of a woman parish-ioner, she became very frightened about being sent to hell. She knew she had made mistakes and done evil at times and would now face the judg-ment of God. She was agitated and scared about God's judgment. During previous conversations with her, she had talked about her children and some of the problems she had experienced with them. I asked her whether she could cast into hell any of her children for the evil they had clearly done. She looked at me and with tears in her eyes said, "No, I could never do that! I love them too much." Then I told her that, regardless of what she had done, God, as a good parent, would never condemn her. Her sense of peace was palpable as we prayed together.

Some people will object that in this fourth opinion there would be no vindication for the just, and there would be no rewards for the good and punishment for the evil. The terrorist bombing and killing of close to three thousand innocent people cannot be forgiven, and it might seem to de-mand either eternal punishment or annihilation. I, myself, have felt deep grief and anger over these events, and I want the perpetrators of these evil deeds to be brought to justice. In order to have true justice we must sepa-rate the good from the evil, and we must decide in many circumstances who is evil and who is good. In the explicate order this is palpably true.

On the other hand, in the implicate order there is a call for a new wholeness which no longer separates but brings together. The adoles-cence of the human race was marked by its tendency to separate nature from the human, the human from God, men from women, whites from blacks, rich from poor, the good from the evil, and on and on. We tended to divide up and conquer, to put the sheep on one side and the goats on the other, Christians against Muslims, nation against nation, tribe against tribe. All of this separateness has led to violence and war. I deeply believe that in resurrected life there will be no separations or divisions. The unconditional love of God will prevail and bring all things together. There is nothing we can do that will make God love us less. When we do evil God does not love us less, but we love God and our neighbor less. There is nothing we can do to make God love us more. When we act justly God does not love us more, but we love God and our neighbor more. The adult values of re-membering and re-integrating, of wholeness and inclusivity, will flourish in the presence of God's unconditional love. Everyone is embraced within the extravagant love of God, but not everyone carries out the message of adult love found in the words of Jesus:

> You have heard it was said, "You shall love your neighbor and hate your enemy." But I say to you, love your enemies, and pray for those who persecute you, that you may be the children of your heavenly Father, for he makes his sun rise on the bad and the good, and causes rain to fall on the just and the unjust. (Matthew 5:43-45)

But, you might say, if there is no heaven or hell and if all people receive the fullness of life with God, what is our motivation for following the commandments and leading a good life? The rewards of heaven should not be the motivation for our following the commandments and leading a good life. The only valid motivation is our love for God and for all God's children and our thirst for justice for all people flowing from the presence of God's love within each of us. The motivation of love and justice must be played out in the present time within the whole Earth community with which we share our lives and not within the future hope for a reward in heaven. Jesus' resurrection as a symbol of new life cannot be understood as an isolated, personal, individual, unique situation; rather, it is a collective event that calls all peoples to search for justice and love within the whole of creation. "Love your enemies and pray for those who persecute you."

Resurrection is also a universal symbolic event that can transform our Earth community and our human family. Resurrection is part of the inner dynamic of the universe, so that in the midst of the chaos, the violence, the terrorist attacks, and the bio-terrorism of our global situation, resurrection will win out. Over and over again in the history of the universe new life has arisen out of death. Since, in the scenario I have chosen, there is no motivation for vindication or rewards in heaven, the human family can look only within itself for the motivation to transform the Earth community and the human family. Salvation emerges from the presence of God within each of us and within our communal lives. If we want to bring love and justice as well as reconciliation, healing, and liberation to the global community, we cannot look outside ourselves for a savior but within ourselves, where we find salvation in the power and presence of God's unconditional love. For those of us who are Christian, this means to have in us the mind of Christ and to immerse ourselves in the heart of Christ's love and compassion.

Resurrection is also a symbol of God's transforming presence within the universe and within the Earth and all its creatures. This transforming presence will be found concretely in the qualities of adulthood and the transition from the Cenozoic Era to the Ecozoic Era. The Cenozoic Era, beginning fifty-five million years ago, was the time when the Earth decked itself with marvelous beauty, mysterious diversity, and puzzling complexity. The varied multitude of living species came into their greatest splendor in this era. But about ten thousand years ago the human family entered into an adolescent phase in which its search for identity led to a gradual separation from nature and an attempt to control the Earth through agriculture and the domestication of animals, resulting in patriarchal societies. This gave rise to greater violence against the Earth and within the human community, and the devastation of the Earth for the apparent welfare of the human community.

Thus, the Cenozoic Era comes to its ending just as does the adolescence of the human species, and we are faced with a choice. On the one hand, we can continue the mystique of our plundering industrial society which is committed to embracing an even more controlling order, a *Technozoic* Era. On the other hand, we can challenge this mystique and awaken to a new consciousness of our mutual relationships within the community of species, a new consciousness of the primacy of the Earth and our dependence on the Earth. For the human community, resurrection means embracing a new Ecozoic Era and a new adulthood in which we move from our human-centered to an Earth-centered norm of reality and value. Patricia Mische describes what is required for us to move into the Ecozoic Era and the adulthood of the human family.

> We are entering a new and dangerous phase in human history and in the Earth's evolution. We can consciously shape the future evolution of the planet. A new maturity is demanded of us. We must become wiser than we've ever been before, for the world is far more complex than our old visions, analyses and structures can accommodate. We must become more conscious and more

holistically spiritual than ever before. Our awareness and our spirituality must be attuned to the sacred presence in all life—to the inner workings of the Spirit in the Earth's processes—lest we destroy our own lifeline out of arrogance.[40]

As the Earth moves into a new era with a mutually enhancing human presence upon the Earth, it can do so only if the human moves out of adolescence and into the maturity of adulthood. In fact, the qualities of the Ecozoic Era are the same as the core characteristics of adulthood, and global resurrection is the call to live out these qualities and characteristics in our personal and communal lives.

- The first quality and characteristic of the Ecozoic Era and the adulthood of the human race is found in embracing the process of *re-membering* nature and the human into one community and *re-integrating* the divine with the human and with nature.

- *Wholeness* found in God, the common womb of the universe, can call the human family together in a new sense of interdependence, and *inclusivity* can do away with the fragmentation of human consciousness. The widespread and pervasive distinctions must give way to the welfare of the Earth community in welcoming all creatures to the common table.

- Humanity will begin to understand that, having first loved ourselves, we can care for others, and our care extends to all species and all of nature. In that way everyone and every species can have a sufficient abundance and all will be enabled to fulfill their own welfare as they serve others.

- The *wisdom of the ages* emerges from many different sources, and we desperately need to mine all of these sources as the human community makes the transition from a Cenozoic Era to an Ecozoic Era and from adolescence to adulthood. No one culture, no one religion, no one nationality, and no one people will have the wisdom to bring this about, but all will contribute to the common good of all.

People who habitually live within the explicate order of material being probably find it hard to imagine a global resurrection and a new

---

40. Mische, "Towards a Global Spirituality," p. 4.

depth of consciousness, while people who habitually discover and live within the implicate order of wholeness can more easily appreciate a global resurrection and a new depth of consciousness. Spirituality and mysticism show us a way, in this life, of becoming more aware of and living within the implicate order. Ira Progoff articulates his sense of immortality in terms of the appreciation of the symbolic experiences that open us to the depths of the psyche, and, in my belief, to the loving presence of God.

> Even more fundamental, the intimation of immortality which is so strong a yearning in man is no longer reduced to being an intellectual belief that must be projected into some nebulous world to come. Immortality becomes present, a condition of reality that is entered now, as the individual orients his existence to the dimension upon which the elemental symbols unfold. The validation of this lies in the continuity of symbolic experiences by which awareness opens in the depth of the psyche.[41]

The explicate order is the more superficial dimension of life, similar to the "flesh" according to Paul's terminology, while the implicate order is the deeper dimension of life, similar to the "spirit" in Paul's terminology. Jesus lived and experienced this deeper, spirit-filled dimension of life and became aware of the powerful presence of God in the implicate order. Jesus' resurrection was the crowning point of his new depth of consciousness. We now move into the biblical story of Jesus, his mission and his message. We will join him in his journey toward a new depth of consciousness in the resurrection, a journey narrated in the light of this resurrection.

---

41. Progoff, *The Symbolic and the Real,* pp. 215–216.

5

THE STORY OF JESUS

Christology in the distinctively Christian sense must, almost by definition, be thought of as a post-resurrection development, an aspect of the Church's thought about how, and through whom, it came to be.[1]

The story of Jesus emerged in the spotlight of the resurrection, and it developed in the context of what we have called *history remembered* and *prophecy historicized*. With the appearance of the synoptic Gospels, the mission and message of Jesus were developed in an effort to show both their continuity with the Jewish tradition and the disciples' expanded faith in the appearance of a new covenant.

The first stage of this development is the Jesus community's faith in the reality of the resurrection and the glorification of Jesus as Lord and Christ. "God has made him both Lord and Messiah, this Jesus whom you crucified" (Acts 2:36). To paraphrase this we can simply say, "This man Jesus, raised from the dead, was made Lord and Christ." The word *Lord, kyrios* in Greek, is a very ambiguous title. In the middle decades of the first century, it could be used as a simple form of address, such as "Sir," or it could be used as a way of addressing a teacher or an authority figure, such as "Master." In the Hebrew tradition, the special word for God is *Yahweh*. Because this sacred name was not to be spoken aloud, the word *Adonai* was used in its place in the public reading of the biblical texts. Later, the Greek translation of *Adonai* was *Kyrios*. As a result of this, the word *Kyrios* (Lord) could be used to refer to Yahweh. Most often, as applied to Jesus, *Kyrios* (Lord) means Master as a sign of respect, or it becomes a title of liturgical invocation and acclamation. Later it comes to mean the glorified and exalted Jesus of the resurrection.

---

1. John Knox, *The Humanity and Divinity of Christ: A Study of Pattern in Christology,* Cambridge University Press, 1967, pp. viii–ix.

STAGE ONE

Made Lord and Christ

This man Jesus

The word *Christ, Messiah* in Hebrew, means the anointed one, and is used in the Hebrew Scriptures as a designation for a king of Israel or for a priest. In Jewish tradition this name gradually acquired the meaning of "one who is to come" who would represent the Israel of the future. In the early Christian community the word Christ identified the historical Jesus as the Messiah of Judaism, but there have always been ambiguities about the meaning of Jesus as the Messiah. Once again the community struggled to find its way between rootedness in its Jewish background and the new experience of the risen Christ.

The second stage in the development of the story of Jesus is found in the reinterpretation of the life and mission of Jesus in the light of the resurrection. As the story is told in the oral tradition and the Gospels it is constantly reinterpreted by filtering out unimportant historical details and filling in new ways of understanding the meaning of Jesus. To use a sports example, on first down the quarterback hands the ball to the running back who gains one yard. On second and third downs he does the same thing to no avail. The team punts, and then gets the ball back. Once more, three fruitless tries at running the ball, they punt, and they get the ball back. The fans are upset and booing. But this time, on second down, the quarterback fakes to the runner and throws a long pass for a touchdown. In light of the touchdown pass, we now know what he was doing. The pass was planned but hidden from the beginning and, in looking back, it is possible to have a new understanding of the team's plans.

To use a biblical example, after the cleansing of the temple in John's Gospel, "Jesus said, 'Destroy this temple and in three days I will raise it up.' The Jews said, 'This temple has been under construction for forty-six years, and you will raise it up in three days?' But he was speaking about the temple of his body. Therefore, when he was raised from the dead, his disciples remembered that he had said this" (John 2:19-22). In the Gospel of John, this conversation moves the reader from the level of the Jewish

STAGE TWO
Interpretation

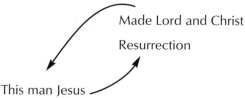

Made Lord and Christ

Resurrection

This man Jesus

temple to the temple of Jesus' body to the risen Christ as the new temple. This type of interpretation is found throughout the Gospels, and it functions not to shed light on the historical character of the story of Jesus but to teach a deeper understanding of Christian life and faith.

The reality that this man Jesus was made Lord and Christ also called for a question about his origin. If Jesus was the exalted and glorified savior, then, as was common in those times, his future notoriety was presaged in his birth narratives. Both Matthew and Luke developed infancy narratives whose purpose was not so much historical as theological. They describe in story language the beliefs of their communities about this man Jesus. The early Christians also began to probe the relationship of the glorified Christ to the overall plan of God. They began to search out the way in which his coming has been a part of the divine plan from the beginning, and to raise the question of the pre-existence of Jesus as found in Paul's letter to the Colossians 1:15-20. Within the context of both Jewish and Hellenistic cultures, these would have been typical questions.

STAGE THREE
Reinterpretation

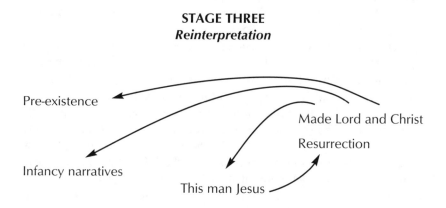

Pre-existence

Made Lord and Christ

Resurrection

Infancy narratives

This man Jesus

With this as a background, we can now proceed to the story of Jesus in four topics: the infancy narratives, discovering a mission, new dimensions of the mission, and the centrality of the reign of God.

THE INFANCY NARRATIVES

These stories of the annunciation, birth, and early life of Jesus do not tell us much about the historical events in the life of Jesus, but they do give us a process that guides us to an awareness of *who* Jesus is and of *how* he came from God. This is similar to the way in which the infancy of many heroes and heroines is described in symbolic language. There is a legend that Thomas Aquinas, during his baptismal ceremony, reached out, grabbed the page with the Lord's Prayer, and ate it. Such a story does not have to be historically accurate to be true. The truth of the story resides in the reality that Aquinas had such a deep knowledge of God that it was as if he had eaten, assimilated, and digested the Lord's Prayer. Similarly, the truth of the stories surrounding the infancy of Jesus resides not in their historical accuracy but in the truth of their message about who Jesus is and how Jesus came from God. The purpose of the infancy stories, therefore, is to show the priority of Jesus by his fulfilling and going beyond the Jewish tradition.

In the annunciation story the words of the angel contain not so much a message to Mary as a message for the early believing community built on the Jewish tradition. Speaking about Jesus, the angel says, "He will be great and will be called Son of the Most High, and the Lord God will give him the throne of David his father, and he will rule over the house of Jacob forever, and of his kingdom there will be no end" (Luke 1:32). Jesus will sit on the throne of David, but he is also the fruit of the Holy Spirit. "The holy Spirit will come upon you, and the power of the Most High will overshadow you. Therefore the child to be born will be called holy, the Son of God" (Luke 1:35).

The visitation story is the coming together of the old and the new in Elizabeth and Mary, and the exchange of greeting between the two covenants is described in the words of Elizabeth. "Most blessed are you among women, and blessed is the fruit of your womb. And how does this happen to me, that the mother of my Lord should come to me? For at the moment the sound of your greeting reached my ears, the infant in my womb leaped for joy" (Luke 1:42-44). Once again the priority of the new covenant in Jesus is shown in the story of the infant John in the womb leaping for joy in celebration of the coming of Jesus. The story of the finding in the temple shows the father, Joseph, being replaced by the Father, God, when Jesus says, "Did you not know I must be in my Father's house?" (Luke 2:49).

Matthew's Gospel opens with a genealogy rooting Jesus in the history of Israel and placing him directly in the line of David. Then he tells a story that, once again, describes the role of the Spirit in the coming of Jesus. "Now this is how the birth of Jesus Christ came about. When his mother Mary was betrothed to Joseph, but before they lived together, she was found with child through the holy Spirit" (Matthew 1:18). The saving role of Jesus is described in the words of the angel to Joseph. "For it is through the holy Spirit that this child has been conceived in her. She will bear a son and you are to name him Jesus, because he will save his people from their sins" (Matthew 1:20-21). Finally, Jesus is seen as the fulfillment of Jewish prophecy found in Isaiah. "All this took place to fulfill what the Lord had said through the prophet: 'Behold, the virgin shall be with child and bear a son, and they shall name him Emmanuel,' which means 'God is with us'" (Matthew 1:22-23).

Who is Jesus? He is the Son of David, the Son of the Most High, and the Son of God. Jesus is the one who fulfills the prophecies, who will usher in a new covenant, and who will save his people from their sins. How did Jesus come from God? Both Luke and Matthew seem to describe the *how* of Jesus' conception as flowing from the power of the Spirit. Luke says, "The holy Spirit will come upon you, and the power of the Most High will overshadow you. Therefore the child to be born will be called holy, the Son of God" (Luke 1:35). Matthew says, "For it is through the holy Spirit that this child has been conceived in her" (Matthew 1:20).

The idea that the divinely chosen leader and savior of God's people would be conceived in some miraculous way is frequently found in the Hebrew Scriptures. Sara became the mother of Isaac when she was beyond the age of childbearing (Genesis 18:9-15). As a result of Isaac's prayer, Jacob was born of the previously barren Rebecca (Genesis 25:21). God remembered the barren Rachel, and she gave birth to Joseph, who later saved Israel from the famine (Genesis 30:1-2, 22-23). The great hero Samson (Judges 13:2, 3) and the prophet Samuel (1 Samuel 1:1-20) were conceived as a result of God's special favor. In the book of the prophet Isaiah we read about the "sign" of a young maiden conceiving and giving birth to a son who will be called Emmanuel. Later in the Greek text (Septuagint) the word "young maiden" was translated as "virgin," and this passage found its way into the Gospel of Matthew.

Why this repetition of miraculous conceptions in the Jewish tradition? Do they have any roots within the history of salvation and the Israelite concept of the relation between God and the chosen people? Repeatedly these stories present the paradox of the divine promise and the salvation of the people of God apparently thwarted by human barrenness. Yet, out of human barrenness comes salvation through the divine initiative and the divine power. The texts of the Bible allow us to resolve the apparent contradiction by showing us that sterility is, for a woman or a man, a consciousness of human limits as well as a manifestation of God's inner power bringing new life out of apparent barrenness. These stories tell us over and over again that both the promise and salvation come through God's initiative. Thus, the Gospel writers used as their model the stories of miraculous conceptions in the Jewish tradition in order to describe the conception and birth of Jesus. The primary meaning and interpretation of the virginity of Mary is to emphasize God's role and God's initiative in freeing the people from their sins.

DISCOVERING A MISSION

Often people think of Jesus as one who knew clearly the mission that God was calling him to fulfill. However, taking Luke as our guide, the story of Jesus unfolds as a process of discovering his mission. This process of Jesus' self-discovery focuses on the role of God's Spirit and Jesus' growing personal awareness of the intimate presence of God as Abba, Father. His mission then flowed from the presence of the Spirit and his personal struggle with his call from God. This struggle and Jesus' growing awareness of God's intimate and loving presence within him are painted in the picture language of Luke in the stories of the baptism, the desert, and the synagogue.

BAPTISM: RELIGIOUS EXPERIENCE OF GOD

> After all the people had been baptized and Jesus also had been baptized and was praying, heaven was opened and the holy Spirit descended upon him in bodily form like a dove. And a voice came from heaven, "You are my beloved Son; with you I am well pleased." (Luke 3:21-22)

This very brief description of the baptism of Jesus contains a wealth of information. The story seems to include Jesus as one of the people being baptized, since there is no special narrative describing Jesus' baptism as in the other synoptic Gospels. He is praying. This simple statement describes the source of his new awareness. In his prayer life during his youth Jesus had developed a deep personal experience of the presence of God within him. This awareness of God, based on his Jewish background as well as his own personal search, led him to a religious experience of God as a loving parent and himself as God's son. The deep spiritual life of Jesus is described in the words of Luke. Jesus' inner life opened itself to God's loving presence, and it was as if "heaven was opened" to him. His sense of his self-identity flowed like the Spirit descending on him in the image of a dove. It was as if God, Abba, actually named Jesus in saying, "You are my beloved Son; with you I am well pleased." This saying was a culmination of a process and a significant turning point in the story of Jesus, and it clearly established his role in the believing community as the Son of God.

DESERT: CLARIFYING THE MISSION

> Filled with the holy Spirit, Jesus returned from the Jordan and was led by the Spirit into the desert for forty days to be tempted by the devil. (Luke 4:1-2)

Once again there is an emphasis on the holy Spirit. Jesus is "filled with the holy Spirit," and the Spirit leads him "into the desert for forty days to be tempted." There is a certain symbolic significance in the story of the desert and the forty days. The Jewish nation spent forty years in the desert where they were tempted. So Jesus here was symbolically replaying the history of the Hebrew people in the desert story. Some say that the forty days in the desert equipped Jesus to overcome the devil, and this might be partially true, but the deeper reason for Jesus' desert experience lies in his continuing discovery of his mission. Jesus was led by the Spirit into the desert in order to clarify and purify his motives for his mission. But why was Jesus tempted?

As people move from self-identity to mission, there is a need to examine their motives. Jesus is tempted to use his mission as the Son of God for his own benefit. "The devil said to him, 'If you are the Son of God, command this stone to become bread.'" Selfishness is always a temptation for one who is called to be a leader, so Jesus says, "It is written, 'One does not live by bread alone.'" Jesus is tempted to use his mission as the Son of God to amass power and glory for himself. "The devil said to him, 'I shall give to you all this power and their glory.'" But Jesus in the depths of his awareness of God's power and presence replies, "You shall worship the Lord, your God, and him alone shall you serve." Certainly someone as precious as the Son of God will be protected by God in all that he does and accomplishes in his mission, even if he throws himself off the parapet of the temple. Yet Jesus' response is: "You shall not put the Lord, your God, to the test."

These temptations picture for us the inner struggle of Jesus and they reinforce the reality of Jesus' humanity. Just because he was God's beloved Son does not mean that he could escape the need to re-examine his motives. His was a mission of immense importance, and the greater the mission the greater the need for clarity and purity with respect to that mission. Moreover, the stories of the baptism and the desert are models for the lives of the believing community. All Christians are called through prayer and the holy Spirit to discover their identity as daughters and sons of God, to be driven out into the desert, and, through temptation, to clarify and purify their mission within the community. Both Jesus and the Christian community are called to face the powers of evil and then to announce the good news to the poor.

SYNAGOGUE: ANNOUNCING THE MISSION

> Jesus returned to Galilee in the power of the Spirit, and news of him spread throughout the whole region. He taught in their synagogues and was praised by all. He came to Nazareth, where he had grown up, and went according to his custom into the synagogue on the sabbath day. He stood up to read and was handed a scroll of the prophet Isaiah. He unrolled the scroll and found the passage where it was written: "The Spirit of the Lord is upon me, because he has anointed me to bring glad tidings to the poor. He has sent me to proclaim liberty to captives and recovery of sight to the blind, to let the oppressed go free, and to proclaim a year acceptable to the Lord." Rolling up the scroll, he handed it back to the attendant and sat down, and the eyes of all in the synagogue looked intently at him. He said to them, "Today this scripture passage is fulfilled in your hearing." (Luke 4:14-21)

This story has all the dimensions of a news release following upon Jesus' inaugural address. After he enters Galilee, news of his return spreads through the whole region. He arrives back home in Nazareth, goes up to the synagogue, and is handed the scroll. The highly praised native son has returned and he reads this powerful passage from Isaiah, a passage that calls to mind the great symbol of the Servant of Yahweh. The Spirit of the Lord is upon this servant, and the Spirit anoints him in seeming reference to the word *Messiah*. Jesus is anointed to bring good news to the poor, liberty to captives, sight to the blind, and to set free the oppressed. This is an astounding inaugural address insofar as it lays out a powerful mission of a suffering servant. And with all in the synagogue looking intently at him, Jesus claims this mission for himself: "Today this scripture passage is fulfilled in your hearing."

Following upon the baptism and the desert, the story of this event in the synagogue lays out the blueprint of Jesus' mission. It is a mission based on his anointing by the Spirit. This mission gives priority to the poor, and it will become a challenge to the political and religious climate of Jesus' day. The outcome of this inaugural day shows us the other dimension of this story (Luke 4:22-30). In a confrontation with the people, Jesus clarifies the meaning of his mission. He speaks of how, although there had been many widows in Israel during a terrible famine, the prophet Elijah went, not to the widows of Israel, but to a foreigner. He also reminds them that, although there were many lepers in Israel during the time of Elisha, the prophet cured only Naaman, the Syrian. The people in the synagogue, realizing that Jesus was referring to them, were filled with fury; they drove him out of the town to a hilltop, and they wanted to hurl him down headlong. But he passed through the midst of them and went away. In a significant way this story, written well after the death and resurrection, gives us a prologue to the mission of Jesus to outcasts, the marginal, and the foreigner, and a bitter foretaste of the ultimate rejection of that mission by the leaders of the people.

NEW DIMENSIONS OF THE MISSION

The mission and message of Jesus are open-ended because, like everything in the universe, they are neither random nor determined, but creative. The emergence of the mission of Jesus has a deep foundation in an emerging universe. If we view the world as "an interconnected web of relationships, with all matter constantly in motion and fundamentally open," then, at the time of Jesus, just as at any other time in human history, "the future was not fixed. The world was full of possibilities for change and creativity."[2]

It Takes a Gang to Make a Messiah

There is a good deal to be learned from examining how Jesus related to a variety of other persons and to God. Christology at the end of the day involves an assessment of the person, works, experiences, relationships, roles, and career of Jesus.[3]

---

2. Joseph Jaworski, *Synchronicity: The Inner Path of Leadership,* San Francisco, Berrett-Koehler Publishers, 1996, p. 160.

3. Witherington, *The Many Faces of the Christ,* p. 5.

We often imagine Jesus as a heroic and charismatic figure who had an in-depth experience of God as Abba and received his mission directly from God. This experience and mission then radiated out from Jesus to the disciples. Jesus was the guide, the master, the teacher, and the Messiah. The Gospel according to Mark hints at a different scenario. There is an interdependence and a web of relationships among Jesus, his disciples, and the various other characters found in the Gospel. Together they experience the presence of God as Abba, and they discover their mission. Such a communal experience is described by Sallie McFague: "We live in a relationship of mutual influence with the other subjects in the Earth community; we do influence them and they do influence us. This interrelationship is so profound, so thorough, and so pervasive that we usually do not see it."[4]

The use of the word *gang* to refer to the many friends, disciples, and enemies of Jesus as well as to those people who were chance acquaintances of Jesus might seem out of place. Usually we think of gangs as the Mafia, drug gangs, or youth gangs, most of whom are unsavory and disreputable people. But in searching for a word for those who influenced and shared the life of Jesus, I looked up the meaning of the word *gang* in an unabridged dictionary. There were two definitions that capture the reality that I want to describe: "an elementary and close knit social group of spontaneous origin," and "a group of persons drawn together by a community of tastes, interests, and activities." Jesus was influenced, first of all, by John the Baptist, then by those called his disciples, and by the many people who, through their questions and their calls for healing, helped to shape his ministry. Finally, this Jesus gang was influenced by its antagonists, such as the scribes and Pharisees, who challenged Jesus and the disciples, and in this way helped them to articulate their mission.

Like his prophetic predecessors of old, John the Baptist stood out as a sign of contradiction. His life style, his powerful preaching, and his message were a revival of that tradition. Albert Nolan writes:

> John the Baptist was the only person in that society who impressed Jesus. Here was the voice of God warning the people of an impending disaster and calling for a change of heart in each and every individual. Jesus believed this and joined in with those who were determined to do something about it. He was baptized by John.[5]

---

4. Sallie McFague, *Super, Natural Christians,* Minneapolis, Fortress Press, 1997, p. 153.

5. Nolan, *Jesus before Christianity,* p. 21.

There are hints of the interrelationship between John and Jesus in the Gospel of Mark. The evangelist starts out his story of the Baptist by putting in the mouth of John the words of Isaiah: "A voice crying out in the desert: 'Prepare the way of the Lord, make straight his paths'" (Isaiah 40:3). Then John describes the mission of Jesus: "One mightier than I is coming after me. I am not worthy to stoop and loosen the thongs of his sandals. I have baptized you with water; he will baptize you with the holy Spirit" (Mark 1:7-8). The Gospels tell us that Jesus was indebted to John for various aspects of his own mission, and that Jesus drew some of his disciples from the early followers of John. There was a mutuality of influence between these two prophets, and this mutuality helped Jesus in his discovery of his message.

In the Gospel of Mark, 7:1-23, there is evidence of the mutual interaction, both negative and positive, between Jesus and both the Pharisees and the disciples. The Pharisees observed some of the disciples eating their meal with unclean hands. By doing so the disciples were contradicting the tradition of the holiness code, and they precipitated a confrontation with the Pharisees. The Pharisees questioned Jesus, "Why do your disciples not follow the tradition of the elders but instead eat a meal with unclean hands?" (Mark 7:5). Jesus responded, "Well did Isaiah prophecy about you hypocrites, as it is written: 'This people honors me with their lips, but their hearts are far from me...' You disregard God's commandment but cling to human tradition" (Mark 7:6-8). In this pericope the disciples precipitate the discussion by eating without having washed. The Pharisees question Jesus. Jesus answers them by moving the focus into a deeper dimension of the heart. When they get home, the disciples question Jesus, and these questions lead Jesus to explain it again.

> He said to them, "Are even you likewise without understanding? Do you not realize that everything that goes into a person from outside cannot defile, since it enters not the heart but the stomach and passes out into the latrine?" (Thus he declared all foods clean.) "But what comes out of a person, that is what defiles." (Mark 7:17-20)

Throughout the Gospel there are many such exchanges with the scribes and Pharisees that lead both Jesus and his gang to see things in new ways and articulate them to the crowds.

Frequently Jesus is led to deepen his understanding of his mission by people who approach him for healing or help. One example is found in the story of the woman with a hemorrhage.

> There was a woman afflicted with hemorrhages for twelve years. She had suffered greatly at the hands of many doctors and had spent all that she had. Yet she was not helped but only grew worse. She had heard about Jesus and came up behind him in the crowd and touched his cloak. She said, "If I but touch his clothes, I shall be cured." (Mark 5:25-28)

Notice that this woman would have been unclean for twelve years because of her hemorrhages. Being unclean, she had to live without ordinary social interchanges, because anything or anyone she touched would become unclean as well. She touched Jesus. Jesus became unclean.

> Immediately her flow of blood dried up. She felt in her body that she was healed of her affliction. Jesus, aware at once that power had gone out from him, turned around in the crowd and asked, "Who has touched my clothes [and made me unclean]?" But his disciples said to him, "You see how the crowd is pressing upon you, and yet you ask, 'Who touched me?'" and he looked around to see who had done it. The woman, realizing what had happened to her, approached in fear and trembling. She fell down before Jesus and told him the whole truth. (Mark 5:29-33)

A woman has touched Jesus. An unclean woman has touched Jesus. Jesus is unclean. What will his reaction be? Righteous anger and revulsion? A rending of his garments? A desire to cleanse himself? No! He says to her, "Daughter, your faith has saved you. Go in peace and be cured of your affliction." This unnamed woman took the initiative and placed Jesus in a dilemma. Rather than condemning her as the law required, he chose to recognize her faith in a loving God. This was a turning point in Jesus' mission as he put her faith and her welfare ahead of the traditions of the elders. It is an example of how Jesus was called by those around him to search more deeply the meaning of his mission.

Another case of someone who calls Jesus to healing is found in the story of the blind Bartimaeus in Mark 10:46-52. Bartimaeus was a blind man who sat by the roadside begging. Jesus with his disciples and a sizable crowd were passing by. Bartimaeus began to cry out and say, "Jesus, son of David, have pity on me." Many of the followers of Jesus rebuked the man, telling him to be silent, but he kept calling out.

> Jesus stopped and said, "Call him." So they called the blind man, saying to him, "Take courage; get up, he is calling you." He threw aside his cloak, sprang up, and came to Jesus. Jesus said to him in reply, "What do you want me to do for you?" The blind

man replied to him, "Master, I want to see." Jesus told him, "Go your way; your faith has saved you." Immediately he received his sight and followed him on the way. (Mark 10:49-52)

Notice that Jesus says, "Your faith has saved you." These are the same words that Jesus spoke to the unclean woman. This theme of tying together faith and healing is found many times in all the synoptics. The following are some other examples: the healing of the centurion's servant in Matthew 8:10 and Luke 7:9; the healing of the paralytic in Matthew 9:2 and Mark 2:5; the healing of the demonic boy in Matthew 17:19-20 and Mark 9:23-25; the pardon of the sinful woman in Luke 7:50; the story of the leper who returned to give thanks in Luke 17:19. My purpose in focusing on this theme of faith and healing is to highlight its dynamics in the development of the gang and to reinforce the necessity of a deep faith in God within the Jesus movement before as well as after the resurrection.

The inner religious experience of God, as symbolized in the baptism of Jesus and the desert temptations, and the dynamic interrelationships with those around him gradually led Jesus to an awareness of his mission. The importance of this network of Jesus with the disciples is hinted at in the Acts of Apostles when the successor of Judas was to be chosen. "Therefore, it is necessary that one of those who accompanied us the whole time the Lord Jesus came and went among us, beginning from the baptism of John until the day on which he was taken up from us, become a witness to his resurrection" (Acts 1:21-22). It takes a gang, an elementary and close knit social group of spontaneous origin, to make a Messiah, and the faith of this Jesus community became the foundation stone of the Christian community of the first century.

JESUS AND THE JUDEAN SOCIAL MAP

Robert Beck, in his book *Nonviolent Story: Narrative Conflict Resolution in the Gospel of Mark*, develops a theory of Jesus' mission in Mark's Gospel as a power struggle between the unclean and the holy, the rigid and the free, the closed and the open. The beginning of this struggle is laid out in the first chapter of Mark in terms of the *holy* Spirit. First, it is found in the words of John, who says, "I have baptized you with water; he will baptize you with the holy Spirit," then in the baptism of Jesus when Jesus saw "the heavens being torn open and the Spirit, like a dove, descending upon him," and finally in the temptation of Jesus when "The Spirit drove him out into the desert." The antagonist, an unclean spirit, appears in the cure of the demoniac. "In their synagogue was a man with an unclean spirit; he cried out, 'What have you to do with us, Jesus of Nazareth? Have you come to destroy us? I know who you are—the Holy

One of God!' Jesus rebuked him and said, 'Quiet! Come out of him!'"
(Mark 1:23-25). Even the unclean spirit recognizes Jesus as the Holy
One. Jesus commands the unclean spirit to come out, and the spirit con-
vulses the man and with a loud cry comes out of him. To come out is to
be set free of the power of evil.

Then comes the cleansing of a leper who would be unclean by reason
of his disease. "A leper came to him, begged him and said, 'If you wish,
you can make me clean.' Moved with pity, Jesus stretched out his hand,
touched him, and said to him, 'I do will it. Be made clean'" (Mark 1:40-
41). Jesus shows the power of holiness over ritual uncleanness. Jesus then
heals a paralytic. One who is rigid is made free and his sins are forgiven,
much to the consternation of the scribes (Mark 2:1-12). Jesus angers
some "scribes who were Pharisees" by eating with tax collectors and sinners who are unclean (Mark 2:13-17). Jesus also challenges the rigid ob-
servance of the sabbath, and by his actions he shows that the rigidity of
the law must give way to the welfare of the human community. On one
occasion his disciples pick heads of grain on the sabbath, and the Pharisees say, "Look, why are they doing what is unlawful on the sabbath?"
Jesus calls for freedom by saying, "The sabbath was made for man, not
man for the sabbath" (Mark 2:23-28). Another time, a man with a withered hand enters the synagogue, and the Pharisees watch closely to see if
Jesus will cure him on the sabbath. "Looking around at them with anger
and grieved at their hardness of heart, he said to the man, 'Stretch out
your hand.' He stretched it out and his hand was restored. The Pharisees
went out and immediately took counsel with the Herodians against him to
put him to death" (Mark 3:5-6).

What do we learn from these dynamic encounters of Jesus? Mark sets
up an opposition, first of all, between the Holy One and the Demonic.
Gradually the narrative moves on to describe Jesus' challenge of the holiness code. Jesus touches the ritually unclean leper and cleanses him.
Jesus heals the rigid paralytic by freeing him from sin and telling him to
take up his mat and walk. Jesus eats with sinners and tax collectors, because Jesus did not come to call the righteous but sinners. Jesus opens the
closed doors of the sabbath and sets free the man with a withered hand.
Jesus' acts are powerful because they challenge the very structure of Jewish social existence and the value of holiness as separation. At the same
time, the Pharisees and Herodians, caught in the web of ritual exclusion,
see Jesus as one who, by his policy of holiness as wholeness, is set on destroying the very existence of the holiness code. They begin to search for
a way of putting Jesus to death.

But the challenge of Jesus reaches even to the outer limits of the
Judean social map. On a journey through the region of the gentiles he encounters a woman who is Greek and a Syrophoenecian by birth.

She begged him to drive the demon out of her daughter. He said to her, "Let the children be fed first. For it is not right to take the food of the children and throw it to the dogs." She replied and said to him, "Lord, even the dogs under the table eat the children's scraps." Then he said to her, "For saying this, you may go. The demon has gone out of your daughter." When the woman went home, she found the child lying in bed and the demon gone. (Mark 7:26-30)

This rather puzzling story has two lessons to teach. As noted above, Jesus' mission was often clarified by the call of the outcasts and the marginal. Here the woman, who must have known something of Judean social customs, goes directly to Jesus and asks him to drive the demon out of her daughter. Jesus' response seems harsh, but perhaps Mark was verbalizing the feelings of the Jewish leaders and perhaps some of Jesus' gang. The woman simply reasserts her request, and Jesus, admiring her response, tells her that the demon has gone out of the daughter. The two lessons are: the character of Jesus' mission is challenged by those who request something from him, and this particular healing has led him to extend the inclusivity of his mission to the gentiles.

It is now time to pull together Mark's examples of Jesus' prophetic ministry into a more intelligible schema. The religious imagination of Jesus' time had fenced off the Judaic world into ritual zones ordering all areas of Jewish life. "A sacred *topography* rippled out in concentric zones from the Holy of Holies in the temple, through the courts of the temple to the Holy City, and then out to the Holy Land and eventually to the unclean pagan nations."[6] This sacred topography can be illustrated by a series of concentric circles beginning with the Holy of Holies and reaching out beyond the boundaries to the pagans.

It will be helpful to quote Beck at some length, because he integrates this map with the various stories in the Gospel of Mark.

In the symbolic maps, the gentiles are off the edge in the zone of the absolutely unclean. Meanwhile the temple, as the site of the Holy of Holies, stands at dead center. Certainly, this positioning of the so-called gentile mission in relation to the journey to Jerusalem makes narrative sense if the journey is interpreted as a deliberate, almost processional march from edge to center...In this regard, the gentile mission represents the extreme case of Jesus' attack on the unclean powers. His ministry to the expendable population that is marked by Judean uncleanness includes the sick, the hungry, the

---

6. Beck, *Nonviolent Story,* p. 66.

JUDEAN SOCIAL MAP

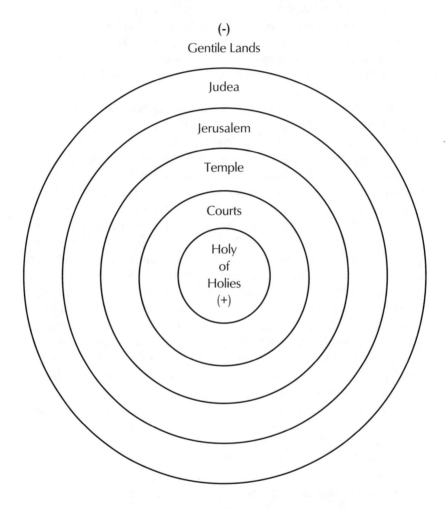

(-)
Gentile Lands

Judea

Jerusalem

Temple

Courts

Holy
of
Holies
(+)

hopelessly marginalized. But his mission to the marginal is not complete until the gentiles too are reached...Mark's priorities relate to his narrative program. That program shows Jesus expanding his assault on the unclean powers through the first eight chapters. Toward the end of chapter 8 he turns his attention toward Jerusalem, moving from the periphery to the center. It is as if he brings a retinue of the various victims of the purity system with him, right to the center. There he turns the purity system inside out.[7]

---

7. Ibid., p. 83.

In chapter 11 Mark chronicles this journey to the center with a triumphant procession led by Jesus seated on a colt. Many people spread their cloaks or leafy branches on the road. "Those preceding him as well as those following kept crying out: 'Hosanna! Blessed is he who comes in the name of the Lord!'" (Mark 11:8-9). Then Jesus entered into Jerusalem and went into the temple area. "He looked around at everything [almost as if planning for the next day's prophetic action in the temple] and, since it was already late, went out to Bethany with the Twelve" (Mark 11:11).

All was ready, and in Mark's Gospel the story of Jesus' action in the temple is described as deliberate and calculated and non-violent.

> They [Jesus and the Twelve] came to Jerusalem, and on entering the temple area he began to drive out those selling and buying there. He overturned the tables of the money changers and the seats of those who were selling doves. He did not permit anyone to carry anything through the temple area. Then he taught them saying, "Is it not written: 'My house shall be called a house of prayer for all peoples'? But you have made it a den of thieves." The chief priests and the scribes came to hear of it and were seeking a way to put him to death, yet they feared him because the whole crowd was astonished at his teaching. When evening came, they went out of the city. (Mark 11:15-19)

In one sense, his non-violent action brings the public ministry of the Jesus community to its culmination and moves the drama on to the impending trial and death of Jesus. Jesus challenges the religious leaders and all the boundaries of the Judean social map, and Beck explains this action in terms of Jesus' prophetic judgment on the purity system.

> Upon arriving at the city, at the conclusion of this journey, Jesus arranges an action of protest and prophetic judgment that we popularly call the *temple cleansing*. The intensity of this paradoxical gesture is difficult to appreciate adequately. After all, the Holy of Holies is categorically least in need of cleansing. It escapes the threat of uncleanness by definition. Its role is to define the unclean as that which is opposed to or removed from it as the center of holiness. It is the standard by which the relative diminishments of purity, graduating into uncleanness, are to be determined. To put the temple under judgment is to place in question the standard itself. Cleansing the temple is no reformist gesture but a deep judgment on the system it represents. In repudiating the central principle of the purity system, Jesus repudiates its entirety.[8]

---

8. Ibid., pp. 83–84.

The purity system and the holiness code of the Jewish society in the early years of the first century embodied some of the characteristics of the adolescence of the human race. As we discussed earlier in chapter 1, adolescence involves a search for identity with the resulting tendency to separate the self from the other. A destructive separateness has persisted throughout the adolescence of the human story. There is nothing wrong with diversity. The Earth revels in its diversity, but separateness ends up pitting one against another and putting one above the other—human over nature, Heaven over Earth, divine over human, spirit over matter, master over slave, ruler over subject, and ritual purity over the unclean. Such separateness was endemic to the society in which Jesus lived.

Adulthood, on the other hand, involves a process of re-membering and re-integrating that which was separate, and it calls for a new social and religious order based on wholeness and inclusivity. Jesus embodies this adulthood in his challenge to the arbitrary boundaries of Jewish society and his call for inclusiveness in all aspects of human life. The unclean, the leper, and the woman with a hemorrhage were made whole. The spiritual and physical healing of the paralytic set him free and enabled him to rediscover his place in society. The man with the withered hand could be made whole on the sabbath. Levi the tax collector was called to the Jesus movement, and Jesus, by eating with the tax collector and the sinners, broke down barriers and showed his respect for all people. The Syrophoenician woman, the hated pagan, led Jesus to heal her daughter and to cross even the barrier between Jews and gentiles. The adult values of re-membering and re-integrating, of wholeness and inclusivity, form the basis of a new society and eventually bring about the hatred of the Pharisees and scribes and chief priests.

THE COMING OF A NEW AGE

The religious and social climate that formed the background of Jesus' life, death, and resurrection was characterized by turmoil and expectation. The atmosphere was electric. While people feared hardships and calamities, they still harbored a hope for a new age. There was hope for a king and a Messiah, a supranational king and savior, an eschatological prophet to prepare for God's coming. The coming of a new age would be a time of great tribulation as described in the Gospel of Matthew in apocalyptic language.

False messiahs and false prophets will arise, and they will perform signs and wonders so great as to deceive, if that were possible, even the elect... Immediately after the tribulation of those days,

> the sun will be darkened, and the moon will not give its
>   light,
> and the stars will fall from the sky,
> and the powers of the heavens will be shaken.

And then the sign of the Son of Man... coming upon the clouds of heaven with power and great glory. And he will send out his angels with a trumpet blast, and they will gather the elect from the four winds, from one end of the heavens to the other. (Matthew 24:24, 29-31)

The Gospel of Matthew contains many references to a new age. John the Baptist spoke of "a voice of one crying out in the desert, 'Prepare the way of the Lord, make straight his paths.'" John wore the clothing of a prophet, camel's hair and a leather belt around his waist. He challenged the Pharisees and Sadducees by saying, "You brood of vipers! Produce good fruit as evidence of your repentance." Then John went on to warn them saying, "Even now the ax lies at the root of the trees. Therefore every tree that does not bear good fruit will be cut down and thrown into the fire. I am baptizing you with water, for repentance, but the one who is coming after me is mightier than I" (Matthew 3:3, 7, 10-11). For John, the day of judgment was here.

In Matthew 22:1-14, the wedding feast is the symbol of the messianic banquet. The king sends his servants out to invite the guests to the feast, but they refuse to come. Then he sends out other servants, saying, "Tell those invited, 'Behold, I have prepared my banquet, my calves and fattened cattle are killed, and everything is ready; come to the feast.'" The invited guests ignore the invitation. Some just go about their business; others lay hold on the servants, mistreat them, and kill them. The invited guests to this eschatological feast are the religious leaders who reject God's invitation to repent and change their lives. Then the king is enraged and sends his troops, destroys those murderers, and burns their city. This is the eschatological destruction of the end times that will usher in a new age of inclusivity. So the servants go out into the main roads and invite to the feast whomever they find. They gather all they find, bad and good alike, and the hall is filled with guests.

It is clear that in Matthew those who refused the invitation were the scribes and Pharisees, the religious leaders of the people, who were not ready or able to enter into the new age. In chapter 23:1-36 Jesus denounces these leaders in the strongest of terms. Here are two examples of the words of Jesus:

> Woe to you, scribes and Pharisees, you hypocrites. You lock the kingdom of heaven before human beings. You do not enter yourselves, nor do you allow entrance to those trying to enter.

> Woe to you, scribes and Pharisees, you hypocrites. You cleanse the outside of cup and dish, but inside they are full of plunder and self-indulgence. Blind Pharisees, cleanse first the inside of the cup, so that the outside may be clean.

In Matthew's Gospel the growing and deepening antagonism between Jesus and the scribes and Pharisees is leading to a climax. Matthew describes that climax in the apocalyptic language of chapter 24. The foreshadowing of the end is found first in Jesus' words about the destruction of the temple:

> Jesus left the temple area and was going away, when his disciples approached him to point out the temple buildings. He said to them in reply, "You see all these things, do you not? Amen, I say to you, there will not be left here a stone upon another stone that will not be thrown down." (Matthew 24:1-2)

Then the Gospel marches before the reader a series of calamities involving false messiahs, wars, and rumors of wars. Nation will rise up against nation, and there will be famines and earthquakes. The faithful will be hated by all nations because of the name of Jesus. Then will come the great tribulation when all will see the desolating abomination spoken of in Daniel. Immediately after the tribulation of those days, the sun will be darkened, and the moon will not give its light, and the stars will fall from the sky, and the powers of the heavens will be shaken. And then the sign of the Son of Man will appear coming upon the clouds of heaven with power and great glory. And he will send out his angels with a trumpet blast, and they will gather the elect from the four winds, from one end of the heavens to the other. The consummation is found in the coming of the Son of Man.

The final reference to a new age in Matthew is found at the moment of Jesus' death on the cross.

> But Jesus cried out again in a loud voice, and gave up his spirit. And behold, the veil of the sanctuary was torn in two from top to bottom. The earth quaked, rocks were split, tombs were opened, and the bodies of many saints who had fallen asleep were raised. And coming forth from their tombs after his resurrection, they entered the holy city and appeared to many. (Matthew 27:50-53)

For the early Christian community, the death of Jesus gradually led to the end of temple worship, and this was symbolized by the rending of the sanctuary veil from top to bottom. Jesus' death was accompanied by the apocalyptic signs of earthquakes, split rocks, and open tombs. The new age was ushered in by the death of Jesus. As we saw in chapter 4, out of the chaos of the crucifixion came the resurrection of Jesus, the source of new life and a new depth of consciousness for the entire Earth community. But the question arises: How did the ministry of the historical Jesus fit in with the historical context of an eschatological expectation articulated in apocalyptic language? Crossan calls the historical role of Jesus *ethical eschatology.*

> *Ethical eschatology (or ethicist)* negates the world by actively protesting and nonviolently resisting a system judged to be evil, unjust, and violent. It is not a question of this group or that government needing some changes or improvements. Ethical eschatology is directed at the world's *normal* situation of discrimination and violence, exploitation and oppression, injustice and unrighteousness...Ethicist is present wherever nonviolent resistance to structural evil appears in this world. And the courage for it derives from union with transcendental nonviolence.[9]

Ethical eschatology calls for opposition to the world as it functions in any place or among any group or in any situation in which there is discrimination, violence, exploitation, oppression, injustice, or unrighteousness. This form of eschatology calls for us to act and not to wait for the intervention of God. This eschatology arises from within the people as the result of an inner change of heart and a new sense of a God of justice and righteousness for the whole Earth and all its creatures and peoples. It calls for a God who opposes systemic evil, not because it is systemic but because it is evil. In our age, ethical eschatology and non-violent resistance to structural evil are found in such diverse people as Mahatma Gandhi, Dorothy Day, and Martin Luther King. The question facing the global community after September 11th is whether nations and leaders of nations will transform this world by rejecting violence and embracing a non-violent ethical eschatology. This will happen only when nations and peoples begin to recognize the centrality of the reign of God in the whole of the universe.

---

9. Crossan, *The Birth of Christianity,* p. 284.

THE CENTRALITY OF THE REIGN OF GOD

> Every New Testament scholar would agree that the central theme
> of Jesus' ministry was the "Kingdom of God."[10]

> Most exegetes and historians also agree that the notion of the
> kingdom of God lies at the heart of the message of Jesus. One
> can take it as a centering point which radiates influence on all of
> the teaching of Jesus.[11]

The theme of the kingdom of God, so central to Jesus' preaching, had
deep roots in the religious history of Israel. It was not an invention of
Jesus or the Gospels. In the Hebrew Scriptures the idea of a kingdom of
God reaches back into the time of Moses and the formation of the people
of God in the promised land. The amorphous group of Hebrews escaping
from Egypt finally ended up self-consciously as a people under the
covenant and the rule of Yahweh. The transformation of the people into a
kingdom ruled by a king acting in the name of Yahweh led to the Davidic
state and the hope for a messianic kingdom. Among the great prophets of
the exile, the image of the kingdom of God begins to express itself more
and more in the hope for an idyllic future with a "new heaven and a new
earth," such as that found in the prophet Isaiah (Isaiah 35). By the second
century B.C.E., this hope begins to transcend the limits of this world and
moves on to a vision of a future resurrection of the just. "Both the
prophetic expectation of a this-worldly rule of justice and the apocalyptic
vision of a future life in the heavenly kingdom are brought together in the
symbol of the reign of God—the proclamation of which was the core
message of the preaching of Jesus."[12]

Looking at this very brief background of the kingdom of God leads
to a deeper concern about the very meaning of the word *kingdom.* In English the word *kingdom* usually carries a political and spatial connotation
that belies the underlying sense of this image. The Hebrew word *malkuth*
and the Greek word *basileia* are more accurately translated as the "reign"
or "rule" of God. The Hebrew and Christian Scriptures describe not a national or politically defined kingdom, but the presence and reign of God
that can transform human social, religious, and political systems into a

---

10. Donald Senior, *Jesus: A Gospel Portrait,* Dayton, Ohio, Pflaum Press, 1975, p.
52.

11. Haight, *Jesus Symbol of God,* p. 97.

12. Raymond Bulman, *The Lure of the Millennium: The Year 2000 and Beyond,*
Maryknoll, N.Y., Orbis Books, 1999, p. 86.

new way of justice and righteousness. Thus I prefer and will use the expression "reign of God" in place of the "kingdom of God" in order to convey the biblical concept of the presence of God within all dimensions of human life. I can also note that the use of "kingdom of heaven" in Matthew flows from the Hebrew hesitancy to use the holy name of Yahweh, and Matthew's terminology is equivalent to "reign of God."

JESUS AND THE REIGN OF GOD

There are three sources for an understanding of Jesus and the reign of God: (1) parables, which are simple stories about familiar things ending often in a reversal of values; (2) miracles, which contain and manifest the power and presence of God; and (3) signs in John, which are wondrous deeds expressing and explaining the meaning of God's presence in Jesus. It is possible in this work to offer only a few examples of each of these three sources and then draw some conclusions.

The *parable* of the good Samaritan (Luke 10:29-37) is a classic story. A scholar asks Jesus, "Who is my neighbor?" In response Jesus tells the story of a man who fell victim to robbers who beat him and left him half dead. Then two Jewish people of some prestige come by. The first, a priest, when he sees the man, passes him by; the second, a Levite, comes to the place and he too passes by. Then a Samaritan traveler, who would ordinarily be despised by Jewish people, approaches the victim and is moved to compassion. He tends to the man's wounds, takes him to the innkeeper, and gives the innkeeper instructions to take care of the victim at the Samaritan's expense. Then Jesus asks the scholar, "Which of these three, in your opinion, was neighbor to the robbers' victim?" He answers, "The one who treated him with mercy." Jesus says to him, "Go and do likewise."

The evangelist tells this story in such a way that the reader is drawn into the plight of the man who was robbed and beaten. Then, as the story continues, the two people with whom the reader would be sympathetic fail to help the victim, and the one with whom the reader would be unsympathetic is compassionate to the victim. Moreover, the scholar, who had asked the question, was forced to admit that the hated Samaritan was the good neighbor. The reign of God is like someone being a compassionate neighbor to those in need.

There are two other brief passages that also show the reversal of values in the reign of God: the parable of the Pharisee and the tax collector in Luke 18:9-14 and the story of the poor widow in Luke 21:1-4. In the parable, both men, the religious Pharisee and the impious tax collector, go up to the temple area to pray. At the end Jesus says, "I tell you, the latter [the tax collector] went home justified, not the former [the Pharisee]; for everyone who exalts himself will be humbled, and the one who humbles himself will be exalted." In the story of the poor widow, Jesus sees the wealthy people putting their offerings into the treasury. A poor widow puts in two small coins. Jesus contradicts the obvious and says, "I tell you truly, this poor widow put in more than all the rest; for those others have all made offerings from their surplus wealth, but she, from her poverty, has offered her whole livelihood." These passages indicate that in the reign of God our accustomed social values are often turned upside down.

In Matthew 13:44 Jesus shows how precious is the reign of God. "The kingdom of heaven is like a treasure buried in a field, which a person finds and hides again, and out of joy, goes and sells all that he has and buys that field." The reign of God is so precious and so important that, in the story of the rich young man (Matthew 19:16-24), Jesus says, "If you wish to be perfect, go, sell what you have and give to the poor, and you will have treasure in heaven. Then come, follow me." When the young man hears this statement, he goes away sad, for he has many possessions. Then Jesus says to his disciples, "Amen, I say to you, it will be hard for one who is rich to enter the kingdom of heaven." The reign of God is the underlying value of the whole of life. It is so precious that we must be willing to sell all that we have in order to discover the presence of God within us.

The *miracles* in the life of Jesus are events that manifest the power and presence of God. They are not interventions of God in the laws of nature, nor are they simply compassionate acts of a compassionate Jesus. The Greek word used to describe a miracle is *dynamis*, which means power. In a miracle, the power and presence of God break through and bring about a transformation, whether of an individual or of society. This dimension of the reign of God is found exemplified in the story of the Gerasene demoniac (Mark 5:1-20). There was a man from the town who was possessed by an unclean spirit. The man had been dwelling among the tombs, and no one could restrain him, even with a chain. In fact, he had frequently been bound with shackles and chains, but he had pulled apart the chains and smashed the shackles. Night and day among the tombs and on the hillsides he was always crying out and bruising himself with stones. At the command of Jesus, the unclean spirits came out of him and entered the swine, which rushed down a steep bank and were drowned. When the townspeople heard about this, they came out and caught sight of the possessed man sitting there clothed and in his right mind. And they were seized with wonder at the power of God which transformed a raging maniac into a man clothed and in his right mind.

In the healing of a paralytic in Matthew 9:1-8, the power of the reign of God appears in the forgiveness of sins as well as in the healing of the paralytic. Here was a man who was rigid and uptight, lying on a stretcher. His friends brought him to Jesus. When Jesus saw their faith, he said to the paralytic, "Courage, child, your sins are forgiven." The scribes accused Jesus of blasphemy, and Jesus said, "Which is easier, to say, 'Your sins are forgiven,' or 'Rise and walk'?" Then Jesus said, "Rise, pick up your stretcher, and go home." The people were struck with awe and wonder at the power of God present in Jesus to both forgive sins and to heal the paralytic. The faith of the man's friends enabled the power of God in Jesus to forgive and to heal.

The miracles in John's Gospel are called *signs,* in Greek *semeian.* The Gospel presents these signs as works of revelation intimately connected with salvation. This means that in this Gospel the focus is not so much on the physical dimension of the miracle, but rather on the revelatory character of a sign that discloses something about the meaning of Jesus and about the meaning of salvation. In John the symbolic element of a sign is primary. There are seven major signs in the Gospel: the changing of water into wine at Cana; the healing of the official's son; the paralytic at the pool; the multiplication of the loaves; walking on the waters; the man born blind; and the raising of Lazarus. A brief discussion of three of these signs will help shed light on their meaning for John's contemporaries and for ourselves.

The changing of water into wine at Cana was the first of the signs (John 2:1-11). The evangelist is calling attention to the replacement of the water prescribed for Jewish purification by the choicest of wines of the new covenant. Then the abundance of wine, one hundred and twenty gallons, is a symbol of the abundance of the messianic kingdom, which not only replaces the old dispensation but also promises the fullness of a messianic future. It reveals the glory of Jesus and calls the disciples to a deeper faith. "Jesus did this as the beginning of his signs in Cana in Galilee and so revealed his glory, and his disciples began to believe in him."

As Jesus was walking along, he saw a man blind from birth (John 9:1-40). The disciples asked him whether it was this man or his parents who had sinned. Jesus answered, "Neither he nor his parents sinned; it is so the works of God might be made visible through him." There follows a story of great dramatic skill that pits the Pharisees against the blind man with Jesus providing the catalyst and the conclusion to the story. The interchange that follows shows that Jesus has not only restored the blind man's sight but also given him spiritual sight and reduced the Pharisees to spiritual blindness. As happens in the signs, the spiritual healing takes the foreground as the story develops, and the words of Jesus form the conclusion of the revelation. "I came into this world for judgment, so that those who do not see might see, and those who do see might become blind."

Lazarus is dead. Mary and Martha call for Jesus. He goes to Bethany and raises Lazarus to new life (John 11:1-44). The story line does not open up the full depths of what Jesus did. Jesus' miracles are signs of who he is and what he gives to us. In none of them is the gift of life more clearly emphasized. Jesus gives life to Lazarus, yet the remarks of Jesus show that the restoration of physical life is important only as a sign of the gift of eternal life. God's power of new life and of resurrection is also found in Jesus himself who says, "I am the resurrection and the life; everyone who believes in me, even if they die, will live, and everyone who lives and believes in me will never die." Finally, the story of Lazarus enacts a sign of the glory of God revealed in Jesus, and shows that the reign of God preached by Jesus will lead us all to eternal life.

The Gospel of John does not speak explicitly of the reign of God in these signs, but its reality is clearly present. Just as in the parables and miracles in the synoptic Gospel, so in John there is an emphasis on the new values found in Jesus and his call for faith. The importance and preciousness of the reign of God are found in the treasure in the field as well as in the superabundance of the wine in Cana. The signs as well as the miracles are events that manifest the power and presence of God. In the miracle of the paralytic in Matthew there is an intimate relationship between physical healing and the forgiveness of sin, and in John between physical and spiritual sight. The parables lead to a new way of thinking; the miracles show the power of God's presence; the signs reveal the deeper presence of God and the spiritual dimensions of life in Jesus.

The parables, the miracles, and the signs all lead us to the power and presence of God. It is the presence of God that will call us and enable us to repent and believe the good news. It is the presence of God that breaks through and manifests itself in the miracles. It is the presence of God that is revealed in the signs of Jesus and in our salvation. The reign of God *is the presence of God* unfolding in our lives and in our communities and churches and nations and in social groups calling us to change our lives and transform the whole of our society. According to Crossan, "Here, clearly, the kingdom of God is not about me but about us, not about individuality but about society, not about heaven but about earth. It is about divine justice here below."[13]

If the reign of God is in reality the presence of God, we can also say that the reign of God *is* God—but God as present to us, God as the revelatory presence to us, and God as the salvific presence to us. Over the past few years, there has been much discussion about whether the reign of God is now or in the future, but for me this is no longer a significant question. The reign of God is wherever and however God is present to us, in the past, in the present, and in the future. "God's reign is his rule, his power, his presence, his glory; it is *God as present* to his people."[14]

13. Crossan, *The Birth of Christianity,* p. 326.

14. Donald J. Goergen, *The Mission and Ministry of Jesus,* Wilmington, Del., Michael Glazier, 1986, p. 230.

The Reign of God in an Emerging Universe

> The presence of God among men which Jesus preached was not
> something new, not a gift that God had saved up for the end of
> time. Jesus merely proclaimed what had always been the case.
> He invited people to awaken to what God had already done from
> the very beginning of time. The eschaton that Jesus proclaimed
> was not a new coming of God but a realization on man's part that
> ever since the creation God had been there among his people.[15]

In an emerging universe, the reign of God is the presence of God. It
is God's inner presence in the unfolding of human history and, in a
deeper sense, in the unfolding of the whole of creation. The flashing forth
of the universe, the formation of our galaxy, and the birth of our Earth
with all of its glory are the result of the reign of God and God's presence
within the universe. Thus, the reign of God is a universal reality that is
found in every nook and cranny of the whole of creation. In a profound
sense the reign of God unfolds as the holy web of relationships that binds
us all to each other and to all of creation. "The reign of God was primarily a way of speaking, one of Jesus' ways of speaking about God, about
God in relationship to humankind... In the end, the reign of God *is* God,
God as near, or as coming in strength, or as ruling, but still God."[16] Or, in
the words of Thomas Sheehan, "The reign of God meant the *incarnation*
of God."[17]

As we have seen, the human race emerges as the Earth becomes conscious. In that new dimension of the Earth, for the first time, creatures are
able to have self-awareness, to reflect on the Earth itself, and to make free
choices. What a marvelous addition to the web of relationships in the universe! Humans can know themselves and they can form relationships
with other humans and with the community of species of the Earth. Humans have the astonishing power to make choices in how they relate to
one another and to the Earth. Moreover, the presence of God is found in a
special way within humans, since humans are able to have a personal relationship with God. What are the consequences of this consciousness
and freedom of choice? The reign of God and the presence of the web of
relationships in the universe are enhanced but also disturbed. It is now
possible for humans to make choices that weaken or destroy the relation-

---

15. Thomas Sheehan, *The First Coming: How the Kingdom of God Became Christianity,* New York, Vintage Books, 1986, p. 68.

16. Goergen, *The Mission and Ministry of Jesus,* p. 229.

17. Sheehan, *The First Coming,* p. 60.

ships among themselves and with creation. Humans can now act in ways that are contrary to the reign of God. For the first time, sin and human evil enter into the story of the universe.

How is that possible? As discussed in chapter 2, the emerging process is neither random nor determined, but creative. Thus the emergence of the human race provides an astonishing new and creative dimension to the Earth. Humans emerge from the inner loving presence of God, but they can simultaneously act contrary to the reign of God and the holy web of relationships. This leads to the perennial debate about human free will and the power of God, a debate that has never been fully unraveled or settled. But such dilemmas are often found in a quantum universe. For example, all being at the subatomic level can be described equally well either as solid particles or as waves. But, beyond that, in the words of Danah Zohar quoted earlier, "quantum 'stuff' is, essentially, *both* wavelike and particle-like, simultaneously."[18] In light of the most basic underlying principles of the universe, it seems reasonable that humans can emerge from the presence of God and simultaneously have freedom of choice, even if the freedom of choice leads to the destruction of the holy web of relationships with others and with creation.

The story of the fall found in the early chapters of Genesis struggles with this same issue of the presence of personal and social evil in a world created by a loving God. This story focuses on the source of the social evils that the ancient Hebrews were actually experiencing within their own communities and in their relationships with other peoples. Using the mythological story of Adam and Eve, Genesis tells us that it is the free choice of humans that causes the breakdown of relationships and the presence of social evil, even though that same gift of freedom, when used positively, is the source of all the new beauty and harmony found in human love and human relationships.

Jesus was certainly aware of the personal and social evils of his time, and he challenged those evils and turned the social and religious systems upside down. When Jesus declares that the reign of God is at hand (Mark 1:15), he is really saying that the reign of God within the entire universe is now manifesting itself in a new way, in an inner conversion of heart and a transformation of society which is good news to the poor. Whenever and wherever God is present and ruling within us as humans, there must be both an inner change of heart and a change in the order of things. Albert Nolan, in his book *Jesus before Christianity*, stresses the fact that the reign of God takes place not in a far-off Heaven but here on Earth.

---

18. Zohar, *The Quantum Self,* p. 25.

The good news of the "kingdom" of God was news about a future state of affairs *on earth* when the poor would no longer be poor, the hungry would be satisfied and the oppressed would no longer be miserable.[19]

When the lives of people and of societies are in accord with the reign of God, there will be a visible and tangible restructuring of relationships, a restructuring that will be good news for the poor, the hungry, the sad, the sick, the lame, the outcasts, and the unclean. The reign of God that is found within the unfolding of the entire universe must be the guiding vision of all peoples.

The people of every nation, every race, and every tribe, in one way or another, are part of God's people and they are all called to share in the reconciling, healing, and liberating presence of the reign of God. The presence of God is so deeply embedded within the universe and within the Earth that to live in tune with the Earth is to live in tune with the reign of God.

---

19. Nolan, *Jesus before Christianity,* p. 58.

6

WHO IS OUR SAVIOR?

Redemption today is often not thought of as coming from some re-
mote God who sends a Savior "from above." Instead, it is seen as
coming from a God within who is "part of" and "along with" people in their sins and sufferings. This is the God who was personi-
fied in the historical Jesus, the God whose Spirit acts in the risen
Christ to free people in all their personal and social struggles.[1]

The traditional doctrine of salvation has had a long and diverse journey through history. Certainly the Jewish tradition saw Yahweh as the
savior who freed the people from slavery in Egypt, and frequently Yahweh's saving power was manifested by such figures as Moses, Joseph,
Samuel, and David. This saving power was evident in the experience of
the Jesus community and the early Christian community. It was embodied
in Jesus as he healed the sick, set the oppressed free, cured the lepers, and
overcame the powers of evil. Salvation was described in many different
ways throughout the centuries of the church, sometimes as redemption, or
atonement, or ransom, or justification, or sacrifice. As Brennan Hill tells
us, "The belief in salvation has had many different meanings over time.
The official church has never formulated a doctrine of salvation; it has
been left to theologians to interpret salvation in many ways to meet the
various needs of different times and places."[2]

As we probe more deeply into the meaning of salvation, we will first
present the Genesis story of the garden of paradise and the fall of our first
parents as well as its reinterpretation in the letters of Paul. Second, we
will discuss the traditional teaching of the Catholic Church on original
sin. Third, we will reinterpret the Genesis story in terms of an emerging
universe. Finally, we will search for the meaning of salvation and the role
of Jesus, as Savior, in an emerging universe.

---

1. Hill, *Jesus the Christ,* p. 248.
2. Ibid., p. 230.

THE GENESIS STORY OF THE FALL

The story of creation in the book of Genesis is based on the cosmology of the Jewish people, and it flows from both the broader Middle and Near Eastern cultures and the specific stories that emerged among the Jewish people. These are stories of faith chronicling the development of the Jewish nation as the chosen people. The style of the creation story is poetic as it describes God calling into being light and darkness and placing a dome in the sky to separate the waters above from the waters below. God called the dry land "Earth" and the basin of water "Sea." Then, at God's command, the Earth brought forth plants and trees, fishes and birds, and animals of all kinds. "Then God said, 'Let us make man in our image and after our likeness'" (Genesis 1:26). According to Genesis 2:7, "The Lord God formed man out of the clay of the earth and blew into his nostrils the breath of life, and so man became a living being." The word that is generally translated as "man" in this text is really a play on words. The Hebrew word for ground or earth is *adama* and the word translated as man is *adam*; the man, *adam*, comes forth from the Earth, *adama*. Thus this text can be more accurately interpreted as saying, "The Lord God formed an *earthling* out of the clay of the earth and blew into its nostrils the breath of life, and so the earthling became a living being." This play on words is consistent with the idea that, in an emerging universe, human beings are the Earth become conscious.

After the creation of human life from the Earth, the Lord God planted a garden in Eden, and settled the earthling in the garden to cultivate and care for it. "The Lord God gave the earthling this order: 'You are free to eat from any of the trees of the garden except the tree of knowledge of good and evil. From that tree you shall not eat; the moment you eat from it you are surely doomed to die'" (Genesis 2:16-17). Then God formed a suitable partner for the earthling from its very flesh, and "The man and his wife were both naked, yet they felt no shame" (Genesis 2:25).

> Now the serpent was the most cunning of all the animals that the Lord God had made. The serpent asked the woman, "Did God really tell you not to eat from any of the trees in the garden?" The woman answered the serpent: "We may eat of the fruit of the trees in the garden; it is only about the fruit of the tree in middle of the garden that God said, *'You shall not eat it or even touch it, lest you die.'*" But the serpent said to the woman: *"You certainly will not die! No, God knows well that the moment you eat of it your eyes will be opened and you will be like gods who know what is good and what is evil."* The woman saw that the tree was

good for food, pleasing to the eyes, and desirable for gaining wisdom. So she took some of its fruit and ate it; and she also gave some to her husband, who was with her, and he ate it. *Then the eyes of both of them were opened, and they realized they were naked*; so they sewed fig leaves together and made loincloths for themselves. (Genesis 3:1-7; italics added)

The man and the woman were placed in the garden of paradise and were given access to all the trees except one, the tree of knowledge of good and evil, in the middle of the garden. Then came the temptation cast in the character of the wily serpent. When the woman told the serpent about God's command not to eat from the tree in the middle of the garden lest they die, the serpent's response was that they would certainly not die. Rather, their eyes would be opened and they would be like God who knows good and evil. The woman ate from the fruit, and so did her husband. Their eyes were opened, and they saw that they were naked. Their nakedness without shame was a sign of their innocence, but their awareness of nakedness was a sign, not of a knowledge like God's, but of a knowledge of their own weakness and sinfulness.

Describing God in human terms, the story goes on to say that the man and his wife heard God moving about in the garden, and they hid themselves. They were afraid because they were naked. "Then God asked, 'Who told you that you were naked? You have eaten then from the tree of which I had forbidden you to eat.'" The man put the blame on the woman, and the woman in turn, blamed the serpent. Then the Lord God said to the serpent:

Because you have done this, you shall be banned from all the animals and from all the wild creatures; on your belly shall you crawl, and dirt shall you eat all the days of your life. I will put enmity between you and the woman, and between your offspring and hers; he will strike at your head, while you strike at his heel. (Genesis 3:14-15)

Obviously, this statement about the enmity between the serpent and the woman is not describing an ensuing relationship between snakes and women. Rather, it is affirming the ongoing struggle within the human race between the powers of evil and the powers of good.

To the woman God said:

I will intensify the pangs of your childbearing; in pain you shall bring forth children. Yet your urge shall be for your husband, and *he shall be your master*. (Genesis 3:16; italics added)

To the man God said:

Cursed be the ground because of you! In toil you shall eat its yield all the days of your life. Thorns and thistles shall it bring forth to you, as you eat of the plants of the field. By the sweat of your face shall you get bread to eat, until you return to the ground, from which you were taken; *for you are from the earth and you will return to the earth.* (Genesis 3:17-19; italics added)

The punishment for the woman was the pain of childbirth, her attraction to her husband, and his mastery over her. These "burdens" should be taken in a symbolic sense to describe the actual role of women in the patriarchal context of the Jewish people during the time of the emergence of this story. The punishment for the man was articulated in strong language: *Cursed be the ground because of you!* The very earth out of which the earthling had come is now cursed by the disobedience of the earthling. This curse was found in those burdens that men bore in their culture, in their personal lives, and in their struggle to survive in a hostile land. The final outcome was a return to the earth from which the earthling had come. The story ends with God expelling the man and his wife from the garden of paradise lest they eat of the tree of life and live forever. God stationed the cherubim and the fiery revolving sword to guard the way to the tree of life.

This brief discussion of the Genesis story of the fall can be summarized in the words of Gerhard von Rad:

With a father's disposition God had purposed every conceivable kindness for man; but his will was that in the realm of knowledge a limit should remain set between himself and mankind ...By endeavouring to enlarge his being on the godward side, and seeking a godlike intensification of his life beyond his creaturely limitations, that is, by wanting to be like God, man stepped out from the simplicity of obedience to God. He thereby forfeited life in the pleasant garden and close to God. What remained to him was a life of toil in the midst of wearying mysteries, involved in a hopeless struggle with the power of evil, and, at the end, to be, without reprieve, the victim of death.[3]

This Genesis story was reinterpreted by Paul in his letter to the Romans, chapter 5. The primitive story is now seen through the prism of the

---

3. von Rad, *Old Testament Theology,* p. 155.

death and resurrection of Jesus. Paul contrasts the sin of Adam with the gift of Christ. The importance of the figure of Adam in Paul's theology is pointed out by James D. G. Dunn.

> Adam plays a larger role in Paul's theology than is usually realized—and even when that role is taken into account it is often misunderstood. Adam is a key figure in Paul's attempt to express his understanding both of Christ and of man. Since soteriology and christology are closely connected in Paul's theology it is necessary to trace the extent of the Adam motif in Paul if we are to appreciate the force of his Adam christology.[4]

Paul begins by outlining humanity's sin through Adam.

> Therefore, just as through one person sin entered the world, and through sin, death, and thus death came to all, inasmuch as all sinned...death reigned from Adam to Moses, even over those who did not sin after the pattern of the trespass of Adam, who is *the type of the one who was to come.* (Romans 5:12-14; italics added)

Paul interprets the Genesis story by affirming that through one person sin and death entered the world, but then he introduces a new concept. Adam is the *type* of the one who was to come. The word *type* is a way of explaining the symbolic interrelationship of persons, institutions, or events of the Hebrew Scriptures with those of the Christian Scriptures. For example, the Israelites in their adventures in the desert are called "types" for the journey of the Christian community; the passage of Israel through the sea is a "type" of baptism. In this way, Paul tells us that Adam was the "type" of Jesus, and in this typology there is both a similarity and a contrast.

> But the gift is not like the transgression. *For if by that one person's transgression the many died, how much more did the grace of God and the gracious gift of the one person Jesus Christ overflow for the many.* And the gift is not like the result of the one person's sinning. For *after the one sin there was the judgment that brought condemnation; but the gift, after many transgres-*

---

4. James D. G. Dunn, *Christology in the Making,* Philadelphia, Westminster Press, 1980, p. 101.

sions, brought acquittal. For if, by the transgression of one person, death came to reign through that one, how much more will those who receive the abundance of grace and the gift of justification come to reign in life the one person Jesus Christ. *In conclusion, just as through one transgression condemnation came upon all, so through one righteous act acquittal and life came to all.* For just as through the disobedience of one person the many were made sinners, so through the obedience of one the many will be made righteous. The law entered in so that transgression might increase but, where sin increased, grace overflowed all the more, so that, *as sin reigned in death, grace also might reign through justification for eternal life through Jesus Christ our Lord.* (Romans 5:15-21; italics added)

One person's sin is negated by one person's gift. The one sin brought condemnation, but the gift brought acquittal. Through one transgression, condemnation came to all, so, through one righteous act, the death and resurrection of Jesus, acquittal came to all. Sin reigned in death, and grace reigns through justification for eternal life through Jesus Christ our Lord. Paul uses this same reverse typology in First Corinthians. "For since death came through a human being, the resurrection of the dead came also through a human being. For just as in Adam all die, so too in Christ shall all be brought to life" (1 Corinthians 15:21-22).

This marvelous typology flows from the early Christians' overwhelming sense of the resurrection of Jesus as the firstfruits of the new life promised by God and experienced in Jesus. Adam, the earthling, was interpreted, not as a historical individual, but as a corporate personality symbolizing the whole of the human race. Corporate or symbolic personality is a characteristic of the Hebrew Scriptures and is often used to identify the nation with an individual.

In Jewish history we find the case of the two brothers, Jacob and Esau, who became symbols of two nations. According to the story, Isaac prayed to Yahweh on behalf of his wife, for she was barren. Yahweh heard his prayer, and Isaac's wife Rebekah conceived. But the children began to struggle with one another inside her. "So she went to consult Yahweh, and he said to her: 'There are two nations in your womb, your issue will be two rival peoples. One nation shall have the mastery of the other, and the elder shall serve the younger'" (Genesis 25:22-23). Esau, the elder son, became the father and later the symbol of the nation of Edom, which was in constant conflict with the nation of Israel, symbolized by Jacob, the younger son, who became its father. In the Hebrew Scriptures both Esau and Jacob took on the role of corporate personalities.

Just as Adam functions as a symbolic person embracing the whole human race, we can and should also say that Jesus, the new earthling, functions, not simply as a historical individual, but as a symbolic personality embracing the Christian community and the new people of God. Paul says that "Christ has been raised from the dead, the firstfruits of those who have fallen asleep" (1 Corinthians 15:20). In the resurrection, Christ becomes the first one of many, and the source of new life for all. But is this role of risen Christ a personal or a symbolic one? Are we talking about an individual or a corporate person? Paul says, "So, too, it is written, 'the first man, Adam, became a living being,' the last Adam a life-giving spirit" (1 Corinthians 15:45). It is difficult to determine just how to interpret the meaning of the risen Christ as the last Adam, but it seems that in this context the risen Christ is a symbolic person. Dunn would seem to support the idea of a corporate person when he says, "The first point which calls for comment is that *when Paul uses Adam language explicitly of Christ he is referring primarily to Christ risen and exalted.* As Adam stands for fallen man, so Christ stands for man risen from the dead."[5] As we said at the end of chapter 4, resurrection is a universal symbolic event that can transform our Earth community and our human family, and so the risen Christ can be a symbolic person who embodies the universal salvific presence of God by which our Earth community and our human family are transformed.

The Genesis story of the fall of our first parents was reinterpreted by Paul to emphasize the significance of Jesus. The story thus entered deeply into Christian life and tradition and was eventually told in new ways by Augustine. As we will see in the next section, this tradition added a new dimension of the fall. Not only did the fall of Adam bring about the expulsion from the garden of paradise, but it was interpreted as a sin of Adam and Eve resulting in an objective and ontological wounding of human nature that was transmitted by propagation to all humankind. The gradual reinterpretation of the fall and its meaning for salvation has continued to be a disputed question, despite the many different ways in which theologians have attempted to explain it. Tracing the history of this controversial teaching is beyond the scope of this book. It is, however, both important and necessary to present the Catholic Church's current interpretation of the fall and the meaning of salvation based on Augustinian and Latin theology and contained in the *Catechism of the Catholic Church*.[6]

---

5. Ibid., p.107 (italics added).

6. As noted earlier, texts taken from the *Catechism* will be identified by their paragraph numbers.

ORIGINAL SIN IN THE CATHOLIC TRADITION

In its section on original sin, the *Catechism of the Catholic Church* discusses the consequences of Adam's sin for humanity.

> How did the sin of Adam become the sin of all his descendants? The whole human race is in Adam "as one body of one man." By this "unity of the human race" all men are implicated in Adam's sin, as all are implicated in Christ's justice. Still, the transmission of original sin is a mystery that we cannot fully understand. (#404)

As happens with all our human efforts to explain the works of God within human life, original sin and its transmission remain a mystery that we cannot fully understand. Despite all the years of theological discussion and articulation of the meaning of original sin, we still do not have an unambiguous way of understanding it. The *Catechism* presents the most current official interpretation of original sin:

> But we do know by Revelation that Adam had received original holiness and justice not for himself alone, but for all human nature. By yielding to the tempter, Adam and Eve committed a *personal sin*, but this sin affected *the human nature* that they would then transmit *in a fallen state*. It is a sin which will be transmitted by propagation to all mankind, that is, by the transmission of a human nature deprived of original holiness and justice. And that is why original sin is called "sin" only in an analogical sense: it is a sin "contracted" and not "committed"—a state and not an act. (#404)

This text from the *Catechism,* which gives a general overview of original sin, tells us that Adam was created in original holiness and justice not for himself alone, but for all human nature. The *Catechism* goes on to describe this state of original justice: "As long as he [man] remained in the divine intimacy, man would not have to suffer or die. The inner harmony of the human person, the harmony between man and woman, and finally the harmony between the first couple and all creation, comprised the state called 'original justice'" (#376).

Adam and Eve, in a state called original justice, committed a personal sin, and this personal sin affected the human nature that they would then transmit in a fallen state. It is important to note that the personal sin of Adam and Eve affected *human nature* itself and not simply individual persons. It is a sin that will be transmitted by propagation to all humankind by the transmission of a human nature deprived of original holiness. The *Catechism* teaches that it is in the very act of propagation of the human race that the sin of Adam is transmitted to all humans. Moreover, the *Catechism* teaches that original sin is a deprivation of original holiness and justice, "but human nature has not been totally corrupted: it is wounded in the natural powers proper to it; subject to ignorance, suffering, and the dominion of death; and inclined to sin—an inclination to evil that is called 'concupiscence'" (#405). This personal sin of our first parents, therefore, causes an objective and ontological flaw in human nature.

The dire effects of original sin, which afflicts all members of the human race, are enumerated in the *Catechism*.

> The harmony in which they had found themselves, thanks to original justice, is now destroyed: the control of the soul's spiritual faculties over the body is shattered; the union of man and woman becomes subject to tensions, their relations henceforth marked by lust and domination. Harmony with creation is broken: visible creation has become alien and hostile to man. Because of man, creation is now subject "to its bondage to decay." Finally the consequence explicitly foretold for this disobedience will come true: man will "return to the ground," for out of it he was taken. *Death makes its entrance into human history.* (#400)

In summary, Adam received original holiness and justice both for himself and for all human nature. Adam and Eve committed a personal sin of disobedience that affected human nature objectively and ontologically and that flaw is transmitted by propagation to all humankind. Human nature is wounded but not totally corrupted, and it is subject to ignorance, suffering, the dominion of death, and an inclination to sin. The harmony between God and the human race has been disrupted and "man" has been expelled from the garden of paradise. Because of the sin of Adam, creation is now subject to bondage and to decay. For the first time, death makes its entrance into human history. Original sin within human nature is called "sin" only in an analogical sense: it is a sin "contracted" and not "committed"—a state, not an act. Finally the source of original sin is the disobedient choice of our first parents.

The *Catechism* moves briefly into a discussion of the interrelationship of Christ and original sin.

> Although to some extent the People of God in the Old Testament had tried to understand the pathos of the human condition in the light of the history of the fall narrated in Genesis, they could not

grasp this story's ultimate meaning, which is revealed only in the light of the death and Resurrection of Jesus Christ. *We must know Christ as the source of grace in order to know Adam as the source of sin.* (#388; italics added)

This final sentence is ambiguous and difficult to understand. Does it mean that only those who now know Christ as the source of grace can fully know Adam as the source of sin? Does it mean that only in knowing the remedy for sin can we know the sin itself? Are Adam as the source of sin and Christ as the source of grace inseparable? This important issue of the relationship between Christ as the savior and original sin will be dealt with at some length as we probe further into the meaning of salvation. However, the *Catechism* does say,

The doctrine of original sin is, so to speak, the "reverse side" of the Good News that Jesus is the Savior of all men, that all need salvation, and that salvation is offered to all through Christ. *The Church, which has the mind of Christ, knows very well that we cannot tamper with the revelation of original sin without undermining the mystery of Christ.* (#389; italics added)

Here we must digress briefly to treat of the meaning of revelation, because the *Catechism* in discussing original sin uses this word to explain certain dimensions of original sin. In #390 the *Catechism* says, "*Revelation gives us the certainty of faith* that the whole of human history is marked by the original fault freely committed by our first parents" (italics added). Revelation in this text seems to be *some thing* and in #404 it also seems to be the source of our knowledge: "But *we do know by Revelation* that Adam had received original holiness and justice" (italics added). The *Catechism* also states that "*we cannot tamper with the revelation* of original sin without undermining the mystery of Christ" (#389; italics added). Revelation in this section of the *Catechism* is something that "gives us the certainty of faith," is a source of our knowledge about original holiness and justice, and is something with which "we cannot tamper."

But, as we saw in chapter 2, revelation in an emerging universe is not something that gives us the certainty of faith; it is also not a *thing* but rather a *relationship* between a human community and the inexpressible presence of God, a grasping after an ultimate mystery which is far beyond our comprehension. The *Catechism* itself tells us that "the transmission of original sin is a mystery that we cannot fully understand" (#404). Revelation is a dynamic relationship between God and humankind who perceive the presence of God through the experience of historical and symbolic events. The Genesis story of original sin was founded on the experience of God's presence within Jewish history; the reinterpretation of this story flowed from the experience of God's presence in the tradition of a Christian community in a "created universe." The presence of God is also found within an "emerging universe" that has been unfolding for fifteen billion years in a dynamic evolutionary process. It is only appropriate that, in the context of such a universe, the experience of God's presence be perceived as an ongoing reality and a deepening relationship between God and the human community. Therefore, as we experience the presence of God in new ways, it is not surprising that we can now look at the origin of sin in a new light, and we can use that new experience as a guide in reinterpreting the meaning of sin and salvation in an emerging universe.

THE ORIGIN OF SIN IN AN EMERGING UNIVERSE

As we have seen, the creation stories in Genesis were not intended to present a historical account of the creation of the world and especially of the creation of Adam and Eve as our first parents, nor were these accounts an effort to explain scientifically the meaning of creation and of the human race. The Hebrew people did not write the biblical accounts as historians or scientists. Rather, they wrote as people of faith who were trying to interpret their lives and their traditions. This interpretation was articulated in terms of their experience of God's presence in the journey of their own lives and that of their ancestors.

They experienced a God who was Yahweh, one who was always with them in their journey despite their failings. They experienced struggle, sin, and violence in their lives despite the presence of their loving God. If God was with them, and if God created them in God's own image, what was the source of the violence, sin, and struggle which were clearly part of the human story? The Genesis story, and especially the story of the fall, is the effort of these people to answer that question using theological and poetic language. God created everything good, and God created the earthling in God's own image. The coming of evil had its source in the disobedience of Adam and Eve. In their desire to be like God by knowing good and evil and so controlling their own lives, humans experienced their limitations and their evil inclinations. Original sin was their way of interpreting the presence of evil in the world.

In an emerging universe, the human family came forth from the Earth about three million years ago and entered upon a journey in conjunction with the rest of the creatures of the Earth. This journey was outlined in chapter 1 in terms of the childhood, adolescence, and adulthood of the human race. In this story there are two sources of the apparent evil within the human family: the limitations of everything in the universe and the free choices of human beings.

It is very difficult for us, as humans, to accept *our limitations and the limitations of everything in the universe.* In our ideal universe, there should be no earthquakes, or droughts, or violent storms. People should be healthy and free of disease, and epidemics should not happen. Societies should not permit hunger, and nations should never go to war. Nevertheless, these things happen and so do the explosion of stars and the burning out of suns. Nature seems violent. Everything in the universe is limited, and these very limitations are part of the emerging process.

There is a story about a king and queen who had a beautiful daughter eagerly sought after by many suitors. The royal parents decided that the successful suitor would have to undergo many trials before winning the hand of the princess. Many young men tried and failed, until one day a stranger appeared. He successfully underwent all the trials (the original telling of the story goes on and on in describing each trial in great detail), the beautiful princess was betrothed to the stranger, and the wedding was planned. There was great excitement in the castle as the wedding day approached. On the day of the wedding ceremony, the stranger and the beautiful princess, still veiled as was the custom, came before the bishop and were duly united in matrimony.

After the celebration and the feast, the newly married couple retired to the bridal chamber. The princess removed her veil and, lo and behold, she was the most ugly person imaginable—she had a crooked nose, beady eyes, fangs for teeth, hair like a floor mop, and a blotched face. The princess explained to her husband that she was under a spell. He had a choice. She could be beautiful by day and ugly at night, or she could be beautiful at night and ugly by day. He chose to have her beautiful by day and ugly at night. She was so ugly that, on the first night in bed the stranger, in his disappointment, just turned his back to her. The next night he turned away from her again. As the days went on the stranger began to see the goodness and virtue of his wife, and one night in bed he turned to her and embraced her. And the spell was broken! She became the beautiful princess, and, of course, they lived happily ever after.

This story contains some profound wisdom; in order to obtain the beautiful we must embrace the ugly. The new creation story tells us not only about the beauty of the Earth but also about what appears to be the ugliness, the chaos, and the shadow side of creation—its limitations. We, as humans, often seek to deny the limitations and the ugliness within our lives and within the Earth community. We try to conquer the Earth in order to do away with all ugliness, pain, discomfort, suffering, and sickness, and in the process we never realize the deeper goodness and beauty within our lives and our community. Only by embracing the chaos and the shadow side can we break the spell and find the beauty of ourselves and our world. "Evolution is an unfolding filled with another kind of eccentricity: the clash of disorder, destruction and extinction."[7]

The ancient Greek philosophers described the four elements as earth, air, fire, and water. According to these philosophers, everything in creation is composed of these elements, which give the world its balance and beauty. But, at the same time, these four elements are the source of most of our natural disasters, such as earthquakes, tornadoes, fires, and floods. In a way, the Greek philosophers seemed to be saying that the very make-up of creation contains the seeds of disaster, and without these violent events the world would not have the same balance and beauty.

Our more recent understanding of the Earth, based on our new science, also paints a picture of destruction and chaos.

Enhanced by modern chemical analysis and radioactive carbon-14 dating techniques, there seems to be the beginning of a consensus that every twenty-six to thirty million years our planet suffers a fate a thousand times worse than if all the world's nuclear arsenals exploded at once.

These periodic catastrophes result in terrible mass extinctions that annihilate 50 to 90 percent of ecologically and genetically diverse global species within intervals of five hundred thousand to three million years. Explosions and catastrophes have been as normal to Gaia's development as fistfights in a Brooklyn schoolyard, and they occur almost as frequently.[8]

The violent dimensions of earth, air, fire, and water, and the Earth's periodic catastrophes are all examples of order coming out of chaos. The chaos and apparent violence in the universe seem to produce not ultimate destruction, but a new order, an evolutionary leap, new life from death.

Judging from the progression of the fossil record and confirmed by the extraordinary diversity of natural development today, anywhere from 10 to 50 percent of the visible biota survives and eventually thrives from even the worst cataclysms. The global ecosystem invariably regenerates quickly and to a higher level of complexity, usually in less time than a hundred thousand years. Though this may seem like an eternity in terms of human civi-

7. Nogar, *The Lord of the Absurd*, p. 144.
8. Joseph, *Gaia: The Growth of an Idea*, p. 104.

lization, to a life form thirty-five-hundred-million years old, one hundred millennia is, at most, a long afternoon.[9]

In a similar way, our human lives and our human relationships are often deepened as we experience our own limitations. The slow process of a grandmother's dying can bring a family together at a new level of love and caring. The darkness of the apparent breakup of a loving relationship can call the lovers to an unanticipated depth of mutuality and friendship. The shadow of a dysfunctional family can often lead its members to heroic efforts to overcome the pain and to learn new ways of relating. The whole concept of finding the beauty by embracing the ugly is also foundational to our Christian tradition. In the words of Jesus, "Amen, amen, I say to you, unless a grain of wheat falls into the ground and dies, it remains just a grain of wheat; but if it dies, it produces much fruit. Whoever loves his life loses it, and whoever hates his life in this world will preserve it for eternal life" (John 12:24-25).

There is a very serious question to be dealt with in connection with chaos and the shadow side. We all know that humans are subject to chaos and that there is a shadow side within all of us. But what about the human violence that seems to be so much a part of our human family and its history? Is this something that we just have to accept? Is this human violence just part of our nature? Are human violence and the violence in the Earth community one and the same? If not, what are the differences?

The violence in nature, such as a pride of lions stalking and killing their prey and the scenes in nature films of bloody battles between species, must be viewed as part of a wider community interaction. In nature, a predator will never destroy the entire species of its prey or the entire species of its competitor. The tensions always found within the community of species ultimately lead to an overall balance. For example, an eagle has very acute eyesight so that it can see a mouse scurrying through the field, and the field mouse can run very quickly so that it can avoid its eagle predator. The outcome is a natural balance between these two species. This is a simple example of the very complex dynamic among the members of an ecological community as limitations and interdependence enhance the welfare of the ecosystem.

On the other hand some human "violence," such as our use of other living creatures for food, flows from our participation in the community of species of which we are members. As part of the community of species, humans, like other living things, can take from the fruit of the Earth what

---

9. Ibid., pp. 203–204.

is necessary for survival. However, this "taking" is limited, because we also must respect the needs and rights of other species. For example, the native peoples would frequently have rituals after the hunt, thanking the animals for providing the necessities of life and promising to kill only what was needed and to use it well.

True human violence, evil, and sin flow from our personal choices. What are the consequences of human consciousness and freedom of choice? It is now possible for humans to make choices that can weaken or destroy the relationships among themselves and with creation. Humans can act in ways that are contrary to the reign of God. With the coming of the human race, sin and human evil enter into the story of the universe. Human choices can be destructive to all of our relationships with ourselves, other individuals, human societies, and nature. Human violence is contrary to the evolutionary drive of the Earth because it upsets the ecological balance by destroying species, polluting the water supply, and wasting natural resources. Human violence does not respect the dignity of other species and other humans. It results in the systemic violence that is so evident in our society and on our city streets, and it often breaks out in warfare that is the most organized and destructive form of human violence. Sin is the tearing of the web of personal relationships, of human societies, and of the community of species.

Human violence and sin are also self-destructive, going contrary to the basic reality of human life and creation. Sin is rooted in our human desire for power and control as well as in our will to conquer the earth. As people are caught up in a spiral of power, the effort to control results in a greater loss of control. The personal, systemic, and ecological violence in our society, as well as the apex of violence in modern warfare, will lead to a life in which "love one another" becomes "destroy one another." The subversion of our human relationships, as well as being self-destructive, impacts our relationship with God. Nothing we can do will ever separate us from the unconditional love of God, but humans can alienate themselves from God as a result of their failure to love God and their neighbor as themselves.

It is necessary for us to embrace the chaos and the shadow side if we are to find new life. But it is equally necessary for us to continue our effort to root out the personal, systemic, and ecological violence in our midst. What will be the source of our redemption from chaos and violence? The new story of creation teaches us that the universe has an inner self-organizing and self-healing power that enables it to bring order out of chaos, light out of darkness, and clarity to the shadow. The redemptive presence of the Creator God is built into the very substance of the universe and will unfold within the dynamics of the universe. "Redemption is planetary (and global) as well as personal. Redemption is about reclaiming the darkness, nothingness, and chaos of our world, and celebrating the negative potential for new life and wholeness."[10]

The redemptive presence of God within the universe is personalized, for us as Christians, in the story of Jesus and in his life-giving death and resurrection. As Jesus began his public life, he saw the evil and violence in the society in which he lived. He saw it as contrary to his deep experience of God as a loving Mother, who wishes to shelter her children under her wings. He challenged the systemic oppression of the poor and the outcasts. Jesus invited his followers and the religious leaders of the times to follow a new ethic of compassion for the poor, of the universality of God's love, and the call to love one another. He, himself, by his commitment to the law of love, was caught up in the violence of his society. By embracing the violence and the ugliness of death on a cross, Jesus, through his resurrection, became a symbol of the redemptive presence of God within the universe and a source of new life for all people.

> History, then, has a capacity for being changed from within; and for the Christian the incarnation is the seed of radical change, of the new. It introduces into the process of time a new future, so that the future of death and oblivion which has been bequeathed to the historical process by distorted and confused human freedom is challenged by a radical alternative: life instead of death.[11]

The concept of original sin in Genesis was the biblical way of accounting for limitations, interdependence, and human violence. If limitations and interdependence are integral and creative dimensions of the universe, and if human violence flows from the free choices of humans, it frees us to reinterpret the idea of original sin in the sense of an objective, ontological flaw within human nature. In an emerging universe, the fact that the human race is "subject to ignorance, suffering, and the dominion of death; and inclined to sin" (#405), which the *Catechism* calls original sin, is simply the inner nature of this emerging universe. The universe is neither random nor determined, but creative. In order to be creative, it must first be chaotic.

Having said all this, there still remains the mystery of evil found in the massive suffering arising from human violence and slavery, in the overwhelming toll of human life flowing from genocide, and in the ongoing devastation of the Earth. We can all cry out with Jeremiah:

---

10. O'Murchu, *Quantum Theology,* p. 136.
11. Douglas John Hall, *God & Human Suffering,* Minneapolis, Augsburg, 1986, p. 111.

Day and night my tears never stop,
for my people are struck,
my daughter crushed by a savage blow.

I see the dead slain in the fields
and people starving on city streets.
Priest and prophet wander about,
not knowing where to turn.

Lord, have you nothing but contempt for Zion?
Have you completely rejected Judah?
Why have you inflicted wounds that do not heal?

We long for peace, we long for healing,
but there is only terror.
We have sinned against you and we know it, God;
We share our people's guilt.
    (Jeremiah 14:17-20)

DOES THE HUMAN RACE NEED A SAVIOR?

In an emerging universe, the answer to this question will be: Yes, No, and Yes.

The first answer is Yes. As we look around our world today, there can be no doubt that the human race needs a savior. We cannot save ourselves by ourselves. The mystery of personal and systemic violence is beyond our power to control or to resist. We need a savior in the sense that the Psalmist and Isaiah describe God as the savior in the following texts: "Restore to us, O God, the light of your presence, and we shall be saved" (Psalm 80). "God indeed is my savior, my trust knows no fear; my strength and my courage is the Lord, yes, God is my savior" (Isaiah 12:2). "God, my love, my safety, my stronghold and defender. God, my shield, my refuge, you give me victory" (Psalm 144). Our living God is not our savior in terms of a divine intervention from without. Rather, God is the inner source of salvation transforming and empowering us from within. During a parish retreat and a discussion of prayer, one woman said, "When we pray for the hungry to be fed, this means that we are asking God to empower us to feed the hungry."

God is the inner source of salvation found throughout the entire universe as seen in the self-organizing principle. According to the self-organizing principle, systems seem to have an inner God-given sense of direction and guidance that enables them to change and restructure themselves from within, and this dynamic is found in all aspects of the universe. A galaxy is a self-organizing system as it takes its spiral form while adapting to the tremendous forces of its neighbors and its own inner dynamics. The water flowing out of a drain is a self-organizing system as it forms a spiral based on the movement of the earth and the force of gravity. A flock of geese is a self-organizing system as it makes its way north to its feeding grounds. The brain is a self-organizing system as it processes millions of pieces of information to form holistic dimensions of reality.

In terms of the emerging universe, salvation can now be described in new terms such as restoration, transformation, reconciliation, and renewal, and it is possible to transfer these new ideas to the social, political, and religious spheres. If God works within the universe, as described in an emerging universe, then this same God works in a comparable way within the personal, social, political, and religious spheres. God's salvific power and presence are made manifest in the self-healing, self-restoring, self-transforming, self-organizing, and self-renewing processes in the universe and in the dynamic web of relationships with others. In an emerging universe, salvation is seen as coming from a God who dwells within the entire universe, and this salvific presence of God in all its manifestations is also found within the human race. As Catherine Mowry LaCugna says, "Sin is broken relationship, the distortion of the image of God in us. Sin, in other words, disorders and fractures our capacity for communion. Salvation reestablishes the image of God in us, and restores right relationship throughout creation."[12]

Broken relationships do not separate us from the unconditional love of God which dwells within each human being. Rather, salvation and new life emerge from within for all those whose lives are transformed by the unconditional love of God. This love of God restores right relationships among the people and within creation. Within us at the deepest level is a desire to be reconciled with each other and find a new sense of wholeness, a desire to be healed by the inner healing center within us, and a desire to discover our inner freedom and use it in service to the whole of society. Moreover, in every race and every religion and wherever and whenever reconciliation, healing, and liberation are found, there is salvation. This salvation unfolds from the loving presence of God within us. Without a doubt, the human race needs God as a savior.

The No answer comes in terms of the necessity for a savior or redeemer who will save us from the effects of original sin like someone who appears suddenly and provides an artificial solution to an insoluble

---

12. Catherine Mowry LaCugna, *God for Us: The Trinity and Christian Life,* New York, HarperSanFrancisco, 1991, p. 284.

difficulty. The traditional interpretation of original sin describes a situation in which Adam and Eve committed a *personal sin* that they then transmitted by propagation to all humankind. By this transmission of sin human nature was deprived of original holiness and justice, the human race was wounded and became subject to ignorance, suffering, the dominion of death, and the inclination to sin. Such a story of a fallen human race whose nature is objectively and ontologically wounded by original sin then calls for a savior who can objectively and ontologically redeem the human race from these negative consequences.

But, in an emerging universe, the love and loyalty of God have always been present, unfolding in the entire universe and especially within the human race. God's unconditional love has never been objectively and ontologically lost, even though humans, through their broken relationships, have lost *their* subjective love of God. In an emerging universe, there is no archeological or historical evidence for such things as a period of original holiness and justice followed by an original sin through which the human race has fallen and become objectively and ontologically wounded. Evil and limitations are certainly present among humans and in their relationships with the rest of creation. There is a need for a savior, but it is not because of an original sin and a fallen nature. Thus, there is no need for Jesus as our savior to redeem us objectively and ontologically from such a sin and its consequences.

The second Yes flows from the reality that, even though the human race has within itself the power and presence of God's love, very often we humans do not tap the resources available to us. As Christians we often have neither the know-how nor the motives to overcome the broken relationships in our lives and to renew the God-given communion and harmony within the human race and with the rest of the Earth community.

First, we need the historical Jesus as a savior to show us the way, to call us to conversion, and to bring us new life; second, we need the crucified Jesus because his death and resurrection is the symbol of the death and resurrection that is found in all dimensions of an emerging universe; third, we need the risen Christ as a symbol of resurrection to enable us to reach new depths of consciousness, and as a corporate person to serve as the head of the Body of Christ and the source of life for the Communion of Saints.

Jesus shows us the way by his deep compassion for all people. He gave people a new sense of dignity by eating with sinners and outcasts and by touching and healing the lepers and the unclean. He challenged the Jewish holiness code of exclusion and invited the poor and the lame, the deaf and the blind into the banquet of God. Jesus also models for his followers a self-giving service to others, a mutual forgiveness, and the restoration of relationships. His sense of inclusion even embraces the pagans and the heathens.

Jesus calls us to conversion. His ringing words in Mark 1:15 echo throughout the centuries. "This is the time of fulfillment. The reign of God is at hand. Repent, and believe the good news." For Jesus, whoever you are and wherever you are, the call for conversion follows you. The call is urgent. Leave your nets and follow me! Don't go back and bury your father. Come follow me! The call to conversion is primary. Go, sell what you have, and come after me! The call for conversion is difficult. Take up your cross and follow me! The call to conversion is constant and never ending.

The call of Jesus is life giving. Jesus says that he came that we may have life and have it abundantly. That new life is found in Jesus' deep experience of the presence of God within him. Jesus could name God as Abba, a loving and intimate Father. Just as the Father has life from within, so does Jesus have the life of God within himself, and Jesus calls us all to that new life. Jesus is the bread of life, and those who share in that life will never hunger or thirst. And the deepest source of that new life is found in Jesus' call to all-embracing love. "You shall love the Lord with all your heart, with all your soul, with all your mind, and with all your strength... You shall love your neighbor as yourself" (Mark 12:30-31). In showing us the way, in calling us to conversion, and in bringing us new life, the historical Jesus embodies the salvific presence of God for us as Christians.

We need the crucified Jesus because the death and resurrection of Jesus symbolize the new life found in dissipative structures within all dimensions of an emerging universe. Death and resurrection haunt the entire story of the universe as creativity emerges out of chaos, as out of the explosion of our mother star came the elements essential to life, and as new stages of evolution emerge after earth catastrophes. Now out of the crucifixion and death of Jesus emerges the resurrection and the promise of new life. "Unless a grain of wheat falls to the ground and dies, it remains just a grain of wheat; but if it dies, it produces much fruit" (John 12:24).

The Jesus community, so overwhelmed by the crucifixion, began to study the Hebrew Scriptures and found in them images that were used to make sense of the death of Jesus. Jesus is the Suffering Servant of Isaiah who was pierced for our offenses and crushed for our sins. It was our infirmities that he bore and our sufferings that he endured. The Servant was to be a light to the nations that God's salvation might reach to the ends of the Earth. In the story of the appearance of Jesus on the road to Emmaus, Jesus says, "How foolish you are! How slow of heart to believe all that the prophets spoke! Was it not necessary that the Messiah should suffer these things and enter into his glory?" (Luke 24:25-26). Paul also describes the meaning of the death of Christ. "For the love of Christ impels us, once we have come to the conviction that one died for all; therefore, all have died. He indeed died for all, that those who live might no longer live for themselves but for him who for their sake died and was raised" (2 Corinthians 5:14-15). Gradually the catastrophe of the crucifixion of Jesus and the glory of his resurrection brought the early church to a belief that the death and resurrection of Jesus is the symbol of God's saving power which gives life to all people.

There is another dimension of the life-giving presence of God in the death and resurrection of Jesus. The early Christian community began to come together and celebrate a memorial of his death and resurrection in a communal meal. Eating and drinking with Jesus was a central experience of the disciples. It is found in stories of feeding of the crowds, of the woman who entered and washed the feet of Jesus while he was at table, of Zacchaeus who climbed the sycamore and invited Jesus to dine with him, of the accusation of the scribes and Pharisees that Jesus ate and drank with sinners, and of the meal on the seashore with the disciples after the resurrection. Especially in the story of the paschal meal celebrated on the night before Jesus died the early church brought together the sacrifice of the paschal lamb in the Jewish tradition with their own memorial meal. As Paul says, "For as often as you eat this bread and drink the cup, you proclaim the death of the Lord until he comes" (1 Corinthians 11:26). The Christian community experienced the life-giving presence of Jesus the Christ in the breaking of the bread and the sharing of the cup, and this became the center of the worship life of Christian believers down through the centuries. Christians need the crucified Jesus as our savior because in his death and resurrection Jesus embodies the life-giving presence of God that is found in all dimensions of an emerging universe.

But we also need the risen Christ as a symbol of resurrection to enable us to reach new depths of consciousness. In chapter 4 we said that resurrection is a universal symbolic event that can transform our Earth community and our human family. Resurrection is part of the inner dynamic of the universe, so that in the midst of the chaos, the violence, the terrorist attacks, and the bio-terrorism of our global situation, resurrection will win out. Over and over again in the history of the universe, new life has arisen out of death. Resurrection is also a symbol of God's transforming presence within the universe and within the Earth and all its creatures. This transforming presence will be found concretely in the qualities of adulthood and the transition from the Cenozoic Era to the Ecozoic Era, as described in chapter 1. In an emerging universe, Christians will begin to realize that the resurrection of Jesus embodies these same dynamics. The risen Christ is the symbol of God's salvific presence in the universe. Resurrection leads us to a new level of consciousness and the universal possibility of finding new life within both the universe and our human situation.

The risen Christ, as we have seen above, became a corporate person symbolizing the Christian community that now shares in the promise of the resurrection. As Paul says, "But now Christ has been raised from the dead, the firstfruits of those who have fallen asleep" (1 Corinthians 15:20). As Christians we are all one in the risen Christ "striving to preserve the unity of the spirit through the bond of peace" (Ephesians 4:3). This new relationship is described by Paul as the Body of Christ. "Living the truth in love, we should grow in every way into him who is the head, Christ, from whom the whole body, joined and held together by every supporting ligament, with the proper functioning of each part, brings about the body's growth and builds itself up in love" (Ephesians 4:15-16).

The risen Christ is also the center and source of what tradition calls the Communion of Saints that embraces all the faithful, whether living or dead. The Second Vatican Council's Constitution on the Church describes this deep interrelationship. "All of us, however, in varying degrees and in different ways share in the same charity towards God and our neighbors, and we all sing the one hymn of glory to our God. All, indeed, who are of Christ and who have his Spirit form one Church and in Christ cleave together" (*Lumen Gentium,* #49). This Communion of Saints and the relationships found within it participate in the broader web of relationships found in the holon theory and quantum nature of the universe.

In the corporate personality of the risen Christ, the Christian community embodies a vision of resurrection and new life which symbolizes the universal saving presence of God in all cultures and all religions and all peoples. John Knox wisely describes the role of Jesus as the creative personal center of God's supreme revealing and redemptive action.

> Jesus became the redeemer of our humanity—or, better, the agent of its redemption—not in virtue of his taking it, but in virtue of what God did in and through the human life, which was not less naturally and inalienably his own for being also, according to "the definite plan and foreknowledge of God," the creative personal center of God's supreme revealing and redemptive action.[13]

Does the human race need a savior? Yes, because in an emerging universe all salvation comes from the God who dwells within the entire universe and within the whole human race. No, because in an emerging universe there is no irrefutable evidence for an original sin through which the human race has become objectively and ontologically wounded, and thus there is no need for Jesus as our savior in order to redeem us ob-

---

13. Knox, *The Humanity and Divinity of Christ,* p. 91.

jectively and ontologically from such a sin and its consequences. Yes, because as Christians we need the historical Jesus as a savior to show us the way, to call us to conversion, and to bring us new life. We need the crucified and risen Jesus whose death and resurrection are the universal symbol of the death and resurrection found in all dimensions of an emerging universe. We need the risen Christ as a universal symbol of resurrection opening us to new depths of consciousness, to a promise of the fullness of life forever, and to a new dynamic web of relationships reaching out to the poor, victims of violence, and refugees, and embracing all cultures, all religions, and all peoples.

> Now to God who is able to accomplish far more than all we ask or imagine, by the power at work within us, to God be glory in the church and in Christ Jesus to all generations forever and ever. Amen. (Ephesians 3:20-21)

7

THE JOURNEY
TO A HIGH CHRISTOLOGY

The Christian gospel, at its simplest, is an announcement of something God has done for us men and our salvation. It is not unlikely that when we use the word "done" in this connection, we have already begun to speak mythologically; but whether that can be said or not, certainly we cannot proceed to describe, even in the simplest terms, *what* God has done in Christ, or to explain *why* he has done it, and just *how* this action has accomplished his purpose—we cannot begin to speak, or even think, of such matters without using mythological terms.[1]

Because we cannot know what God is, but rather what God is not, we have no means for considering how God is, but rather how God is not.[2]

The basic question of this chapter is the following: How did Jesus, an itinerant peasant preacher and healer in Galilee, become for the Christian community the Wisdom of God, the Word of God, the Lord, and the divine Son of God? To phrase it more simply, how did the Christian community, as found in its various writings, move from a low Christology to a high Christology? Within the community of scholars "low" Christology focuses more on the humanity of Jesus and the use of titles based on the Jewish tradition and the reinterpretation of that tradition, such as Messiah, prophet, servant, lord, Son of God. "High" Christology focuses more on the divinity of Jesus and the development and deeper interpretation of the person of Jesus through the use of more exalted titles, such as, the Wisdom of God, the Word of God, Lord, the divine Son of God.

---

1. Knox, *The Humanity and Divinity of Christ,* pp. 3–4.
2. Thomas Aquinas, *Summa Theologica,* I, 3, Intro.

At the beginning of chapter 5 several diagrams helped us to visualize the gradual development of how Jesus was understood in the early Christian community. Such an understanding enabled the early Christians to reflect on the stories of Jesus and reinterpret them in the light of the glorified and risen Christ. As often happens with heroes, the early community developed the story of the infancy of Jesus with the purpose of clarifying his mission and his message. But beyond these infancy narratives, people began to question the ultimate origin of Jesus. Did Christ exist in the beginning before the world was created? Did he then come down and enter into human history by being born of the Virgin Mary? Such stories would not have been beyond the comprehension of people in the first century of Christianity, because stories of the coming and going of the gods were common. A divine figure comes down from Mount Olympus, interacts with humans, and then returns to heaven. Such a story, however, is incomprehensible to many people who live in an emerging universe. We have a whole different view of the universe, of God's relationship to the universe, and of the meaning of salvation within human history. How can the story of Jesus be integrated into a new vision of the universe?

STAGE THREE
Reinterpretation

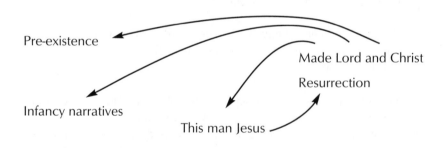

First of all, we must probe the Christian Scriptures to see whether in fact there is a belief in the pre-existence of Christ. We will examine the title "Son of God" in the New Testament; we will explore the meaning of a pre-existent Christ in the letters of Paul and in his use of the Jewish tradition of the Wisdom of God; finally, we will treat of the Word of God in the prologue to John's Gospel. Second, in the light of this biblical discussion, we will search for the meaning of the divinity of Jesus in an emerging universe.

THE PRE-EXISTENCE OF CHRIST

THE SON OF GOD

What could it have meant to their hearers when the first Christians called Jesus "son of God"? All the time in a study like this we must endeavor to attune our listening to hear with the ears of the first Christians' contemporaries. We must attempt the exceedingly difficult task of shutting out the voices of early Fathers, Councils and dogmaticians down through the centuries, in case they drown the earlier voices, in case the earlier voices were saying something different, in case they intended their words to speak with different force to their hearers.[3]

In the earliest Christian Scriptures the distinctive relationship of Jesus to God is found in the use of the titles "Son of God" and "the Son." While Jesus never referred to himself as the "Son of God," it is certain that he spoke to God as *Abba*, Father. Jesus' awareness of God, based on his Jewish background as well as on his own personal search, led him to a religious experience of God as a loving parent and himself as God's son. In the Gospel story of his baptism, Jesus' inner life opened itself to God's loving presence, and it was as if "heaven was opened" to him. Jesus' sense of self-identity flowed like the Spirit descending on him in the image of a dove. It was as if God, Abba, actually named Jesus in saying, "You are my beloved Son; with you I am well pleased." Dunn says, "It is excessively difficult therefore to avoid the conclusion that *it was a characteristic of Jesus' approach to God in prayer that he addressed God as 'abba' and that the earliest Christians retained an awareness of this fact in their own use of 'abba.'*"[4]

Beyond this, the Christian writings give evidence that the resurrection of Jesus was considered to be the event by which he became God's son. In the very beginning of Paul's letter to the Romans he says:

Paul, a servant of Jesus Christ, called to be an apostle, set apart for the gospel of God which God promised beforehand through his prophets in the holy scriptures, the gospel concerning his Son, who was descended from David according to the flesh *and*

---

3. Dunn, *Christology in the Making,* pp. 13–14.
4. Ibid., p. 26.

> *appointed Son of God in power according to the Spirit of holi-*
> *ness by his resurrection from the dead,* Jesus Christ our Lord.
> (Romans 1:1-4; italics added)

Another early text is found in the Acts of the Apostles. "And we bring
you the good news that what God promised to the fathers, *this he has ful-*
filled to us their children by raising Jesus; as also it is written in the second psalm, 'You are my Son, this day I have begotten you'" (Acts 13:32-
33; italics added). The use of this psalm as the Jewish background for the
title "Son of God" is an example of prophecy historicized. A prophecy—
You are my Son, this day I have begotten you—is historicized in the resurrection of Jesus. Paul also connects the title of Son to the life-giving death
of Jesus. "Indeed, if, while we were enemies, we were reconciled to God
by the death of his Son, how much more, once reconciled, will we be
saved by his life" (Romans 5:10). The title of "Son of God" is very commonly used in a variety of ways to explicate the relationship of Jesus to
the Father and to the salvific plan of God. Finally, Jesus as the Son of God
becomes the type of the redeemed community who share in this sonship.

> But in the fullness of time, God sent forth his Son, born of a
> woman, born under the law, to redeem those who were under the
> law, so that we might receive the adoption as sons. And because
> you are sons, God has sent the Spirit of his Son into our hearts,
> crying, "Abba! Father!" So through God you are no longer a
> slave but a son, and if a son then an heir. (Galatians 4:4-7)

The synoptic Gospels further develop the use of the title "Son of
God." In Mark this title is not used frequently, but it is used at the most
critical moments in the story of Jesus. The first words of this Gospel,
serving almost like the headline, state its message. "The beginning of the
Gospel of Jesus Christ, the Son of God" (Mark 1:1). The Gospel moves
on to the baptism when the Spirit descends upon Jesus like a dove, and a
voice speaks to Jesus from heaven, "You are my beloved Son; with you I
am well pleased" (Mark 1:10-11). Then comes the story of the transfiguration when the voice speaks to the disciples. "And a cloud overshad-
owed them, and a voice came out of the cloud, 'This is my beloved Son,
listen to him'" (Mark 9:7). Finally, at the foot of the cross and after the
death of Jesus, the centurion speaks to us and says, "Truly this man was
the Son of God!" (Mark 15:39). Mark's chief emphasis is clearly on Jesus
as the Son of God whose intimate relationship with God as Abba and
whose anointing with the Sprit at the baptism place Jesus within a trinitarian view of God.

In the infancy narratives, Jesus as the Son of God is found described in the stories of his physical conception itself, implicitly in Matthew and explicitly in Luke. The story in Matthew tells us of Joseph who, in his confusion over Mary's pregnancy, is visited by an angel. "Do not be afraid to take Mary your wife into your home. For it is through the holy Spirit that this child has been conceived in her" (Matthew 1:20). This is clearly portrayed as a conception resulting from the power of God's Spirit, and Matthew's intention is to give an account of a divine origin for Jesus. The story in the Gospel of Luke is more direct. The angel describes Jesus by saying that "he will be great and will be called the Son of the Most High, and the Lord God will give him the throne of David his father" (Luke 1:32). Then the angel explains to Mary that "the holy Spirit will come upon you, and the power of the Most High will overshadow you. Therefore the child to be born will be called holy, the Son of God" (Luke 1:35). Jesus is the Son of the Most High and he will take the throne of David. Once again there is the presence of God's Spirit in the conception of the child, and because of this divine presence the child will be holy and will be the Son of God.

In these readings, the title "Son of God" is first bestowed on Jesus in terms of his resurrection and glorification and later it is used in relationship to his reconciling death on the cross. Jesus is revealed as the Son of God at both his baptism and his transfiguration, and finally the infancy narratives portray Jesus as the Son of God in their description of his conception and the divine origin of that conception. The title "Son of God" emerged during the early period of the church's history and it is a title that focuses on Jesus' special relationship to God. The title in this earliest period of Christianity was not the expression of a belief in a personal pre-existence of Jesus as the Son of God. Rather, Jesus was a Son of God, one specially chosen and loved by God, designated to be Messiah, and filled with God's presence and power. However, in the letters of Paul and especially in the use of the Jewish Wisdom tradition, the sense of some type of pre-existence seems to emerge, and later in this chapter we will find a deeper meaning of the title "Son of God" in John's Gospel.

THE LETTERS OF PAUL AND THE WISDOM TRADITION

The debate about the pre-existence of Jesus centers on several passages in the writings of Paul. For our purposes it will be adequate to consider two of these passages: Philippians 2:5-11, in which Paul speaks of Jesus emptying himself and being born in the likeness of a human, and Colossians 1:15-20, in which Paul describes Jesus in terms of the Wisdom of God.

Philippians 2:5-11.   Scripture scholars today believe that these verses in Philippians were based on the hymn of an earlier Christian community, and that Paul used this hymn with several minor changes. Here is the passage as we know it today.

> Have this mind among yourselves which you have in Christ Jesus, who, though he was in the form of God, did not count equality with God a thing to be grasped, but emptied himself, taking the form of a servant, being born in human likeness. And being found in human form Christ Jesus humbled himself and became obedient unto death, even death on a cross. Therefore God has greatly exalted him and bestowed on him the name which is above every name, that at the name of Jesus every knee should bow, in heaven and on earth and under the earth, and every tongue confess that Jesus Christ is Lord, to the glory of God the Father. (Philippians 2:5-11)

There has been a tendency among scholars as well as preachers to interpret this passage as the expression of a belief in the pre-existence of Christ Jesus. This belief is based on the following statement in the text: "though he was in the form of God, did not count equality with God a thing to be grasped, but emptied himself, taking the form of a servant, being born in human likeness." On one occasion I was preaching a parish mission, and the pastor and I discussed this text. He was absolutely convinced that Paul intended to tell us that Christ Jesus was equal to God and then Jesus emptied himself by being born as a human. When I suggested an alternative interpretation, which I will discuss below, he got agitated and upset. If my interpretation was correct, he said, it would challenge the way he understood and preached about this passage. At the end of our discussion, he said he was devastated by this interpretation. Jerome Murphy-O'Connor writes of this tendency.

> The conviction that the hymn speaks of the pre-existence of Christ is so deeply rooted that it is taken completely for granted...The mere fact that pre-existence can be used as a criterion (for exegesis) underlines the solidity of the consensus, and leads one to expect that it is clearly rooted in the text. A surprise, however, awaits anyone who dispassionately looks for the evidence.[5]

---

5. Jerome Murphy-O'Connor, "Christological Anthropology in Phil. 2:6-11," in *Revue Biblique* 83 (1976) 30.

It is my hope that we can dispassionately look for the evidence. The interpretation offered by James D. G. Dunn is very different from that of many biblical scholars and the pastor mentioned above. He bases his exegesis on the idea of an Adam Christology, which develops the contrast between the first Adam who was the source of sin and death and the second Adam, Jesus, who is the source of grace and new life.

> It seems to me that Phil. 2:6-11 is best understood as an expression of Adam christology, one of the fullest expressions that we still possess. We have already seen how *widespread* was this Adam christology in the period before Paul wrote his letters—a fact not usually appreciated by those who offer alternative exegeses of the hymn.[6]

The citation from Philippians begins with these words: "Have this mind among yourselves which you have in Christ Jesus, who, though he was in the form of God, did not count equality with God a thing to be grasped." The subject of these verses is Christ Jesus, and Paul says, in most English translations, that Christ Jesus was in the form of God. However, the Greek word for *form* is *morphe*, which is synonymous with the word *image*. Thus, being in the form of God is equivalent to being in the image of God. Paul is saying that, just as Adam was created in the image of God, so Christ Jesus was in the image of God. Both are in the image of God, but Jesus did not "grasp" after equality to God, while Adam, on the contrary, wanted to be equal to God by knowing good and evil. Once again we find similarities and contrasts between Jesus and Adam. Both are created in the image of God, but Adam by his disobedience wanted to be like God, while Jesus on the contrary emptied himself.

The passage goes on to say that Christ Jesus "emptied himself, taking the form of a servant, being born in human likeness. And being found in human form he humbled himself and became obedient unto death, even death on a cross." Now Paul says that Jesus emptied himself, in Greek *kenosis*, taking the form of a servant. The "form of a servant" refers to what Adam became as a result of original sin. As we saw in chapter 6, Adam before the fall was described as being in a state of original innocence, but after the fall Adam was told that by the sweat of his face he would eat his bread. So, Paul says, Christ Jesus emptied himself, being born in the likeness of an ordinary human after the fall.

This language seems to assume a pre-existent Christ Jesus who freely emptied himself and took the form of a servant, being born in human

---

6. Dunn, *Christology in the Making*, pp. 114–115.

likeness. But this is not necessarily so, because the language is primarily determined by the contrast between Adam and Christ. "The language was used *not* because it is first and foremost appropriate to *Christ,* but because it is appropriate to *Adam,* drawn from the account of Adam's creation and fall."[7] Moreover, Paul is not describing a chronology of events; rather, the poetic style calls for and describes what in fact happened to Christ Jesus in contrast to Adam. It was simply Paul's way of describing the character of Christ's mission and ministry to his readers and it was probably not intended as a metaphysical assertion about the pre-existence of Jesus.

Paul goes on to say that Christ Jesus went beyond this by humbling himself and, in contrast to Adam's disobedience, became obedient to death, even a death on the cross. Therefore Paul is saying that Christ Jesus, who was the image of God, emptied himself by coming in the form of an ordinary human and then humbled himself by obedience unto death. "The hymn states of Jesus what the other expressions of Adam christology (particularly Rom. 5; 8:3 and Heb. 2:9-18) also state of Jesus, that *he freely chose to embrace the death that Adam experienced as punishment.*"[8]

> Therefore God has greatly exalted him and bestowed on him the name which is above every name, that at the name of Jesus every knee should bow, in heaven and on earth and under the earth, and every tongue confess the Jesus Christ is Lord, to the glory of God the Father. (Philippians 2:9-11)

Because of Jesus' humility and obedience, God bestowed on him the name which is above every name, and every tongue will confess that Jesus Christ is Lord. The use of the word *Lord* in this passage does not mean Lord in the sense of "Yahweh" but in the sense of a royal king. We find a hint of this exaltation in Psalm 110, a royal hymn, in which God appoints the king. "The Lord says to my lord: 'Take your throne at my right hand, while I make your enemies your footstool.' The scepter of your sovereign might the Lord will extend from Zion. The Lord says: 'Rule over your enemies!'" (Psalm 110:1-3). Isaiah speaks in the name of God, "By myself I swear, uttering my just decree and my unalterable word: To me every knee shall bend; by me every tongue shall swear" (Isaiah 45:23). As so often happens in the Christian writings, the authors have reached back into the Hebrew Scriptures for the language that is then knitted into their experience of Christ Jesus and the Christian life.

---

7. Ibid., p. 120.
8. Ibid., p. 118.

This whole passage begins by saying, "Have this mind among your-selves which you have in Christ Jesus." Paul then articulates the mind of Christ for us and tells us that we are the image of God, and that we should not try to be equal to God by lording it over others or wanting to decide what is good or evil. We should empty ourselves and humble ourselves in obedience to all that emerges in our life, even unto death. Then we will share in the exaltation and glory of God that belongs to us as humble and obedient daughters and sons of God.

What about the question of the pre-existence of Christ Jesus which is so often connected with this text in Philippians? This interpretation based on Adam Christology does not discover in the text a pre-existent Christ who is later born in the likeness of man. It does not affirm that the empty-ing involves a heavenly man who leaves behind his previous existence to become human. Rather, it affirms the true humanity of Jesus as the image of God, who, in contrast to Adam, does not grasp at being equal to God, but humbles himself in obedience even to death. This passage from Philip-pians has as its purpose not a teaching on pre-existence, but the affirma-tion of the humility and obedience of Jesus and his glorious resurrection.

Colossians 1:15-20.   In their struggle to explain their belief in the role of the risen Christ in both salvation and creation, the early Christian com-munity found in the figure of Sophia/Wisdom an appropriate way of doing so.[9] Perhaps the clearest and most significant description of the risen Christ is found in the use of the Jewish Wisdom tradition. The fol-lowing text from Paul's letter to the Colossians illustrates the connection between Jesus and the Wisdom of God. The words in italics are based on the Wisdom literature itself.

> He [the risen Christ] is the *image of the invisible God*, the *first-born of all creation.* For in him *were created all things in heaven and on earth*, the visible and the invisible, whether thrones or do-minions or principalities or powers; *all things were created through him* and for him. He is *before all things, and in him all things hold together.* He [the risen Christ] is the head of the body, the church.

> He is the beginning, *the firstborn* from the dead, that in all things he himself might be preeminent. For in him *all the fullness of God was pleased to dwell,* and through Christ to reconcile all things

---

9. For an excellent presentation of the relationship of Jesus and Sophia, see Eliza-beth Johnson, *She Who Is,* pp. 150–169.

for God, making peace by the blood of the cross, whether those on earth or those in heaven. (Colossians 1:15-20; italics added)

The following texts from Proverbs and Wisdom address the meaning of Wisdom and it is clear that Paul drew upon the very wording of these texts to describe the risen Christ.

The Lord begot me as *the firstborn,* the forerunner of God's prodigies of long ago; from of old I was poured forth, at the first, before the earth. When there were no depths I was brought forth, *when there were no fountains or springs of water; before the mountains were settled into place, before the hills, I was brought forth.* (Proverbs 8:22-25; italics added)

For Wisdom is mobile beyond all motion, and she penetrates and pervades all things by reason of her purity. *For she is an aura of the might of God and a pure effusion of the glory of the almighty;* therefore nought that is sullied enters into her. *For she is the refulgence of eternal light, the spotless mirror of the power of God, the image of God's goodness. And she, who is one, can do all things, and renews everything* while herself perduring. (Wisdom 7:24-27; italics added)

The language that was used in Colossians to describe the glorious risen Christ reflects the language from the Wisdom literature, and clearly the role of Wisdom is being attributed to Christ. When we say that the risen Christ embodies the fullness of God's Wisdom, are we speaking of the historical Jesus or about Christ as a *corporate* or *symbolic* person? Corporate personality is a characteristic of the Hebrew Scriptures, and is often used to identify the nation with an individual. And so the risen Christ, who embodies the fullness of God's Wisdom, can be a symbolic person who also embodies the universal salvific presence of God by which our Earth community and our human family are transformed. Elizabeth Johnson describes it in this way.

The fundamental nature of Christian identity as life in Christ makes clear that the biblical symbol of Christ, the one anointed in the Spirit, cannot be restricted to the historical person Jesus nor to certain select members of the community but signifies all those who by drinking of the Spirit participate in the community of disciples.[10]

10. Johnson, *She Who Is,* p. 162.

We can now apply the text from Colossians to the risen Christ as both a historical person and a symbolic person.

> He [the risen Christ] is the *image of the invisible God*, the *first-born of all creation*. For in him *were created all things in heaven and on earth*, the visible and the invisible, whether thrones or dominions or principalities or powers; *all things were created through him* and for him. He is *before all things, and in him all things hold together*. He [the risen Christ] is the head of the body, the church. (Colossians 1:15-18; italics added)

The risen Christ, like Wisdom, is called *the image of the invisible God*. Wisdom is the immanence of God found in all of creation and now made manifest in the life, death, and resurrection of Christ Jesus. The risen Christ is *the firstborn of all creation*, not necessarily in a temporal sense, but in terms of sovereignty over all creation. The passage is referring to the preeminence of Christ and to his coming rule over all creation in the eschaton. In God's plan the risen Christ is to be the fullest expression of God's wise ordering of the world and its history. In other words it was God's intention that all things were to be created in and through and for Christ. Thus, it is not necessary to say that Jesus in a temporal way existed before all creation. The risen Christ embodies the fullness of the Wisdom of God and through his resurrection becomes the archetype of God's Wisdom.

Paul continues his description of the risen Christ.

> He is *the beginning, the firstborn from the dead, that in all things he himself might be preeminent*. For in him *all the fullness of God was pleased to dwell,* and through Christ to reconcile all things for God, making peace by the blood of the cross, whether those on earth or those in heaven. (Colossians 1:18-20; italics added)

The second part of the Colossian passage says that the risen Christ is *the beginning, the firstborn from the dead, that in all things he himself might be preeminent*. Through his resurrection the risen Christ is truly the beginning and the firstborn from the dead, and the preeminence of Christ flows from this exalted state. The passage then says that *in the risen Christ all the fullness of God was pleased to dwell*. God himself is the all-permeating fullness and source of all being unfolding within the entire universe. But how does the fullness of God unfold? In the Wisdom tradition God's fullness unfolds through the all-pervasive presence of Wisdom, and in the Pauline tradition the risen Christ embodies this same all-pervasive Wisdom of God. Elizabeth Johnson says, "Whoever espouses a wisdom Christology is asserting that Sophia in all her fullness was in Jesus so that in his historicity he embodies divine mystery in creative and saving involvement with the world."[11] Dunn espouses the same view. "What he [Paul] was saying is that Wisdom, whatever precisely that term meant for his readers, is now most fully expressed in Jesus—*Jesus is the exhaustive embodiment of divine wisdom; all* the divine fullness dwelt in him."[12]

Do we find the pre-existence of Christ in this passage from Colossians? In Jewish tradition, Wisdom is the personification of the creative and salvific power of God, but Wisdom is not seen as a separate being or a divine person. Therefore, a pre-existence of Christ as an actual being with God in the beginning prior to creation is not found in this passage. Rather, the pre-existence of Christ in this passage is a poetic personification of Wisdom. All creation was summed up in the risen Christ as the archetype of Wisdom and as the symbol of the universal presence and power of God. Dunn summarizes this conclusion:

> Once again then we have found that what at first reads as a straightforward assertion of Christ's pre-existent activity in creation becomes on closer analysis an assertion which is rather more profound—not of Christ as such present with God in the beginning, nor of Christ as identified with a pre-existent hypostasis or divine being (Wisdom) beside God, but *of Christ as embodying and expressing (and defining) that power of God which is the manifestation of God in and to his creation.*[13]

THE JOHANNINE COMMUNITY

The Gospel of John is the product of what is commonly known as the Johannine community, and the story of this community is fundamental to an understanding of the Gospel. John's Gospel involves the interplay of *historical memory* and a *community autobiography*. The Johannine community included eyewitnesses to the life of Jesus who were aware of the synoptic Gospels. At the same time, these historical memories were interwoven with the community's own experiences of conflict with the Jews and of the incorporation of new converts.

---

11. Elizabeth Johnson, "Redeeming the Name of Christ," in *Freeing Theology,* ed. Catherine Mowry LaCugna, HarperSanFrancisco, 1993, p. 127.

12. Dunn, *Christology in the Making,* p. 195.

13. Ibid., p. 194.

In the early period the Johannine community consisted of Jews whose belief in Jesus involved a relatively low christology. Later there appeared a higher christology which brought the Johannine community into sharp conflict with Jews who regarded this as blasphemy, and this friction pushed the Johannine group to even bolder assertions.[14]

The pre-Gospel era of this community, from the mid-50s to the late 80s of the first century, began with mid-century Jews who had accepted Jesus as the Messiah. We might call them Christian *Jews*. They followed the message of Jesus, but they gradually began to separate themselves from the temple worship and to develop their own worship patterns. Their new beliefs and practices led to conflicts with the more traditional Jewish leaders. In the story of the Samaritan woman in John 4:4-42 one also finds evidence of Samaritan converts entering into the Johannine community.[15] Raymond Brown says that "the combination of a different christology, opposition to the Temple cult, and Samaritan elements... would have made the Johannine believers in Jesus particularly obnoxious to more traditional Jews."[16] Thus the Johannine community was expelled from the synagogue as found in the story of the blind man in John 9:22.

By the time that the Gospel of John was written, ca. 90 C.E., the Johannine community might be described as *Jewish Christians.* The struggles with the Jews as well as conflicts with other Christian believers pushed the Johannine community into a deepening belief in a higher Christology, including an elevated appreciation of Jesus' divinity. In defending their communal identity, they had to maximize the differences between their beliefs and those of the synagogue. The recognition of this reality "shows a community whose evaluation of Jesus was honed by struggle, and whose elevated appreciation of Jesus' divinity led to antagonisms without and schism within."[17] There remained an adolescent dualism that separated the human race into believers and non-believers, those who already have eternal life and those who are condemned. There was a sharp edge to the Johannine community which required a strong orthodoxy and which caused eventual divisions within the community. With this brief survey of the emergence of the Johannine community, we can move on to unearth the community's higher Christology as contained in the prologue to John's Gospel.

---

14. Raymond E. Brown, *The Community of the Beloved Disciple,* New York, Paulist Press, 1979, p. 25.

15. See also Acts 8:4-8.

16. Brown, *The Community of the Beloved Disciple,* p. 39.

17. Ibid., p. 24.

This prologue is a powerful message couched in the form of a hymn. It uses poetic material that may have been composed independently of the Gospel and later incorporated into the Gospel. Clearly it is a hymn to the living Word of God and the embodiment of that Word in Jesus, the only Son of God. The following is the text of the prologue using the verses that focus on the Word of God and Jesus as the only Son of God.

> In the beginning was the Word,
> and the Word was with God,
> and the Word was God.
> He was in the beginning with God.
> All things came into being through him,
> and no created thing came into being without him . . .
>
> And the Word was made flesh and pitched his tent among us.
> And we saw his glory, the glory as the only Son of the Father,
> full of grace and truth . . .
>
> From his fullness we have all received, grace upon grace.
> Because while the law was given through Moses,
> grace and truth came through Jesus Christ.
> No one has ever seen God.
> The only Son, God, who is at the Father's side,
> has revealed him. (John 1:1-3, 14, 16-18)

The phrase "Word of God" was commonly used in the Jewish tradition. In chapter 1 of Genesis the Word of God was present and active in the creative process; God's Word brought all things into being. The Word of the Lord came down upon the prophets, and they spoke that word to the people and to the nations. "Word" carries the sense of a revelation, as in a word revealed in creation or a word spoken by the prophet. In the early Christian community, the message about Jesus and the good news preached by the apostles was called the word of the Lord. "So when they had *testified and proclaimed the word of the Lord*, they returned to Jerusalem and preached good news to many Samaritan villages" (Acts 8:25; italics added). The word, in Hebrew *Dabar*, carries the meaning of action. It is not just an intellectual term but also a dynamic term, one which effects what it speaks. In the following text from Isaiah it also takes on a poetic dimension.

> For just as from the heavens the rain and snow come down and
> do not return there till they have watered the earth, making it fer-
> tile and fruitful, giving seed to him who sows and bread to him

who eats, so shall my word be that goes forth from my mouth; it shall not return to me void, but shall do my will, achieving the end for which I sent it. (Isaiah 55:10-11)

In the prologue John brings together these various meanings of the term *word* and describes the Word as a person present with God. "In the beginning was the Word, and the Word was with God, and the Word was God. He was in the beginning with God. All things came into being through him, and no created thing came into being without him." The Word was God, and through this Word all things came into being. But is the Word really a "person" or is it a "personification" of the creative, revelatory, and salvific acts of God, just as we found previously with Wisdom?

But if on the contrary, OT and LXX[18] talk of the Word and Wisdom of God is of a piece with the much wider and more varied personifications of other divine functions and actions, as it is, then we must conclude that their treatment of the Word and Wisdom of God is simply another example of the vigorous metaphorical style of Israel's spokesmen.[19]

In using both Word and Wisdom it is doubtful whether the vision of the Jewish tradition ever goes beyond a powerful literary personification of the immanent power and revelation of God. But the next section of the prologue calls us to a new and deeper meaning of the Word of God. "And the Word was made flesh and pitched his tent among us. And we saw his glory, the glory as the only Son of the Father, full of grace and truth." Now the Word of God takes on a more personal character by becoming flesh and pitching his tent among us. In Sirach we find a similar story as Wisdom sings her own praises:

From the mouth of the Most High I came forth, and mistlike covered the earth. In the highest heaven did I dwell, my throne on a pillar of cloud . . . Then the Creator of all gave me his command, and he who formed me chose the spot for my tent, saying, "In Jacob make your dwelling, in Israel your inheritance." (Sirach 24:3, 4, 8)

The Word or Wisdom pitching a tent among the people is really not without precedent in the Jewish Wisdom tradition, but in verse 14 of

---

18. OT means Old Testament, and LXX means the Septuagint version of the Bible.
19. Dunn, *Christology in the Making,* p. 220.

John's prologue, the Word, as a "person," has become flesh in an innova-
tive and different way. This seems to support the idea of a pre-existent
Word becoming flesh, and the Word who became flesh is named in the
next verses to be Jesus Christ. If that is true, then the Word of God, as
Jesus Christ, is, in fact, a real person who lives among us and embodies
all that belongs to the power and presence of the Word of God. Dunn concludes by saying "The revolutionary significance of v. 14 may well be
that it marks *not only the transition in the thought of the poem from pre-
existence to incarnation, but also the transition from impersonal personification to actual person.*"[20]

The prologue now turns its attention to Jesus Christ and, in particular,
to Jesus as the Son of God.

> And we saw his glory, the glory as the only Son of the Father,
> full of grace and truth...
> From his fullness we have all received, grace upon grace.
> Because while the law was given through Moses,
> grace and truth came through Jesus Christ.
> No one has ever seen God.
> The only Son, God, who is at the Father's side, has revealed him.
>   (John 1:14, 16-18)

In the synoptic Gospels the title Son of God was interpreted in terms
of a low Christology, which means that there was a special relationship between God as Father, Abba, and Jesus as the beloved Son of God. Referring to Psalm 2, which says, "This day I have begotten you, and I am your
Father," Paul says that Jesus was made the Son of God in his resurrection.
Now in the prologue, however, John says that Jesus Christ is the *only* Son
of the Father, full of grace and truth. Moreover, from the fullness of this
only Son we have all received. There is a uniqueness here in John's description that has not been found before. Then comes the twofold compari-
son with Moses. Moses gave the Jewish nation the law, but Jesus gives his
people grace and truth; no one, not even Moses, has ever seen God, but the
only Son, God, who is at the Father's side and has revealed him.

The vision of the Son of God who is at the Father's side raises the
issue of Jesus' pre-existence and the reality of his descent from heaven. In
the synoptics, Jesus is presented as one who walked this earth and then
was taken up to God. As the Son of Man he would return to judge the living and the dead. In John's interpretation, during his earthly ministry Jesus
had already *come down* from God to serve as a judgment. "The one who

---

20. Ibid., p. 243.

comes from above is above all...He testifies to what he has seen and heard, but no one accepts his testimony. For the one whom God sent speaks the words of God" (John 3:31-32, 34). "I came from the Father and have come into the world. Now I am leaving the world and going back to the Father" (John 16:28). Edward Schillebeeckx explains the meaning of this *coming down.* "In speaking of the *katabasis* or descent from heaven, that is, of the sending of Jesus by the Father, John is not presenting a theology of the Trinity but a christology. Because of his pre-existence, the *earthly Jesus* has the gift of the knowledge and power of salvation."[21]

But this descent is followed by ascent. "No one has gone up to heaven except the one who has come down from heaven, the Son of Man. And just as Moses lifted up the serpent in the desert, so must the Son of Man be lifted up, so that everyone who believes in him may have eternal life" (John 3:13-15). The lifting up, that is the exaltation, of the Son of Man takes place in the death of Jesus. John speaks of the death of Jesus as his glorification and his return to heaven. In the last supper discourses Jesus summarizes this descent and ascent in one brief statement. "I came from the Father and have come into the world. Now I am leaving the world and going back to the Father" (John 16:28). Belief in the pre-existence of Jesus enabled the Johannine community to complete the circle of God's plan of salvation in the descent of the Word made flesh from heaven and his glorification and return to the Father. "According to the Gospel of John, the pre-existence of Jesus explains the real and complete significance of the final phase of the life of Jesus: his exaltation (death) and his resurrection or glorification."[22]

We have now reached the end of our brief sketch of the journey toward a high Christology. The question that was posed is the following: How did Jesus, an itinerant peasant preacher and healer in Galilee, become the Lord, the Wisdom of God, the pre-existent Word of God, and the divine Son of God? The journey began with the earthly ministry of Jesus of Nazareth and his message of the coming reign of God and the good news to the poor. Jesus was crucified, and this man Jesus was raised from the dead and became the Lord and the Messiah. The resurrection was the crucial hinge on which a new interpretation of the person and message of Jesus turned. The writings of Paul move the journey along by treating Jesus as the new Adam, who, through his obedience, reversed the deadly fall of Adam. Paul also used the Jewish Wisdom tradition to describe Jesus as the embodiment of the Wisdom of God. The journey

---

21. Edward Schillebeeckx, *Christ: The Experience of Jesus as Lord,* New York, Seabury Press, 1980, p. 223.

22. Ibid., p. 324.

found its high point within the Johannine community and the Gospel of John. This high Christology sits atop a table with four legs, and it is dependent on those four supports for its emergence and for its stability.

The first leg is the very context of the Johannine community and its struggles with what John calls "the Jews." The very existence of the Johannine community depended on its ability to distinguish the community's Christian beliefs from current Jewish beliefs. This struggle eventually led to making Jesus the Messiah and more than a Messiah. The community's Christian identity over against "the Jews" was its first priority.

The second leg is the use of the Word of God concept found in the prologue to the Gospel. This enabled the Johannine community to build on the Pauline ideas of the New Adam and Jesus as the Wisdom of God. It also opened up the possibility of moving from a personification of the Word to the Word made flesh in the person of Jesus. This, however, did not finalize the concept of the pre-existence of Jesus, but it called for *the third leg*. The prologue now brings in a new sense of the Son of God when the author calls him the *only* Son of the Father. The prologue states, "No one has ever seen God. The *only* Son, God, who is at the Father's side, has revealed him." The Word of God has now become a person who is the only Son of the Father.

The fourth leg of the table is the concept that Jesus, who was at the Father's side, was sent down from heaven, and would return to heaven. The idea of the descent and ascent of Jesus, an idea that was not uncommon among first-century thinkers, was a necessary dimension of belief in a pre-existent Jesus. The Word of God was made flesh in Jesus, that is, by his coming down from the Father and entering into human history. These words are attributed to Jesus himself. "I came from the Father and have come into the world. Now I am leaving the world and going back to the Father" (John 16:28).

This fourth leg, however, loses its coherence in the twenty-first century among people who have thoroughly imbibed the modern scientific world view because, as Schillebeeckx says, "Descending and coming down are primarily connected with the picture of the world drawn in antiquity: above, here, below. Heaven, that is, where God dwells, is the highest storey [*sic*] of our universe."[23] In the context of a vastly different picture of the world, the table supporting the pre-existence seems likely to fall. The descent of the Son who came into the world from the Father and will leave the world and go back to the Father is no longer a credible interpretation of the role of Christ. We must seek to find a way of reinterpreting the role of Jesus within the context of an emerging universe.

---

23. Ibid., p. 322.

Before proceeding, we can summarize our conclusions on the pre-existence of Jesus by saying that, from a biblical point of view, there is no unambiguous passage in the Bible to prove that Jesus pre-existed his coming on Earth. The strongest passage is found in John's prologue which is based on a three-level cosmology, and which, in an emerging universe, is no longer an appropriate image. The New Testament does describe Jesus as pre-existent in the mind and intention of God. In an emerging universe, on scientific grounds, however, there is no overall divine plan for the universe. The emergence of Jesus, as of all beings, is neither random nor determined, but creative. In the inner unfolding of God in Jesus, both as an individual and as a corporate person, he embodied the biblical personification of divine Wisdom and the Word of God.

JESUS IN AN EMERGING UNIVERSE

The exalted Johannine christology is not some abstract test of orthodoxy that has nothing to do with community living. If it is crucial to believe that Jesus is the pre-existent Word of God who has come from God and is of God, it is because then we know what God is really like—He really is a God of love who so loved the world that he was willing to give of Himself, in His Son (3:16; 1 John 4:8-9), and not merely send someone else.[24]

The most significant aspect of an emerging universe is the presence of the unconditional love of God unfolding within the universe as an internal cause, rather than as an external cause intervening in a created universe. Three topics flowing from an emerging universe will be discussed in this section: first, the presence of God and its impact on the meaning of Jesus; second, the divinity of Jesus in an emerging universe; and third, the uniqueness of Jesus. We will conclude with some final thoughts.

THE PRESENCE OF GOD

In chapter 2 the difference between a "created" universe and an "emerging" universe was discussed at some length. It will be helpful to repeat some of the basic ideas developed in that chapter. When we say that the universe is "created," we are describing a process in which God created the world out of nothing and all at once. The word *created* stresses the transcendence of God as well as the continuing presence of God; it im-

---

24. Brown, *The Community of the Beloved Disciple,* pp. 60–61.

plies a God who created the universe from the outside as the efficient cause of everything. God rules the world through a plan called "Divine Providence," and creatures are secondary causes in carrying out this plan.

When we say that the universe is "emerging," we are referring to a process in which the whole universe emerges in a time-development sequence from within. The language of emergence stresses the immanence of God; it implies a God who acts from the inside out, unfolding as an internal cause. It does not speak of mediators, but of the immediate internal presence of the power, energy, and love of God. There are common elements in the concepts of a created universe, such as the fact that both see God as the source of all being and present to all creatures. The difference lies in *how* God is the source and *how* God is present. In an emerging universe God is the source of all being, not as an external cause, but as an internal cause. In an emerging universe the inner presence of God is found in the very unfolding and emerging of the universe and not in some external divine plan.

In chapter 5 we saw that, in an emerging universe, the reign of God is the presence of God. The flashing forth of the universe, the formation of our galaxy, and the birth of our Earth are the result of the reign of God and God's presence within the universe. Thus the reign of God is a universal reality that is found in the whole of the cosmos. In a profound sense the reign of God unfolds as the holy web of relationships that binds us all to each other and to all of creation. When Jesus declares that the reign of God is at hand (Mark 1:15), he is really saying that the reign of God within the entire universe is now manifesting itself in a new way, in an inner conversion of heart and a transformation of society which is good news to the poor. Whenever and wherever God is present and ruling within us, as humans, there will be both an inner change of heart and a change in the political, social, and religious order of things. The presence of the unconditional love of God is so deeply embedded within the universe and within the Earth that to live in tune with the Earth is to live in tune with the reign of God.

Moreover, the presence of God within creation also unfolds as revelation and salvation. In chapter 2 we defined revelation as the *presence of God* perceived in historical and symbolic events as interpreted and expressed in symbols and rituals within a community. Faith is our loving response to God's invitation based on our experience of God's presence in the various events and symbols of our individual and communal lives. Thus, revelation and faith are interconnected insofar as revelation is found in the presence of God in our human experience, and faith is our spirit-filled response to this presence of God.

In an emerging universe, salvation can now be described in new terms such as restoration, transformation, reconciliation, and renewal, and it is possible to transfer these ideas to the social, political, and religious spheres.

If God works within the universe, as described in an emerging universe, then this same God works in a comparable way within the social, political, and religious spheres. In an emerging universe salvation comes from a God who dwells within the entire universe, and this salvific presence of God is found equivalently within the human race in all its manifestations. Revelation and salvation are two dimensions of the presence of God unfolding in the universe. If revelation is not salvific, it is not true revelation. If salvation is not revelatory, it is not true salvation. Both revelation and salvation are intimately bound up with and emerge from our experience of the human community and the entire community of species.

THE DIVINITY OF JESUS

Jesus' role in salvation is one of the major issues relating to the divinity of Jesus. The soteriology of the early theologians and ecumenical councils of the church was frequently based on their belief in the divinity of Jesus and on the need for a savior. Original sin, as interpreted by Catholic tradition, is an offense against God and because of this original sin "[human nature] is wounded in the natural powers proper to it; subject to ignorance, suffering, and the dominion of death; and inclined to sin—an inclination to evil that is called concupiscence" (*Catechism of the Catholic Church,* #405). As a result, the savior and redeemer must have been human in order to redeem humans and must have been God in order to atone for the infinite offense of sin and to overcome the objective and ontological wounding of human nature.

Gerald O'Collins explains it this way: "The overriding concern for salvation and their experience of it led Christians to maintain that two basic conditions make it possible for Jesus to do this for them: he must be truly human and truly divine to function as their effective Saviour."[25] Then O'Collins quotes the second-century theologian Irenaeus.

If a human being had not overcome the enemy of humanity, the enemy would not have been rightly overcome. On the other side, if it had not been God to give us salvation, we would not have received it permanently. If the human being had not been united to God, it would not have been possible to share in incorruptibility. (*Adversus haereses*, 3. 18. 7: see 3. 19. 1)

Finally, O'Collins concludes by saying, "Without the incarnation of the *Son of God*, divine redemption would be impossible. Yet without a

---

25. Gerald O'Collins, *Christology,* Oxford University Press, 1995, p. 155.

genuine *incarnation*, the battle against the diabolic forces of evil would not be won from the inside."[26]

Athanasius, the Bishop of Alexandria in the fourth century, used a similar argument to support the divinity of the historical person of Jesus Christ. "For since by men death had laid hold of men, so for this reason, by the incarnation of God the Word, were effected the overthrow of death and the resurrection of life... This, therefore, is the primary cause of the incarnation of the Saviour."[27]

But what if the origin of sin is found in the intrinsic limitations of all creatures and in the free choices of human beings? In this interpretation there is no need to atone for and redeem us from an original sin. If the limitations and interdependency of all creatures are the origin of the natural evils in the world, and if human violence flows from the free choices of humans, there is no original sin, in the sense of an objective, ontological flaw within human nature. God's unconditional love has never been objectively and ontologically lost, even though humans, through their broken relationships, can lose *their* subjective love of God. In an emerging universe there is no evidence for such a thing as an original holiness and justice, and there is no evidence for an original sin through which the human race has fallen and become objectively and ontologically wounded. There is certainly evil in human relationships and there are limitations in our relationships with the rest of creation. There is a need for a savior, but it is not because of an original sin and a fallen nature. Thus, there is no necessity for Jesus to be God in order to redeem us objectively and ontologically from such a sin and its consequences.

In the *Summa* of Thomas Aquinas there is a very interesting text that relates to this issue. He asks whether, if man had not sinned, God would have become incarnate. The answer to this question was hotly debated in the thirteenth century, with most theologians saying that if man had not sinned God still would have become incarnate. Thomas went against the common teaching and answered:

> Hence, since everywhere in the Sacred Scripture the sin of the first man is assigned as the reason of the Incarnation, it is more in accordance with this to say that the work of the Incarnation was ordained by God as a remedy for sin; so that, had sin not existed, the Incarnation would not have been. And yet the power of

---

26. Ibid., p. 155.

27. Athanasius, *Contra Gentes and De Incarnatione,* ed. Robert W. Thompson, Oxford, The Clarendon Press, 1971, p. 159.

God is not limited to this; even had sin not existed, God could have become incarnate.[28]

As you can see, Aquinas, who usually speaks with care, left himself a way out by saying that we cannot limit the power of God, even if we try.

There is another very important dimension to this discussion of the divinity of Jesus in the context of an emerging universe. We must return to the human story found in chapter 1. In the adolescence of the human race, from ten thousand years ago until today, it became clear that separation and separateness were major characteristics of an adolescent human race. The use of fire and the power of words helped humans establish their species identity, yet the process of establishing a clear species identity tended toward isolating the human within itself over against the non-human components of the larger Earth community. Just as an individual develops his or her ego by distinguishing "self" from "other," humanity distinguished itself from the rest of nature. The separation of the human from nature while seeking our species identity also impacted the relationship of humans to the divine. Moreover, the cosmology of the biblical and Western world reinforced the separation of the human and the divine. From biblical times throughout the Middle Ages, both learned and ordinary folks shared a creation story that placed Heaven above, separated from the Earth below. God was found in Heaven along with the spirits and the angels. The Earth was the home of the human race and all its creatures. As we lost our intimacy with the Earth, we lost our intimacy with the divine; the human and the divine, as we might say, lived on different planets.

The Christian community emerged during this adolescent stage of the human story with its separation of the human from the divine. As this community experienced the resurrection and glorification of Jesus, it more and more experienced the risen Christ as the very presence of God. Yet this experience was at odds with its cultural and religious sense of the separation of the human from the divine. If there is a separation between God in heaven and humans here on Earth, how could God and Jesus be brought together?

As we have seen above, the Christian Scriptures used many different ways of describing the relationship between Jesus and God, and these descriptions approached the issue from many diverse perspectives. But no single answer emerged, and in the end there remained a great ambiguity concerning how to conceptualize the divinity of Jesus. This ambiguity is found in the title, Son of God, in the use of Wisdom in Paul, and in the de-

---

28. Thomas Aquinas, *Summa Theologica,* Part III, Q. 1, Art. 3.

velopment of the Word of God in John. Several other texts in John which seem to treat Jesus as divine and pre-existent remain equally ambiguous. The Baptist says, "He is the one of whom I said, 'A man is coming after me who ranks ahead of me because he existed before me'" (John 1:30). In what way does Jesus exist before John? In prophecy? In the mind of God? As the eternal Word? We can ask the same questions of the passages where Jesus seems to claim the divine name, I AM. "Amen, amen, I say to you, before Abraham came to be, I AM" (John 8:58). In what way did the author of this Gospel interpret this saying? Were these meant to be Jesus' own words, or was this the interpretation of the Johannine community? Are the words meant to be taken literally, metaphorically, or poetically? There is polyvalence in all these texts, and the magnitude of the claim to be God cannot be unambiguously proved by such poetic texts.

In the history of the first five centuries this ambiguity led to a series of heresies and church councils ending with the Council of Chalcedon, which provided the classical doctrine of the two natures in one divine person articulated in the philosophical language of a specific time and culture. When lecturing on these issues, the question often surfaces about whether Jesus is true God and true man. I usually answer by asking another question: What does it mean to say that Jesus is true God and true man? For most people, these are words without meaning. Some people can quote the Council of Chalcedon, which declares that "the one self-same Christ, only-begotten Son and Lord, must be acknowledged in two natures."[29] In other words, Jesus is one person with both a divine nature and human nature. This declaration still leaves us unsettled. We have some sense of what it means to be human because of our concrete experience of our own and other people's human nature. Even so, we cannot exhaust the meaning of our humanness. What it means to be divine or to have a divine nature is something totally beyond our concrete experience and our ability to comprehend. In the text quoted at the beginning of this chapter, Aquinas reiterates the limitations of our understanding of God. "Because we cannot know what God is, but rather what God is not, we have no means for considering how God is, but rather how God is not."[30]

The basic issue for us is that in these councils, as well as in medieval theology, it was common to make a distinction or a separation between nature and person. Jesus, a pre-existent *person*, the Son of God, with a *divine nature,* came down and was united to a *human nature* resulting in a divine person with two natures. The presupposition is that the divine person and the human nature were separate, and thus it took a special act of

---

29. Gerard Van Ackeren, S.J., et al., *The Church Teaches,* New York, B. Herder Book Co., 1955, p. 172.

30. Thomas Aquinas, *Summa Theologica,* I, 3, Intro.

God to bring them together—the *incarnation*. But what if the human and the divine were never separated? In an emerging universe God is fully present within the whole of the universe as the source of all being, not by an external efficient causality, but by an internal causality. God cannot be partially present. In an emerging universe, the inner presence of God is found in the very unfolding of the universe by God's internal causality. In an emerging universe, everything and every one is inseparable from God and there is no way that God can be separated from the human.

Roger Haight describes this intimacy as it relates to God's presence in Jesus.

> God's presence to Jesus must be regarded as a presence within his humanity. By this I mean that the divine in Jesus does not appear over and above Jesus' being a human being, but rather precisely within the way Jesus was human, the way he lived and taught. Jesus' divinity was not added on top of his humanity, nor was his humanity an abstract human nature added on to or assumed by his divinity. The divine is not apparent in Jesus in any recognizable way, because it does not subsist in him apart from or separate from the integrally human life that Jesus lived.[31]

This in no way means that God is identical with the universe. God is other than and more than the universe, but God is inseparable from the universe. As Jesus says in the Gospel of John, "The Father is greater than I" (other than and more than) and "The Father and I are one" (inseparable). It is possible for each of us to say the same thing with the same meaning: the Father is greater than I (other than and more than), and the Father and I are one (inseparable).

The descent of the Word of God, as described in John's prologue, is not necessary, because God is already present in Jesus. What is necessary is that the Word of God emerges in Jesus from within in all its fullness! The Word is made flesh in Jesus, not by an extrinsic action of God, but by an emergence from within, which is always the case in an emerging universe. Likewise, since there is no separation between God and the human person, the Word is also made flesh in us by the emergence of the Word from within us. As we have seen, because of the immediate presence of God, the universe itself can be imagined as God incarnate; we can also say that, because of the immediate presence of God in humans, humans are God incarnate in a special way insofar as humans can consciously know and love and worship the living God. The unconditional love of

---

31. Haight, *Jesus Symbol of God,* p. 293.

God, manifested in the coming of the only Son, also dwells within us all as we read in the First Letter of John:

> Beloved, let us love one another; for love is of God, and anyone who loves is born of God and knows God. Anyone who does not love does not know God; for God is love. In this way the love of God was made manifest among us, that God sent his only Son into the world, so that we might live through him. In this is love, not that we loved God but that God loved us, and we also ought to love one another. No one has ever seen God. If we love one another, God abides in us and God's love is perfected in us. By this we know that we abide in God and God in us, because God has given us God's own Spirit. (1 John 4:7-13)

THE UNIQUENESS OF JESUS

If the love of God and the Word of God are present and unfolding within every human being as well as Jesus, then how can Jesus be in any way unique? First of all, we must make a distinction between what I call *exclusive uniqueness* and *inclusive uniqueness*. Exclusive uniqueness is found when something embodies a uniqueness that excludes everything and everyone. Human beings possess a unique power of consciousness and free choice which, as far as we know, is not possessed by any other creature. We can say that the Grand Canyon is unique in the sense that, as far as we know, no other natural wonder shares its beauty and awesomeness. Inclusive uniqueness is found when someone embodies a uniqueness that includes everyone else and is possessed by everyone else. The soloist in a choir has a certain uniqueness, but the music is really being performed by everyone in the choir. A priest has a certain uniqueness as the presider in the celebration of the Eucharist, but the Eucharist is really celebrated by the whole worshiping community. It is my view that the uniqueness of Jesus is an inclusive uniqueness.

The uniqueness of Jesus is found first in the resurrection. Jesus of Nazareth, a powerful peasant preacher and healer, challenged the Jewish holiness code and the leaders of the Jewish people in the midst of a social crisis of Roman commercialization. Because of his call for change and transformation he was finally crucified outside the city of Jerusalem. His crucifixion and resurrection became the catalyst out of which emerged a new level of consciousness and a deeper sense of faith. In an emerging universe, the resurrection of Jesus is symbolic of a qualitatively new moment in history and a deeper level of human consciousness flowing from the chaos of the crucifixion.

In the resurrection Jesus was transformed by an act of God, and at the same time the Jesus community was transformed. Their experience of the risen Jesus confirmed for them his mission and message, and it gave them new life and the impetus to make his mission and message their own. A deeper level of consciousness enabled the Jesus community to experience the meaning of death as new life, a re-entry into the consciousness of God, and a communal call to new life for all peoples. Bob Veitch of the "First Friday Group" wrote the following about the power and significance of the resurrection of Jesus:

> The Jesus story is really the resurrection story and the message is that there is life after death—eternal life, with Abba, a life of love and joy. The resurrection of Jesus makes the story live for his followers. If Jesus lives, all may live. This is a very powerful message to the poor who, up until this time, had little hope alive or dead.

The resurrection is not something that happened only to Jesus; it is not something that happened only to the Jesus community or the early Christian community; it is something that is happening to us. We are all called to transformation, to a personal experience of resurrection life, to a dynamic response of faith, and to a mission to all people. In an emerging universe, resurrection can be seen as a new depth of consciousness that has the potential of transforming humanity from adolescence into adulthood at a moment when the adolescence of the human race is so apparent in the reliance on violence on the part of both terrorists and those who oppose terrorism.

Resurrection is also a universal symbolic event that can transform our Earth community and our human family. Resurrection is part of the inner dynamics of the universe, so that in the midst of the chaos, the violence, the terrorist attacks, and the bio-terrorism of our global situation, resurrection will win out. Over and over again in the history of the universe this new life has arisen out of death. Now there is an opportunity for the new story of an emerging universe and the chaos currently experienced in the lives of many peoples and nations to open up to us a quantum leap into a new depth of consciousness and a new experience of life. As Jesus is raised so shall we be raised. The uniqueness of the resurrection of Jesus is an inclusive uniqueness. The words of Kenan Osborne bear repeating:

> Jesus' resurrection, from this Jewish background, cannot be understood as an isolated, personal, individual, unique situation. If

Jesus did rise bodily from the dead, then his resurrection is at the same time related to the bodily resurrection of others...and the opposite is true as well—the resurrection of others is related to the resurrection of Jesus.[32]

Second, the uniqueness of Jesus is also found in his role as a corporate or symbolic person. Just as Adam functions as a corporate personality symbolizing the whole human race, we can and should also say that Jesus, the new earthling, can be interpreted as something more than simply a historical individual. Jesus is a corporate personality symbolizing the Christian community and the new people of God. Dunn says that "the first point which calls for comment is that *when Paul uses Adam language explicitly of Christ he is referring primarily to Christ risen and exalted.* As Adam stands for fallen man, so Christ stands for man risen from the dead."[33]

The risen Christ is a symbolic person within the Christian community, which now shares in the promise of the resurrection. The risen Christ is also the center of what tradition calls the Body of Christ and the Communion of Saints that embraces all the faithful whether living or dead. This Communion of Saints and the relationships found within it participate in the broader web of relationships found in the holon theory and quantum nature of the universe. As mentioned in chapter 4, there is a deep web of relationships within our human lives. This web of relationships bonds us not only to those people who have impacted our lives in a variety of ways, but also to the whole of creation. Our bonding changes us and we are one in a unity that can reach beyond the grave. After death, the web of relationships that is my individual conscious self does not cease to exist. Rather, it becomes part of a larger whole, the larger web of relationships, a new holon that embraces all of space and time and the whole of creation within the infinite love of the Creator God.

All things were to be created in and through and for Christ, and all creation was to be summed up in the risen Christ as the archetype of Wisdom and the corporate symbol of the universal presence and power of God within all creation. In the symbolic personality of the risen Christ the Christian community embodies a vision of resurrection and new life and calls for the universal saving presence of God in all cultures and all religions and all peoples. We should not forget the words of Elizabeth Johnson, who points out that "the biblical symbol of Christ, the one anointed in the Spirit, cannot be restricted to the historical person Jesus nor to cer-

---

32. Osborne, *The Resurrection of Jesus,* pp. 91–92.
33. Dunn, *Christology in the Making,* p. 107.

tain select members of the community but signifies all those who by drinking of the Spirit participate in the community of Disciples."[34]

Third, the uniqueness of Jesus is found in his role in the worship of the believing community. In chapter 5 we said that it takes a gang to make a Messiah, and we can say now that it takes a community of believers to bear witness to Jesus as the symbol of God. Their experience of the presence of God in Jesus calls the community to share in the life of Jesus and in the coming of the Holy Spirit. The Pentecost experience continually witnesses to God's presence within the community. This experience of the presence of God within Jesus by the believing community also results in giving Jesus a central role in the worship of the community. By its very nature the Christian community is called to ritualize its faith and its witness to Jesus. Rituals, symbols, and sacraments are essential dimensions of deeper consciousness, so much so that only with a vibrant and life-giving liturgical life will the church be able to foster, develop, and live out its spirituality and carry out its servant role in society. Central to the life of any religion are the rituals that express symbolically the mystery of the presence of God within the community. The depth of this mystery and of our relationship to God is so powerful that words alone are inadequate. Communities have an inner life involving a communal memory and a particular energy field. It is only in symbolic rituals that the community can adequately articulate this inner life with its memory and energy field.[35]

The presence of God in Jesus became central to the ritual experience of the early Christians. This is especially clear in the tradition of eating and drinking with Jesus and uniquely in the paschal meal. As the paschal meal was transformed into the last supper and then into the ritual celebration of the death and resurrection of Jesus, it became a reminder of the powerful presence of God unfolding within Jesus. The ritual of baptism also arose as an initiation ritual within the community, and it celebrated the new life that is found in the risen Christ and in the community. In these rituals the community gave witness to Jesus as the symbol and model of the salvific and revelatory presence of God within the community. Jesus is unique because of his resurrection, which is the very center of the worship life of the community. Jesus is unique because in the symbols and sacraments of the church he manifests for us the real presence of God within himself, within the whole human race, and within all Earth's creatures.

In the words of John Knox,

---

34. Johnson, *She Who Is,* p. 162.
35. See my *The Holy Web,* p. 118.

the uniqueness of this man lies in the fact that, in him and in what happened through him and in response to him, the God of heaven and earth, of all nature and history, made himself known, in mighty power and with reconciling and saving effect, in an action unique and supremely significant. Through this man—living, dying, risen—God brought into being a redeemed humanity.[36]

In a similar way, as people absorb the new creation story, they celebrate that story in rituals and symbols. People are coming together in such rituals as the national celebration of Earth Day, the various solstice rituals around the country, and the dances and nature rituals of the Native Americans. The powerful revised ceremonies of the Easter Vigil use such earth symbols as fire, water, light, and darkness. These rituals embody our closeness to the Earth, our unity in the Earth, and our dependence on the Earth. We are absorbed into a whole web of relationships with and in all of creation. These rituals call us to confess our new and deeper sense of identity, not as humans ruling over creation, but as members of the community of species sharing in the bounty of the Earth. We are the Earth become conscious. We are co-creators in the search for a new adult phase of human life that stresses collaboration and mutuality, justice and equal rights, wholeness and world peace. The full flowering of this self-awareness will guide us into social and political action for the welfare of our Earth and the equitable distribution of the Earth's sustainable resources among all creatures.

FINAL THOUGHTS

An emerging universe provides us with a new and powerful way of depicting our experience of the world and the presence of God in that world. The presence of God always unfolds from within, whether in the cosmic drama of the formation of galaxies, in the gradual evolution of species here on Earth, or in the inner consciousness of the human race. In an emerging universe, a God who intervenes in the great cosmic flow of creativity seems out of place. The holon theory shows how the tension between self-preservation and self-adaptation leads to self-transcendence. The emerging process from within is neither determined nor random; it is creative. In an emerging universe, God is the source of all being, not by an external efficient causality, but by an internal causality. This new concept flows from the quantum make-up of the universe, and it calls us to think in new ways about the universe and the presence of God within the universe.

---

36. Knox, *The Humanity and Divinity of Christ,* p. 114.

The message of an emerging universe is crucial at this stage of history where we find a human race that is deeply divided and racked with violence and war, an Earth that is devastated by the encroachments of human greed and selfishness. This message can also give us an agenda for the twenty-first century. The first item on the agenda is the human story itself and the movement from adolescence to adulthood. The second item is the possibility of new life and a new depth of consciousness as found in the resurrection.

In our discussion of the human story in chapter 1 we described the passage from childhood to adolescence to adulthood. The human race is now on the cusp between adolescence and adulthood, and the outcome will be either a leap into adulthood or a fall into oblivion. The characteristics of adolescence are separateness, patriarchy, and the desire of man to become God. These characteristics have been a source of ego and mental development as well as of poverty, famine, exploitation, and violence. We must go beyond adolescence and call each other to an adult awareness of wholeness and inclusivity, a new sense of power as service to others, and a willingness to learn from the wisdom of the ages. Adulthood demands conversion and a change of heart, a willingness to challenge violence and search for non-violent conflict resolution. Jesus' message of the primacy of love, his willingness to embrace all people, his courage in confronting the powers of evil, and his breaking down of the artificial barriers that divide people can serve as a role model for this generation. His mission described in the Gospels is one of service to the poor, the outcasts, and the prostitutes; it is one of feeding the hungry, welcoming the stranger, and freeing the captives.

Simultaneously with the movement toward adulthood the Earth is experiencing the transformation from a Cenozoic Era to an Ecozoic Era. The Cenozoic Era, which began about fifty-five million years ago, was the time when the Earth decked itself with marvelous beauty, mysterious diversity, and puzzling complexity. But now a distorted myth of *progress* has brought about a potential destruction of all that beauty and diversity. A new consciousness is now necessary, a consciousness that will guide our society in embracing an Ecozoic Era and moving from our human-centered to an Earth-centered norm of reality and value. We cannot change the outer world without also changing our inner world. A desolate Earth will be reflected in the desolate depths of the human. The comprehensive objective of the Ecozoic is to assist in establishing what Swimme and Berry call "a mutually enhancing human presence upon the Earth,"[37] and this can be done only if the human race moves out of adolescence and into the maturity of adulthood.

---

37. Swimme and Berry, *The Universe Story,* p. 250.

The message of Jesus shows us that the dignity of the human race is not found in its ability to control and dominate the Earth, nor is it found in the marvels of technology. Rather, our dignity is found in our intimate loving relationships within and among ourselves and with the whole community of species. His preaching models a love of nature, as is evident in his frequent use of the earth and seeds and animals in his parables. Jesus' focus on the reign of God can be interpreted to mean that to live in tune with the universe is to live in tune with the reign of God. What can be the inner source of salvation that will enable humans in the twenty-first century to move toward adulthood and the transition to an Ecozoic Era?

There are probably many answers to this question, but, in the context of Jesus in an emerging universe, an inner source of salvation can be discovered in the resurrection of Jesus. Jesus' life, death, and resurrection model for us a living example of a dissipative structure which moves from turbulence to chaos to creativity. Jesus' preaching and his challenging of the religious and political leaders of his day led to a disturbance of the social balance in Israel. This escalated into a call for the violence of his crucifixion and death. Out of the chaos came new life in the resurrection. In our world today there is a religious and political chaos—the intransigent violence among the Israelis and the Palestinians, the tribal wars in Africa, the war in Afghanistan, the violence of terrorist and anti-terrorists alike, the conflicts among religious and ethnic groups, the turmoil within the Catholic Church over clergy sexual abuse and the subsequent failure of its leadership, the fear within the hearts of many Americans as they discover their vulnerability.

There is chaos in the Earth communities. But chaos is the beginning of creativity. Death opens out into resurrection. The resurrection of Jesus can be the icon of new life for the individual, the nation, and the Earth. Resurrection is the pattern that promises new life for the individual because of the loving presence of God within every single person. We have within us the source of new life. Because of the presence of God within the holy web of relationships among all people and within all of creation, the resurrection of Jesus brings us to a new depth of consciousness that can overcome our fears and give us new hope. We are never alone and we are never without the promise of life—spring always follows winter. Resurrection calls for action. Jesus' resurrection was a dynamic catalyst for the early Christian community. It transformed a group of frightened disciples into exuberant and spirit-filled missionaries. That same power is still present within and among us. Resurrection often lies dormant within us, but it can be a powerful life-giving source flowing from within us. It can call us to transform our lives in such a way that we can be a mutually enhancing human presence upon the Earth.

The universe continues to emerge, our Earth continues to emerge, and the human community continues to emerge. Because of the unconditional love of God within us, there is no doubt in my mind that the human race will move into adulthood and this Earth will be transformed in a new Ecozoic Era. Life on Earth will never be a paradise, humans will never be like God knowing good and evil, but God's inner presence in all of creation will show its power and love and salvation in new life for individuals, nations, and the Earth.

The following text from Psalm 119:145-152 summarizes my prayer at this point in my own personal story:

My heart begs you, Lord,
hear me, so I can keep faith.
I beg you, make me free,
So I can live your laws.

I faced you in the cold night,
praying, waiting for your word.
I kept watch through the night,
repeating what you promise.

Hear me, loving God;
let your justice make me live.
The wicked close in on me;
to them your law is foreign.

But you, Lord, are closer still;
your law is my whole truth,
learned when I was young,
fixed for all time.

BIBLIOGRAPHY

Armstrong, Karen, *A History of God,* New York, Alfred A. Knopf, 1993.

Athanasius, *Contra Gentes and De Incarnatione,* ed. Robert W. Thompson, Oxford, The Clarendon Press, 1971.

Beck, Robert, *Nonviolent Story: Narrative Conflict Resolution in the Gospel of Mark,* Maryknoll, N.Y., Orbis Books, 1996.

Berry, Thomas, *The Dream of the Earth,* San Francisco, Sierra Club Books, 1988.

——, *The Great Work: Our Way into the Future,* New York, Bell Tower, 1999.

Bohm, David, *Wholeness and the Implicate Order,* New York, Routledge & Kegan Paul, 1980.

Boismard, Marie-Emile, *Our Victory over Death: Resurrection?* Collegeville, Minn., The Liturgical Press, 1999.

Borg, Marcus, *Meeting Jesus Again for the First Time,* New York, HarperCollins, 1994.

Brock, Rita Nakashima, *Journeys by Heart: A Christology of Erotic Power,* New York, Crossroad, 1992.

Bronowski, Jacob, *The Ascent of Man,* Boston, Little Brown, 1973.

Brown, Raymond E., *The Community of the Beloved Disciple*, New York, Paulist Press, 1979.

Bulman, Raymond, *The Lure of the Millennium: The Year 2000 and Beyond,* Maryknoll, N.Y., Orbis Books, 1999.

Catechism of the Catholic Church, Mission Hills, Calif., Benziger Publishing Company, 1994.

Chopra, Deepak, *Ageless Body, Timeless Mind: The Quantum Alternative to Growing Old,* New York, Harmony Books, 1993.

Crossan, John Dominic, *The Birth of Christianity: Discovering What Happened in the Years Immediately after the Execution of Jesus,* HarperSanFrancisco, 1999.

———, *Jesus: A Revolutionary Biography,* New York, HarperCollins, 1995.

Dunn, James D. G., *Christology in the Making,* Philadelphia, Westminster Press, 1980.

———, *The Evidence for Jesus,* Philadelphia, Westminster Press, 1985.

———, *Jesus and the Spirit,* Philadelphia, Westminster Press, 1975.

Edwards, Denis, *Human Experience of God,* New York, Paulist Press, 1983.

———, *Jesus and the Cosmos,* New York, Paulist Press, 1991.

———, *Jesus the Wisdom of God: An Ecological Theology,* Maryknoll, N.Y., Orbis Books, 1995.

Ferguson, Marilyn, *The Aquarian Conspiracy,* New York, St. Martin's Press, 1980.

Gebara, Ivone, *Longing for Running Water: Ecofeminism and Liberation,* Minneapolis, Minn., Fortress Press, 1999.

Goergen, Donald J., *The Death and Resurrection of Jesus,* Wilmington, Del., Michael Glazier, 1988.

———, *The Jesus of Christian History,* Wilmington, Del., Michael Glazier, 1992.

———, *The Mission and Ministry of Jesus,* Wilmington, Del., Michael Glazier, 1986.

Haight, Roger, *Jesus Symbol of God,* Maryknoll, N.Y., Orbis Books, 1999.

Hall, Douglas John, *God & Human Suffering,* Minneapolis, Minn., Augsburg, 1986.

Haughton, Rosemary, *The Passionate God,* New York, Paulist Press, 1981.

Hill, Brennan, *Jesus the Christ: Contemporary Perspectives,* Mystic, Conn., Twenty-Third Publications, 1991.

Jaworski, Joseph, *Synchronicity: The Inner Path of Leadership,* San Francisco, Berrett-Koehler Publishers, 1996.

Jaynes, Julian, *The Origin of Consciousness in the Breakdown of the Bicameral Mind,* Boston, Houghton Mifflin, 1976.

Johnson, Elizabeth, *Friends of God and Prophets,* New York, Continuum, 1998.

——, "Redeeming the Name of Christ," in *Freeing Theology,* ed. Catherine Mowry LaCugna, HarperSanFrancisco, 1993.

——, *She Who Is: The Mystery of God in Feminist Theological Discourse,* New York, Crossroad, 1994.

——, *Women, Earth, and Creator Spirit,* New York, Paulist Press, 1993.

Joseph, Lawrence E., *Gaia: The Growth of an Idea,* New York, St. Martin's Press, 1990.

Kaspar, Walter, *Jesus the Christ,* New York, Paulist Press, 1976.

Kautsky, John H., *The Politics of Aristocratic Empires,* Chapel Hill, N.C., University of North Carolina Press, 1982.

Keck, L. Robert, *Sacred Eyes,* Boulder, Colo., Synergy Associates, 1995.

——, *Sacred Quest: The Evolution and Future of the Human Soul,* West Chester, Pa., Chrysalis Books, 2000.

Keen, Sam, *The Passionate Life: Stages of Loving,* San Francisco, Harper & Row, 1983.

Kingsolver, Barbara, *Animal Dreams,* New York, Harper Perennial, 1991.

Knox, John, *The Humanity and Divinity of Christ: A Study of Pattern in Christology,* Cambridge University Press, 1967.

Kubler-Ross, Elisabeth, *On Life after Death,* Berkeley, Calif., Celestial Arts, 1991.

LaCugna, Catherine Mowry, *God for Us: The Trinity and Christian Life,* New York, HarperSanFrancisco, 1991.

Lane, Dermot, *The Reality of Jesus,* New York, Paulist Press, 1975.

Lenski, Gerhard E., *Power and Privilege: A Theory of Social Stratification,* New York, McGraw-Hill, 1966.

McFague, Sallie, *Super, Natural Christians,* Minneapolis, Minn., Fortress Press, 1997.

Mische, Patricia, "Towards a Global Spirituality," in *The Whole Earth Papers,* no. 16, 1982.

Moran, Gabriel, *The Present Revelation: In Quest of Religious Foundations,* New York, Seabury Press, 1972.

Morwood, Michael, *Is Jesus God? Finding Our Faith,* New York, Crossroad, 2001.

——, *Tomorrow's Catholic: Understanding God and Jesus in a New Millennium,* Mystic, Conn., Twenty-Third Publications, 1997.

Murphy-O'Connor, Jerome, "Christological Anthropology in Phil. 2:6-11," in *Revue Biblique* 83 (1976).

Murray, John Courtney, S.J., *The Problem of God,* New Haven, Yale University Press, 1964.

Nogar, Raymond J., *The Lord of the Absurd,* New York, Herder and Herder, 1972.

Nolan, Albert, *Jesus before Christianity,* Maryknoll, N.Y., Orbis Books, 1992.

O'Collins, Gerald, *Christology,* Oxford University Press, 1995.

O'Murchu, Diarmuid, *Quantum Theology,* New York, Crossroad, 1997.

———, *Reclaiming Spirituality,* New York, Crossroad, 1998.

Osborne, Kenan B., *The Resurrection of Jesus: New Considerations for Its Theological Interpretation,* New York, Paulist Press, 1997.

Polkinghorne, John, and Michael Welker, eds., *The End of the World and the Ends of God: Science and Theology on Eschatology,* Harrisburg, Pa., Trinity Press International, 2000.

Prigogine, Ilya, *Order Out of Chaos,* New York, Bantam Books, 1984.

Progoff, Ira, *The Symbolic and the Real,* New York, McGraw-Hill, 1973.

Quinn, Daniel, *Ishmael: An Adventure of the Mind and Spirit,* New York, Bantam Turner Book, 1992.

———, *My Ishmael,* New York, Bantam Books, 1997.

Riley, Gregory J., *Resurrection Reconsidered: Thomas and John in Controversy,* Minneapolis, Minn., Fortress Press, 1995.

Ruether, Rosemary Radford, *Gaia and God: An Ecofeminist Theology of Earth Healing,* HarperSanFrancisco, 1992.

Schillebeeckx, Edward, *Christ: The Experience of Jesus as Lord,* New York, Seabury Press, 1980.

———, *Church: The Human Story of God,* New York, Crossroad, 1991.

———, *Jesus: An Experiment in Christology,* New York, Seabury Press, 1979.

Schoonenberg, Piet, "Trinity—the Consummated Covenant, Theses on the Doctrine of the Trinitarian God," in *Studies in Religion* 5 (1975–1976).

Schüssler Fiorenza, Elisabeth, *In Memory of Her: A Feminist Reconstruction of Christian Origins,* New York, Crossroad, 1983.

Schweizer, Eduard, *The Holy Spirit,* Philadelphia, Fortress Press, 1980.

Senior, Donald, *Jesus: A Gospel Portrait,* Dayton, Ohio, Pflaum Press, 1975.

Sheehan, Thomas, *The First Coming: How the Kingdom of God Became Christianity,* New York, Vintage Books, 1986.

Swimme, Brian, *The Hidden Heart of the Cosmos,* Maryknoll, N.Y., Orbis Books, 1996.

Swimme, Brian, and Thomas Berry, *The Universe Story,* HarperSanFrancisco, 1992.

Tarnas, Richard, *The Passion of the Western Mind,* New York, Harmony Books, 1991.

Toffler, Alvin, "Science and Change," foreword to *Order Out of Chaos,* by Ilya Prigogine, New York, Bantam Books, 1984.

Toolan, David, *At Home in the Cosmos,* Maryknoll, N.Y., Orbis Books, 2001.

Ulanov, Ann, and Barry Ulanov, *Religion and the Unconscious,* Philadelphia, Westminster Press, 1975.

Van Ackeren, Gerald, S.J., et al., *The Church Teaches,* New York, B. Herder Book Co., 1955.

von Bertalanffy, L., *General System Theory,* New York, Braziller, 1969.

von Rad, Gerhard, *Old Testament Theology,* Volume 1, The Theology of Israel's Historical Traditions, New York, Harper and Row, 1962.

Weber, Renee, "The Physicist and the Mystic—Is a Dialogue between Them Possible? A Conversation with David Bohm," in *The Holographic Paradigm and Other Paradoxes,* ed. Ken Wilber, The New Science Library, 1982.

Welch, John, O. Carm., *Spiritual Pilgrims,* New York, Paulist Press, 1982.

Wessels, Cletus, *The Holy Web: Church and the New Universe Story,* Maryknoll, N.Y., Orbis Books, 2000.

West, Thomas H., *Jesus and the Quest for Meaning,* Minneapolis, Minn., Fortress Press, 2001.

Wheatley, Margaret J., *Leadership and the New Science,* San Francisco, Berrett-Koehler Publishers, 1994.

Wheatley, Margaret J., and Myron Kellner-Rogers, *A Simpler Way,* San Francisco, Berrett-Koehler Publishers, 1996.

Wilber, Ken, *Sex, Ecology, Spirituality: The Spirit of Evolution,* Boston, Shambhala, 1995.

Witherington, Ben, *The Many Faces of the Christ: The Christologies of the New Testament and Beyond,* New York, Crossroad, 1998.

Woods, Richard, Mysterion: *An Approach to Mystical Spirituality,* Chicago, Thomas More Press, 1981.

Zohar, Danah, *The Quantum Self: Human Nature and Consciousness Defined by the New Physics,* New York, Quill/William Morrow, 1990.

Zohar, Danah, and Ian Marshall, *The Quantum Society: Mind, Physics, and a New Social Vision,* New York, Quill/William Morrow, 1994.

INDEX